Occupy Pynchon

Occupy Pynchon

POLITICS AFTER *GRAVITY'S RAINBOW*

Sean Carswell

The University of Georgia Press
Athens

An earlier version of chapter 2, "*Vineland* and the Insomniac Unavenged," was previously published as "A *Vineland* Guide to Contemporary Rebellion" in *Orbit: Writing around Pynchon* 1, no. 1 (2012). An earlier version of chapter 7, "A Snappy 'Ukulele Accompaniment," was previously published as "Thomas Pynchon's Ukulele" in the *Journal of American Culture* 38, no. 3 (2015). Both chapters have been significantly revised.

Paperback edition, 2019
© 2017 by the University of Georgia Press
Athens, Georgia 30602
www.ugapress.org
All rights reserved
Set in Adobe Garamond Pro by Graphic Composition, Inc. Bogart, GA

Most University of Georgia Press titles are
available from popular e-book vendors.

Printed digitally

The Library of Congress has cataloged the hardcover edition of this book as follows:
Names: Carswell, Sean, 1970– author.
Title: Occupy Pynchon : politics after Gravity's Rainbow / Sean Carswell.
Description: Athens : The University of Georgia Press, 2017. | Includes bibliographical
    references and index.
Identifiers: LCCN 2016043637 | ISBN 9780820350882 (hardcover : alk. paper) | ISBN
    9780820350899 (ebook)
Subjects: LCSH: Pynchon, Thomas—Criticism and interpretation. | Politics in literature. |
    Government, Resistance to, in literature.
Classification: LCC PS3566.Y55 Z5768 2017 | DDC 813/.54—dc23 LC record available at https://
    lccn.loc.gov/2016043637

Paperback ISBN 978-0-8203-5684-6

For David Downing

CONTENTS

CHAPTER 1. Pynchon in Zuccotti Park: An Introduction   1

CHAPTER 2. *Vineland* and the Insomniac Unavenged   19

CHAPTER 3. *Mason & Dixon* and the Ghastly Fop   49

CHAPTER 4. *Against the Day* and a World Like Ours, with One or Two Adjustments   80

CHAPTER 5. *Inherent Vice* and Being in Place   121

CHAPTER 6. *Bleeding Edge* and Getting Constructively Lost   139

CHAPTER 7. A Snappy 'Ukulele Accompaniment   158

CHAPTER 8. Occupy the Novel: A Conclusion   176

Notes   187
Works Cited   191
Index   199

Occupy Pynchon

CHAPTER I

Pynchon in Zuccotti Park

An Introduction

ON SEPTEMBER 17, 2011, a group of activists responded to a call from *Adbusters* to assemble on Wall Street and bring a tent. Originally, protestors planned to encamp in Chase Manhattan Plaza. Police were informed of the protest, so when the activists arrived, they found the area behind barricades and police protection. An alternate plan had been made. Word got around that activists should reconvene in Zuccotti Park. It was a pleasant day. Activists gathered around the park, talked about economics, democracy, injustice, and other issues. Astra Taylor, in her piece "Scenes from an Occupation," reflects, "It was kind of nice to be at a protest and, instead of marching and shouting, to be talking about ideas. It felt as if the script had changed" (3). When evening fell, several activists pitched tents and stayed the night. An occupation was born.

The events in Zuccotti Park triggered several more occupations of parks and plazas throughout the world. As Sarah van Gelder explains, "In a matter of weeks, the occupations and protests had spread worldwide, to over 1,500 cities, from Madrid to Cape Town and from Buenos Aires to Hong Kong, involving hundreds of thousands of people" (2). Mainstream media sources were quick to criticize the movement as lacking a purpose. Several activists responded with corrections to this. According to Bernard Harcourt, the movement was not one of civil disobedience. In other words, activists were not accepting the legitimacy of existing political and economic structures and advocating for specific changes. It was, instead, a movement of political disobedience in which activists refused to accept the established power system and sought different, more just ways of living. In this respect, it was less of a protest. They were not hammering away at a specific issue. It was a demonstration. They were showing an alternative way of approaching society.

Even without a specific set of demands, the events that inspired the occupations were clear. One percent of the population of the United States held an inordinate amount of wealth and political power. The government was made up of members of this 1 percent. They rigged the system so that wealth would flow away from the rest of the population and into a few hands. They also pro-

{1}

mulgated a specific ideological viewpoint that can be classified as neoliberalism: the belief that capitalism is synonymous with endless accumulation and that the concerns of the marketplace take priority over all concerns. The activists in the various encampments were, in many cases, people who played by the rules, worked hard, earned college degrees, and were struggling under the weight of a debt-based economy. They had lost their homes in the subprime mortgage crisis. They struggled to pay student loans from state universities that had lost much of their government support. They saw banks get tremendous taxpayer bailouts while the social safety net was systematically dismantled. They were frustrated with their own alienation from civic engagement. Outside of being able to vote for one of two candidates from the 1 percent every couple of years, they had largely been excluded from the democratic process. The lockdown of Chase Manhattan Plaza demonstrated this disenfranchisement. In his contribution to "Scenes from an Occupation," Eli Schmidt observes, "The event seemed to be predicated on the idea that the act of assembling was threatened, that the gathering was a justification of itself" (Taylor 2). In this regard, perhaps the most pressing demand of Occupy was the demand for democracy itself; perhaps the greatest legacy of Occupy is its demonstration that real democracy is a tremendous threat to the existing power structure.

Occupy activists theorized the need to resist demands. Colleen Asper, paraphrased by David Graeber in *The Democracy Project*, observes, "Often the power of a work of art is precisely the fact that you're not quite sure what it's trying to say" (21–22). In this way, works of art are able to communicate larger, more far-reaching concepts. Rather than specifically advocating for issues that most Occupy activists agreed with—higher taxes for the 1 percent, a repeal of Citizens United, and so on—the lack of a demand allowed observers to contemplate the deeper issues of injustice and disenfranchisement. Michael Taussig builds on this idea in his essay "I'm So Angry I Made a Sign": "They see OWS as primitive and diffuse because it has no precise demands—as if the demand for equality were not a demand, at once moral and economic, redefining personhood and reality itself" (39). And so, without a precise demand, Occupy demonstrated acts of participatory democracy. Like second-wave feminist movements and various anarchist collectives, demonstrators set up spaces built around consensus rather than voting or top-down hierarchy. They developed the occupations to be horizontal in structure and leaderless. Everyone was enfranchised. Everyone had a veto. Everyone could speak and be heard.

I did not participate in Occupy. I watched from a distance. At the time, I had been teaching courses on Thomas Pynchon. I was finishing up scholarship on Pynchon's conceptions of power and resistance. One thing that struck me about Occupy was how closely it relates to Pynchon's post–*Gravity's Rainbow* novels. The occupation of Zuccotti Park could find its literary precedent in the Becker-Traverse reunion in *Vineland* or in the Yz-les-Bains community in *Against the Day*. Like Pynchon, Occupy complicates contemporary notions of sovereignty. The demonstrations were not, specifically, attacking the federal government of the United States. After all, Occupiers set up encampments in Hong Kong, Buenos Aires, Madrid, Cape Town, and various other places that are not directly under the control of the U.S. government. Instead, Occupy seemed to envision sovereignty similar to how Pynchon demonstrates it in his novels: a network of shared power among multinational corporations, national governments, and supranational agencies. This is one of the reasons Zuccotti Park—a privatized public space—was such an appropriate arena for the demonstration. Like Pynchon, Occupy-style protests sought to include a multitude of political perspectives all confronting the 1 percent, but not necessarily agreeing on a unified platform. W. J. T. Mitchell explains this in "Image, Space, Revolution: The Arts of Occupation": "In Tahrir Square the Muslim Brotherhood camped next to Coptic Christians, radical fundamentalists, secular liberals, and Marxist revolutionaries. Right-wing Zionist settlers joined the anti-Zionist ultra-orthodox along with secular Jews and even a few Palestinians on Rothschild Boulevard in Tel Aviv, and Tea Partiers showed up at Occupy rallies across the United States" (104). I have no reason to believe that Thomas Pynchon was among the diverse voices in Zuccotti Park or any of the sites of the Occupy movement. However, his post–*Gravity's Rainbow* novels in many ways predict Occupy. Putting these works in conversation with the demonstrations articulates much about contemporary power, inequality, injustice, and revolution. Because *Vineland* is Pynchon's first novel to follow the neoliberal revolution of the 1980s, which created the global capitalist culture that catalyzed resistance movements like Occupy, this conversation begins with *Vineland*.

Reconsidering *Vineland*

It is a familiar story among readers of Thomas Pynchon: after a seventeen-year absence from novel writing accompanied mostly by silence from a reclusive author, Thomas Pynchon followed up his masterpiece, *Gravity's Rainbow*, with the largely disappointing novel *Vineland*. The story is so established among Pynchon scholarship and criticism—even among the Pynchon websites and wikis—that we can easily mistake it for a fact. While there is some truth to this story, it dismisses *Vineland* too easily.

Certainly, I agree with the first half of the story. *Gravity's Rainbow* is an incredible novel. Perhaps "masterpiece" is too strong of a descriptor. Every fan of Pynchon's work can decide for herself which work is Pynchon's greatest. Nonetheless, *Gravity's Rainbow* catapulted Pynchon from a promising young novelist to a major American author whose work came to be a defining voice of sixties counterculture and postmodernism. The novel was awarded the 1974 National Book Award. The judges for the Pulitzer Prize unanimously selected *Gravity's Rainbow* for the 1974 prize before the advisory board dubbed the novel rambling and obscene and refused to award a Pulitzer for fiction that year. *Gravity's Rainbow* paved the way for Pynchon to be selected for both the prestigious Howells Medal (which he declined) and a MacArthur fellowship (which he accepted). Additionally, the novel drew hundreds of thousands of worldwide fans to Pynchon's work.

There is no doubt in my mind that *Gravity's Rainbow* is a wonderful novel. It is dazzling in its scope; it demonstrates an encyclopedic breadth of knowledge. The novel explores Herero uprisings, British spy novels, rocket science, mysticism, the dodo bird—everything. Pynchon seamlessly combines this wisdom with drug-fueled paranoia and comic absurdity. There is one scene in the novel in which the protagonist, Tyrone Slothrop, attempts to escape from U.S. Army Ordnance officer Major Marvy (leader of Marvy's Mothers) in a hot-air balloon smuggling custard pies into occupied Berlin. The setup alone is comic absurdity: the alliterative names of Major Marvy's Mothers, the act of smuggling custard pies (which, once mentioned, must be thrown into someone's face), and the hot-air balloon as a getaway vehicle. The scene that follows fulfills the promise of the setup. Slothrop and Schnorp, the balloon captain, manage to win an aerial confrontation with Marvy's Mothers using only custard pies and balloon ballasts as weapons. Major Marvy does get a pie to the face. The scene is so much more than comic absurdity, though. It delves into Teutonic mythology. It links Rolls Royce, General Electric, Harvard, the Office of Strategic Services (the predecessor to the CIA), and Nazi scientists together in a global political and economic network. Pynchon demonstrates a breadth of knowledge about World War II military aircraft, hot-air balloons, and various forms of weaponry—all in less than ten pages. The scene can exist as a microcosm of the entire novel for its ability to juggle the comic, the political, the spiritual, and the academic. *Gravity's Rainbow* continues to exist as one of the few novels to treat contemporary global culture with the depth and breadth of knowledge and understanding necessary for unpacking meaning within this culture.

When *Vineland* followed up *Gravity's Rainbow*, critics and academics alike could not be blamed for expecting Pynchon to use the intervening decades—not to mention the money from the MacArthur fellowship—to create a work of fiction that rivaled *Gravity's Rainbow* in both scale and scope. Instead,

Pynchon narrowed both, focusing largely on the United States (and, more often than not, California), exploring mostly the 1960s and 1980s through the point of view of a few (for Pynchon) characters. The initial response to the novel was largely negative.

Critics were quick to pan *Vineland*. Brad Leithauser, in the *New York Review of Books*, is perhaps the most succinct in summarizing a widely held criticism of the book when he notes, "[I]n view of our expectations the book is a disappointment" (7). Leithauser goes on to explain, "*Vineland* falters in a convincing variety of ways—perhaps chiefly through its failure in any significant degree to extend or improve upon what the author has done before" (7). Leithauser's disappointment was shared by the *National Review*'s J. O. Tate, who characterizes the book as "a bore and a chore" (59), by the *New Republic*'s Edward Mendelson, whose first adjective describing the novel is "tedious" (40), and by *Newsweek*'s Malcolm Jones, who bemoans, "By the time the climax arrives, it's such a relief to see the end of this overwrought tale that it almost doesn't matter who's left standing" (66). Even *The Progressive*, a longtime bastion of tendentious political writing, laments that *Vineland*'s "politics is available but a little too pat" (Bluestein 42). Indeed, with the exception of Salman Rushdie's rave in the *New York Times* and Terrence Rafferty's praise in the *New Yorker*, most of the reviewers of *Vineland* run the gamut from slightly miffed to outright hostile.

Leithauser concluded his review by hoping "that time will reveal [*Vineland*] to have been a lighthearted interlude, one completed while its author was intent on a more substantial . . . work" (10). The activity of Pynchon scholars seems to have seconded Leithauser's hope. A quick survey of *Pynchon Notes* reveals that, while nearly half the scholarship on Pynchon in the 1992 issue is dedicated to *Vineland*, scholarship on the novel quickly takes a backseat to Pynchon's first three novels. This forms a stark contrast to the celebration with which scholars and critics alike greeted Pynchon's subsequent work, *Mason & Dixon*.

I joined my fellow Pynchon fans in celebrating the release of *Mason & Dixon*. Why wouldn't I? It is a novel that demonstrates a return to the precedents set by *Gravity's Rainbow*. There are dozens and dozens of characters in *Mason & Dixon*. The novel wanders from continent to continent. It is encyclopedic in breadth. It blends together the disparate worlds of spirituality, economics, politics, and literature. It conveniently seconds as a doorstop for even the heaviest door on the windiest day. Nonetheless, as I mention above, I disagree with critics and scholars who overlook *Vineland*.

As a general rule of literary scholarship, we should probably reexamine any idea that becomes too accepted. A good example of this lies in the scholarship surrounding *Moby-Dick*. For years, scholars characterized the chapter in which Ishmael meditates on the whiteness of the whale as an enigma. Perhaps it was a religious vision. Perhaps it was a reaction to the darkness in American gothic novels. Perhaps it was a prose poem or a suggestion of the infinite just beyond our grasp. For 140 years, scholars were nearly unanimous in ignoring the possibility that a meditation on whiteness could be about race. This ignorance is even more striking when one considers that *Moby-Dick* was published within months of both the passage of the Fugitive Slave Act and the publication of *Uncle Tom's Cabin*. It came out amid the backdrop of the slave revolts that would trigger the passage of the Thirteenth Amendment. Critics also ignored the basic fact that it is a novel about a multicultural whaling crew chasing whiteness until it leads to their ultimate annihilation. It was not until the emergence of critical whiteness studies and groundbreaking scholarship done by both Toni Morrison in *Playing in the Dark* and Valerie Babb in *Whiteness Visible* that race was folded back into the mainstream discussion on *Moby-Dick*. In doing so, they opened exciting new passages into the book that is considered by many to be the Great American Novel. It should not have taken nearly a century and a half to get there, however. A mere five years after the publication of Melville's novel, James McCune Smith, writing for the abolitionist magazine *Horoscope*, examines the "Whiteness of the Whale" chapter in particular to demonstrate that the novel is, inherently, about racial equality.

A similar example can be found in the dismissal of *Vineland*. One reviewer in particular, Salman Rushdie, declares *Vineland* to be "a major political novel about what America has been doing to itself, to its children, all these many years" (BR37). When Rushdie discusses what "America has been doing to itself," he is referencing historiographical revisions of 1960s rebellion and the rise of neoliberal ideology fostered in the 1980s by the likes of Margaret Thatcher, Ronald Reagan, and Deng Xiaoping. And, just as literary scholars steeped in the theories of New Criticism were unable to view the racial examinations of whiteness in *Moby-Dick*, the frames of sixties counterculture and postmodernism restrict the view of Pynchon's confrontation with neoliberalism in *Vineland*.

In Sascha Pöhlmann's introduction to a collection of essays on *Against the Day*, he warns readers of the danger inherent in attempting to shoehorn Pynchon's work into postmodern theory. Pöhlmann argues that, while *Gravity's Rainbow* "is still the defining text of postmodernism in literature" (*Against the Grain* 10), Pynchon's subsequent works move beyond the theory and its constructs (however loosely defined postmodernism's constructs are). Likewise, I argue that Pynchon's politics are informed by sixties radicalism, and his first three novels stand as significant texts exemplifying that radicalism. However, it would be a mistake to attempt to force Pynchon's complex political views into the confines of sixties radicalism. Instead, beginning with *Vineland*, Pynchon creates a model for viewing contemporary power systems and the forces that oppose them.

As I mention above, I believe it is a mistake to overlook *Vineland*, to confuse Pynchon's return to the stylistic devices of *Gravity's Rainbow* in *Mason & Dixon* with a return to serious literary writing. Pynchon never took a break from serious literature. For all the humor in *Vineland*, it is a serious text, a lens through which all his subsequent texts can be viewed. That is part of the project of this study. I will argue that *Vineland* marks a significant turning point in Pynchon's oeuvre, specifically with regard to Pynchon's politics. Previous to *Vineland*, Pynchon's work was concerned largely with the radicalism of the sixties and seventies as a resistance to totalitarian powers. Pynchon's early works tend to feature paranoid characters swept up in a conspiracy beyond their comprehension and hurtling toward fragmented and ultimately dismal ends. With the publication of *Vineland*, this paranoia gives way to a more fully articulated global system of power. Pynchon's five most recent novels (*Vineland, Mason & Dixon, Against the Day, Inherent Vice,* and *Bleeding Edge*) feature an examination of neoliberal capitalism's exploitative system of privatization, deregulation, militarization, and free-market fundamentalism. The novels also seek sites for resistance to this exploitative system. The purpose of this study, then, will be to elaborate on the global systems of power that Pynchon constructs in his five most recent novels and to examine the possibilities Pynchon explores for resistance to and advancement beyond these systems of power.

Occupy Pynchon gains added relevance when weighed with global movements that sprung up subsequent to the publication of *Inherent Vice* in 2009. Pynchon's conception of twenty-first-century resistance can serve as a model for understanding the Arab Spring, the Occupy Wall Street Movement, and various other global uprisings. Ultimately, by unpacking Pynchon's conceptions of global power and resistance, this study leads us to ways of using, in literary studies, the notions of participatory democracy that characterized the Occupy movement.

Of course, Pynchon has always written about power structures and opposition. From his earliest short stories like "Under the Rose," he has used historical narratives to criticize global systems of power. He has done this throughout most of his works by using expansive narratives to explore an increasingly connected world on a political, social, cultural, and economic level. While Pynchon has done this both before and after *Vineland*, his three novels that precede *Vineland* (as well as the short stories and newspaper articles he wrote before 1990) all end on a fairly dismal note. Pynchon is critical of global systems of power throughout; however, his first three novels afford little room for resistance. Pynchon hints about pockets of resistance, certainly. The Whole Sick Crew of *V.* are somewhat of a reconstituted familial community similar to the communities in which Pynchon places so much value in his later works. A "Counterforce" is established at the end of *Gravity's Rainbow* that will, to some extent, confront the political and economic powers that dominate the characters in the novel. These two examples, however, differ from the sites of resistance in Pynchon's later works mostly with regard to their scale—they are brief moments instead of sustainable alternatives—and their potential. Both the Whole Sick Crew and the Counterforce leave little hope for a lasting movement of resistance. Instead, Pynchon's first three novels are steeped in paranoia in part because the characters have little recourse against power structures. The characters recognize that a network of government agencies and multinational corporations exists and maintains power over their lives, yet the characters lack the insight necessary to understand this network well enough to counter it. However, beginning with *Vineland*, the paranoia lessens as the characters begin to find pockets of resistance.

Vineland does not, then, represent a clean break for Pynchon. All his novels carry anarchist sympathies. All his endings have been read as hopeful by some scholars and bleak by others. All his work confronts global, networked power. However, *Vineland* came out within a different cultural context. *The Crying of Lot 49* preceded much of the activism that has come to characterize the late 1960s and early 1970s. *Gravity's Rainbow* was published in the thick of political activism. In the intervening decades, global sovereignty experienced one of the world's most successful and destructive revolutions: the neoliberal revolution. As described by David Harvey in *A Brief History of Neoliberalism*, a new ideology came to dominate global discussions of sovereignty. Harvey explains this ideology: "It holds that the social good will be maximized by maximizing the reach and frequency of market transactions, and it seeks to bring all human action into the domain of the market" (3). Under the tutelage of politicians like Margaret Thatcher, Ronald Reagan, and Deng Xiaoping, social safety nets began to shrink. Ideas of freedom came to mean the freedom of multinational corporations to exploit land and labor in pursuit of endless accumulation. These ideas run directly counter to Pynchon's subtle anarchism. On a smaller scale in his first three novels and a much larger scale in his subsequent ones, Pynchon seeks avenues for freedom within a culture where neoliberalism is hegemonic. Since this revolution occurred after the publication of *Gravity's Rainbow*, the novel and the ones before it cannot respond to it (though, at times, they seem to predict it). Pynchon's post–*Gravity's Rainbow* novels are also post-neoliberal revolution novels. Because these novels confront neoliberal ideology directly, I have focused on them.

Empire and Multitude

To better understand concepts of power in both Occupy and Pynchon's work, it is helpful to utilize the terms that Michael Hardt and Antonio Negri articulate in *Empire*. Pynchon's description of a global network of sovereignty exemplifies Hardt and Negri's conception of an "Empire" consisting of government agencies, multinational corporations, and international financial institutions that work like governments but beyond the jurisdiction of national rule. This is not an empire in the eighteenth- and nineteenth-century model, which is characterized by governments and their militaries colonizing a foreign region to exploit it for its natural resources. Instead, it is Empire without a single sovereign. This Empire works as a network with various negotiations of power occurring between a limited number of players who contend for a greater share of it while ensuring that power does not expand beyond this network. Since the 1944 Bretton Woods agreements, "post-Fordist" neoliberal capitalism has been driven by this global network. It has been characterized by organizations like the World Bank, the World Trade Organization, the International Monetary Fund; by multinational corporations whose members are instrumental in drafting trade and tariff treaties that allow for the exploitation of labor while facilitating profits of these corporations; and various "First World" governments who work largely in concert with big business. This capitalism is a far cry from the myth of laissez-faire economics largely because capital and governments are so frequently inseparable. In fact, as scholars like Wendy Brown and David Harvey demonstrate, the purpose of contemporary national governments seems to be largely economic. Under neoliberalism, every aspect of society becomes saturated by the logic of the marketplace.

From his earliest novels, Pynchon has explored this Empire of late capitalism. It is the power system that Stencil seeks to understand in *V*. It is Them who manipulate Tyrone Slothrop throughout *Gravity's Rainbow*. It battles (and perhaps co-opts) the Tristero that haunts Oedipa Maas in *The Crying of Lot 49*. This Empire continues throughout his later novels. Brock Vond in *Vineland* is Empire's hired thug, perpetually vying for greater power. Mason and Dixon travel throughout the nascent Empire, witnessing the slavery and exploitation that fuel and empower it. Dixon observes that these chartered companies—with their attendant exploitation—are becoming the new shape of the world. *Against the Day* traces various anarchists, revolutionaries, mathematicians, ukulelists, and fictional balloonists through the rise of nineteenth-century economic liberalism's race toward the annihilation that was World War I. Several of these characters recognize the devastating outcomes of economic liberalism—capital's material effects—and organize to oppose it. Doc Sportello of *Inherent*

Vice is the private detective engaged in investigating—though not necessarily hired to investigate—the massive reach of Empire as it is represented in the fictional organization the Golden Fang. And, finally, Maxine Turnow of *Bleeding Edge* investigates Empire as it infiltrates the Internet during the early twenty-first century tech boom in Manhattan.

Utilizing Hardt and Negri's conception of Empire helps articulate exactly how the global systems of power that Pynchon criticizes operate and also how effective sites of resistance can emerge. Because Empire is indelibly tied to neoliberal capitalism, my study relies on several scholars and theorists whose work overlaps Hardt and Negri's yet approaches Empire from different directions. To better understand Empire, one must also recognize Wendy Brown's argument that at the core of Empire's power is an unquestioned neoliberal ideology that insists every aspect of life must be subject to the rule of the marketplace. Brown's notion complements David Harvey's *A Brief History of Neoliberalism*, which traces the rise of this neoliberal ideology and suggests that the core to opposing it lies in a discussion of the concept of freedom. As mentioned above, Harvey argues that, in a neoliberal society, freedom comes to denote the freedom of economic elites to exploit labor and land as a means of accumulating massive fortunes. Harvey petitions for a more egalitarian concept of freedom, one that is based on social relations and mutual benefits instead of endless accumulation. Finally, because Pynchon is primarily a historical novelist, understanding the contemporary neoliberalism that he confronts requires an exploration into the historical predecessor of neoliberalism, economic liberalism. Karl Polanyi's seminal work *The Great Transformation* elucidates the transition of global economies from economies of social relations—which were the core of all economic systems prior to the industrial revolution—to economies of gain. Polanyi provides the framework for understanding the pseudospiritual aspects of capital, with its Invisible Hand mystically guiding markets. Polanyi argues against this concept of unregulated markets, concluding that, if a market were truly unregulated, it would lead to annihilation. Polanyi supports this conclusion by demonstrating the ways in which insufficiently regulated markets in the nineteenth century were the catalyzing factor behind the twentieth century's two world wars. Polanyi also develops the notion of double movements or countermovements, which are resistance movements that spontaneously arise to oppose unregulated financial markets and economies of gain.

These double movements or countermovements lead to the second useful concept from Hardt and Negri: the multitude. Hardt and Negri envision the multitude as the site of resistance against Empire. Breaking from Marxist and Enlightenment ideologies, Hardt and Negri resist the notion of the multitude as a unified whole. Instead, the multitude consists of discursive voices with various concerns. Key to the concept of the multitude is the idea that the many who construct the multitude never lose their singularity; they remain many. Nonetheless, they are united in their exploitation by Empire and by the neoliberal capitalism that drives it. They must resist the network of Empire by remaining a horizontal network without a single goal or sovereignty. The most concrete example of the multitude Hardt and Negri present in their critical trilogy resides in the protests against the World Trade Organization in Seattle in 1999. During these protests, environmentalists, labor union activists, anarchists, antiwar activists, and various other diverse (and at times seemingly contradictory or antagonistic) groups worked in concert against a common site of exploitation: the Empire as represented by the WTO. The groups retained their singularity. Identity was never surrendered to a unified concept like "the people" or "the masses." Instead, labor opposed Empire on the grounds of labor exploitation, and environmentalists protested Empire on the grounds of environmental exploitation, but they worked together opposing the common exploiter.

Since the publication of their critical trilogy, Hardt and Negri have continued to clarify their definition of the multitude by examining resistance movements that arose in 2011 in Egypt, Spain, Greece, and the United States. In "The Fight for 'Real Democracy' at the Heart of Occupy Wall Street," Hardt and Negri link the occupation of Tahrir Square in Cairo and Syntagma Square in Athens with encampments in Madrid's Puerta del Sol, Barcelona's Plaça Catalunya, and New York's Wall Street as well as with the extended protests at the Wisconsin capitol. While Hardt and Negri acknowledge that the specific grievances of the protestors in each case are different, they resist a common oppression. In all cases, the protestors recognize that "politics has become subservient to economic and financial interests" and that representative democracy as it has been constructed in these states is merely a pretense. Hardt and Negri assert, "These movements have all developed according to what we call a 'multitude form' and are characterized by frequent assemblies and participatory decision-making structures." They further observe that no leaders have arisen from these protests. The protestors have instead developed a "horizontal network structure" in which real, participatory democratic experiments are taking place. While in some cases the protestors did have specific messages (Egyptians rallying around a cry of "Mubarak must go," Wisconsinites joined in defense of collective bargaining rights), in all cases protestors agitated against the exploitative power of Empire and in favor of a new form of participatory democracy that allows for a multitude of singularities.

Understanding this concept of the multitude is key to understanding the shift that occurs in Pynchon's work beginning with *Vineland*. Pynchon's novels have always featured a multitude of characters from marginalized social positions. However, prior to *Vineland*, these characters are disparate and fragmented. To use Pynchon's term from *Gravity's Rainbow*, his characters compose the "preterite": those who exist outside the boundaries of society, who are cast off, forgotten, abandoned. This is best exemplified by Tyrone Slothrop at the end of *Gravity's Rainbow*, when he himself seems to fragment and disperse as if he were a rocket that exploded. There is little sense among the preterite that they exist as a network or that, despite their diverse perspectives, they have an understanding of a dominant global system of power to resist. Hardt and Negri's definition of the multitude is based on a reworking of Marx's notions of both the public commons and the proletariat. Whereas for Marx the proletariat was the source of resistance to capital, the multitude is a much broader concept, more appropriate for the complex global networks of contemporary capitalism. This sense of the multitude first appears at the end of *Vineland*, when the disparate characters gather for the Becker-Traverse family reunion. The reunion expands the notion of a family beyond bloodlines. In attendance are a motley collection of Wobblies, communists, activists, snitches, madmen, punk rockers, drug dealers, Vietnam veterans, and even a few dead people thrown in for good measure. All these characters retain their singularity but (either consciously or unconsciously) share their need for the commons as a site of resistance against private capital's Empire. Their occupation of the woods and the horizontal, participatory nature of their community mirrors W. J. T. Mitchell's reflection on the Occupy movement, which demonstrates that "spaces of actually existing democratic equality are a danger to the political status quo" (xiii). Significantly, it is in the face of this assembly of the multitude where the imperial Brock Vond meets his insurmountable resistance. The fact that this resistance occurs in the Northern California backcountry on land that has no clear owner—property that is seemingly neither public nor private property—suggests another form of commons for the multitude. In this case, it is a representation of what Marx classified as the global commons. David B. Downing articulates these commons as "local spaces of *relative* autonomy from direct capital appropriation of surplus value and from private property as regulated by law" (28). This commons is the literal site of resistance at the end of *Vineland*. It will also prove to be the figurative site of resistance—and, beyond resistance, advancement—throughout Pynchon's five most recent novels. Here, for the first time, Pynchon leaves readers with a sense of hope at the end of one of his novels.

The four novels that succeed *Vineland* differ from the three novels that precede it by exploring the possibilities for resistance represented in the multitude. In this study, I seek to articulate this site of resistance and expand it into several arenas of social injustice. As I mention above, Hardt and Negri's (as well as Pynchon's) representation of the multitude is dependent on a construction that rejects unification and embraces multiple singularities. Along these lines, my investigation of Pynchon's site of resistance includes an exploration into issues of gender (particularly with respect to *Vineland* and the intergenerational relationships between mothers and daughters as represented by Sasha Gates, Frenesi Gates, and Prairie Wheeler), issues of race (spanning all five novels but perhaps most salient in *Mason & Dixon*, which confronts the burgeoning concepts of race with respect to Native Americans, Africans, and African Americans), and issues of sexuality (as represented by openly lesbian characters in the nascent United States in *Mason & Dixon* and the several openly gay or lesbian characters in *Against the Day*). These singularities are all intertwined with class when considered through the lens of the multitude.

Perhaps the most powerful aspect of examining global issues of gender, race, sexuality, and class through the concept of the multitude lies in both Pynchon's and Hardt and Negri's concept of the inside and outside of society. Hardt and Negri reject the notion of an inside and an outside of society. Starting with *Vineland*, Pynchon likewise rejects this notion. Instead of constructing a worldview that suggests certain people reside in the center or mainstream of society while others are marginalized or on the fringes, Pynchon and Hardt and Negri construct a worldview that holds no center, no mainstream. Instead, it is a network of autonomous beings with diverse perspectives who often act with or against one another. From this perspective, an exploration into gender, race, sexuality, and class avoids the trappings of placing these issues on the margins of society. Gender, race, sexuality, and class issues are treated as inextricable injustices shared in a common exploitation. Further, like Pynchon's five novels that succeed *Gravity's Rainbow*, my study goes beyond social criticism and into the arena of resistance and sites for negotiating social justice.

Approaches to Pynchon's Power and Resistance

The chapters that follow adhere to a basic pattern of exploring, first, the systems of power that Pynchon confronts in each of his novels and, second, the sites of resistance Pynchon proposes. While all six chapters expand on notions of Empire and the multitude, I approach these notions from different entryways, utilizing different theorists, and attempting to expand and complicate the machinations of contemporary power and resistance. In chapter 2, I begin to trace the shift in Pynchon's oeuvre with the novel *Vineland*. I expand upon the argument that the power structure in Pynchon's novels is very much in line with Hardt and Negri's concept of the Empire and that Pynchon constructs a multitude in *Vineland* which can serve as a model of resistance to Empire. I explore these notions in *Vineland*, first, by presenting Empire as engaged in a series of civil wars as a means of restricting civil rights; second, by examining the multitude's complicity in perpetuating Empire; third, by analyzing the failure of violent revolution; and finally, by providing a positive site for resistance. Specifically, I locate this positive site for resistance at the Becker-Traverse family reunion and in the social and economic alternatives suggested by the Sisterhood of Kunoichi Attentives. As I mention above, the Becker-Traverse family reunion works as a site of resistance by seeking a Marxist commons as a meeting place, bringing together a network of individuals who are notable in their differences yet have the ability to work cooperatively to resist Empire, and by reconstructing a familial community that may be tied together by circumstances of birth, socioeconomic factors, and places in a system of power but nonetheless form a system of nurture, support, and cooperation. The family reunion also provides room for the wise elder of the family, Jess Traverse, to deliver a speech that presents a counternarrative to Empire's history of resistance movements. Jess's history links these movements together and validates the work that groups like the Wobblies, sixties activists, and punk rockers have done.

The Sisterhood represents another site of resistance to Empire. It resides in a social business: one that is complicit with corporate society but recognizes that complicity and moves beyond it; one that rejects consumerism by refusing to sell consumables and by rejecting the notion of spirituality as a commodity; one that accepts payments beyond the typical system of cash currency; one that exists for mutual profit instead of exploitative profit; one that reconstructs notions of family and community to provide a safe harbor; and one that rejects competition in favor of cooperation. Through these sites of resistance, Pynchon resurrects the American left, which, though seemingly destroyed during the Reagan years, still has the potential to resist the corporate takeover of the American promise.

Chapter 3 further explores the concepts of power and resistance, this time focusing on *Mason & Dixon*. By following the eponymous characters Mason and Dixon through the slave colonies of Dutch South Africa, Pennsylvania, and Maryland, I examine the interrelationship between Empire and slavery as well as the depth of injustice and exploitation that exists beyond chattel slavery in a system of global commodity culture. Pynchon's use of chartered companies—the eighteenth-century predecessor to contemporary multinational corporations—demonstrates the political and economic power that built the Empire. He demonstrates how, beginning in the eighteenth century, chartered companies' power permeated every aspect of human society. They controlled the direction of scientific inquiry, they produced and distributed products to which consumers became addicted, and they reorganized land and labor under their ideology. Pynchon's representations of the so-called Founding Fathers further elucidates the ways in which the construction of the United States was inextricably linked to the shadier sides of commerce. Pynchon presents a burgeoning United States founded less by an ideology of freedom and equality and more by wealthy landowners seeking to expand their wealth at the expense of women, slaves, Native Americans, and contract employees like Mason and Dixon. By doing so, Pynchon complicates labor and exploitation. He goes beyond the simple notion that chattel slavery is unethical. Instead, he links the exploitation of divorcing labor from the wealth it produces with the injustice of global economic systems.

I further examine Pynchon's use of the subjunctive as a means to confront the ideology of neoliberalism. For Pynchon, the subjunctive—or the imagined as real—provides a site for counternarratives. As Mason and Dixon voyage deeper into the American continent, they encounter a supernatural world that the American Empire will devour. It's a world where mechanized ducks fly faster than the human eye can detect, golems wander the countryside, men turn into werebeavers (similar to werewolves, but the human morphs into a different animal form), vegetables grow large enough for families to carve out homes in the center of them, and inhabitants are haunted by ghost visions and memories of mythical worms. This subjunctive world of tall tales and ghost stories becomes a magical realm in which the locals can disseminate the values of their culture through stories that represent their multitude of singularities. This subjunctive world is where Pynchon reinserts the magic that preceded the Age of Reason into the history of America. Pynchon's forays into the subjunctive allow him to control which magic is reinserted into the narrative. As opposed to "the magic system" that consumer capitalism promulgates through its marketing arms, Pynchon presents a magic system in which discursive voices are written back into the narrative of colonial times, in which Pynchon is able to promote a value system that radically differs from the one produced by multinational corporations and national governments. Ultimately, Pynchon does not provide a single clear proposal for a more just world. He does not even provide a few clear proposals from which the reader can choose. Instead, *Mason & Dixon* narrates a series of subjunctive testimonies that serve to trigger the reader's imagination regarding what a world beyond Empire could look like.

In chapter 4, I concentrate on Pynchon's most encyclopedic novel, *Against the Day*. I begin the examination with Pynchon's concept of bilocation, which means, literally, being in two places at the same time. I argue that Pynchon creates a bilocation between the time period when the novel is set (the end of the nineteenth and beginning of the twentieth century) and the time when the novel was released (the early twenty-first century). The specific focus of this bilocation is (1) the economic liberalism and anarchism that opposed it during the novel's historical time period and (2) contemporary neoliberalism and Pynchon's construction of a resistance to it. Exploring this bilocation gives form to the project Pynchon has been undertaking since *Vineland*: envisioning a future that wrests wealth and power from the opulent few who helm national governments, multinational corporations, and supranational organizations; a future that moves the contemporary ideology away from the free market/neoliberal utopian ideal of accumulation of wealth; a future that replaces this power system and ideology with a life based on social relations constructed out of reconstituted family systems and communities; a future, in short, that reflects goals of the Occupy movement.

My investigation begins with Pynchon's use of fiction to envision new worlds and to give ideas the form and freedom they need to play themselves out logically. I move from there to an exploration of political violence. I acknowledge the immense violence in the novel and Pynchon's sympathy for the disenfranchised characters who employ violence as a means of resistance but argue that Pynchon ultimately dismisses this violent resistance as futile. Pynchon also seems to take an ethical stance against political violence, demonstrating the impossibility of separating the means of a revolution from its ends. Nonetheless, Pynchon must give political violence freedom to reach these conclusions in his novel.

Along the lines of freedom, chapter 4 investigates notions of freedom in a neoliberal society, questioning the neoliberal hegemonic view that freedom equates to free markets. Pynchon seems to work toward the goal of replacing the neoliberal concept of freedom (which can be further defined as the freedom to accumulate goods) with a freedom that creates more meaningful social relations. *Against the Day* builds on constructions of alternative possible societies that Pynchon began in *Vineland* and *Mason & Dixon*. In particular, *Against the Day* situates a vision for a better society with freedoms based on the concepts of nomadism, spiritual journeys, immaterial labor, intellectual inquiry, and community. His conclusions should by no means be read as a simple prescription for a new way to live. As I demonstrate below, Pynchon's subjunctive future is a flawed one. It is predicated on humans having the freedom to make choices regarding the specific forms of their nomadism, immaterial labor, and intellectual inquiry. These characters act human and at times make selfish and petty choices. They are often self-destructive. Social relations are distressed as a result. Further, due to the bilocation of the novel, the reader cannot ignore that this historical novel's future is, to some extent, the twenty-first century's past. The resistance of the Traverse family in *Against the Day* will not result in a utopia of the multitude. Or, if it eventually does, it must do so after it first withstands the twentieth century's Second World War, attacks on organized labor, witch hunts, and neoliberal takeovers that threatened to destroy the American left. Nonetheless, Pynchon is substituting his imperfect but improved vision of the future for neoliberalism's failed vision of a utopia inspired by unregulated markets.

In chapter 5, I focus on *Inherent Vice*. With so many of the initial critics and scholars approaching *Inherent Vice* as a pastiche built from the work of Raymond Chandler, I begin my investigation of the novel by noting the similarities between the novel and not only Chandler's *The Long Goodbye* but also the Coen brothers' pastiche of *The Long Goodbye*, *The Big Lebowski*. I borrow from Christian Moraru's notion of rewriting to recognize not only the similarities between the novels and film but to examine the differences. Much of the significance of Pynchon's thematic argument in *Inherent Vice* can be teased out by exploring his deviations from the texts he rewrites. Examining Pynchon's interplay with the tropes of detective fiction and his meandering from the form's conventions affords a deeper understanding of not only the novel but the novel's place in Pynchon's construction of contemporary resistance. The end result situates Pynchon's site for resistance as lying in an incremental drifting away from notions of public and private property and into a living example of an economic system based on the commons.

Chapter 6 turns to Pynchon's most recent novel and the first work by Pynchon written after the global participatory democracy movements that emerged in 2011. *Bleeding Edge*'s Maxine Turnow takes a journey into DeepArcher that mirrors Doc's adventures in the fog of *Inherent Vice*. While Doc has the advantage of sixties optimism, Maxine approaches her investigations into power and resistance with a twenty-first-century apprehension. She finds room for resistance in immaterial labor and cyberspace commons, and she gets wrapped up in the most complete representation of Empire in any Pynchon novel. Through it all, Linda Hutcheon's postmodern concept that we are all complicit in the very systems we condemn informs Maxine's actions and provides a means of investigating conflicting ideologies. Ultimately, like Maxine, we negotiate a space between conspicuous consumption and total asceticism—searching for a way to live a contemporary life that is less than a sellout and more than a hermitage.

In this search, Maxine finds hope in the unlikeliest of places: the Deep Web and her sons' computer games. Ziggy and Otis construct an alternate Manhattan in the Deep Web, Zigotisopolis, a place where big-money developers, dotcom venture capitalists, and sanitized gentrification are replaced with community spaces and reconstructed families. Much like the Occupy movement itself, it reclaims space that was once public, then privatized—Zuccotti Park for Occupy, the Deep Web for Ziggy and Otis—and reverts it to the commons. Like Occupy, Ziggy and Otis delegitimize power through their occupation of this space. Their alternative does not make demands of this delegitimized power structure. It instead demonstrates a subjunctive world where democracy, autonomy, horizontal power, and consensus rule the day.

Chapter 7 seeks to tie together the complex notions of power and resistance running through Pynchon's oeuvre by examining the 'ukuleles in Pynchon's novels. This enigmatic little instrument appears in every novel of Pynchon's after *The Crying of Lot 49*. It appears in a variety of contexts and cannot be read as a unified metaphor. Nonetheless, when one considers the history of the 'ukulele as a cultural artifact, it becomes a useful motif for Pynchon's explorations into Empire and the multitude. Ultimately, the 'ukulele instructs a method of resistance by constructing a culture that reclaims the artifacts of global commodity culture and repurposes them. It also answers the selfishness of economies of gain and accumulation with the mutual benefits of an economy of social relations.

Finally, I conclude this study with a suggestion for where all this research on Pynchon can be expanded outside of Pynchon studies. I introduce a heuristic that affords scholars a means of beginning with Hardt and Negri, moving through economic and literary theory, and applying criticism of global consumer capitalism to contemporary fiction. I explore similar engagements with power and resistance in the works of Japanese author Haruki Murakami and Scottish author Ali Smith, then suggest passageways into the works of authors Paul Murray, David Mitchell, Kiran Desai, and others. I apply notions of participatory democracy promulgated by the Occupy movement in its contemporary, global format. By doing this, I hope to facilitate a shift in the study of resistance in Pynchon's novels. Scholarly explorations of Pynchon's engagement with sixties counterculture have been ubiquitous and thorough. However, as Francesca Polletta argues in "Participatory Democracy's Moment," many of the resistance movements of the sixties tended to be as hierarchical as the system they opposed. This vertical alignment tended to be one of sixties counterculture's fatal flaws. Polletta argues that resistance movements become more democratic when they adopt horizontal structures. Much of the scholarship on Occupy echoes this notion. The purpose and value of this study resides in understanding this evolution from sixties counterculture to contemporary movements for participatory democracy and Pynchon's evolution in response to the neoliberal takeover. In the end, I am searching for new, exciting ways to find pockets of autonomy and social justice that challenge the ubiquitous, smothering ideology of neoliberalism.

CHAPTER 2

Vineland and the Insomniac Unavenged

THE FINAL PAGES of *Vineland* (1990) mark a shift in Thomas Pynchon's oeuvre. Relative to his first three novels, *Vineland* ends on a more hopeful note. Protagonist Prairie Wheeler has successfully completed her search for her mother, despite the interference of the diabolical federal agent Brock Vond. In a playful allusion to *Star Wars*, the Darth Vader–like Brock descends from the sky and tells Prairie, "I'm your father." Prairie quips back, "But you can't be my father . . . my blood type is A. Yours is preparation H" (376). This exchange immediately precedes the end of Brock's power and the beginning of Prairie's liberation. Brock dies shortly thereafter and is escorted to an underworld by a pair of shady tow truck drivers. Peace reigns among the Wobblies, communists, activists, snitches, madmen, punk rockers, and drug dealers who, along with Prairie, populate the Becker-Traverse family reunion. Even the dog comes home with a face full of feathers from the blue jays that attacked in the novel's opening paragraph. This ending gives hope, specifically, for a resistance to the power structure represented by Brock Vond. The irony of Pynchon lighting his spark of hope for resistance in 1984 is salient. Beyond the irony, though, and beyond the mixed and often negative reception that *Vineland* received upon its publication, the novel provides an entry into ideas that Pynchon goes on to explore and expand in his next four novels. *Vineland* catalyzes Pynchon's articulation of power and resistance in a globalized society. Though the novel precedes Michael Hardt and Antonio Negri's critical trilogy *Empire*, *Multitude*, and *Commonwealth*, it is helpful to explore Hardt and Negri's concepts of Empire and the multitude in conjunction with this shift in Pynchon's oeuvre. Reading Pynchon through the lens of Hardt and Negri clarifies Pynchon's conceptions of power and resistance. It also helps alleviate David Harvey's justified criticism that Hardt and Negri offer no concrete model for resistance through the multitude. The power structure in Pynchon's novels is very much in line with Hardt and Negri's concept of Empire, and Pynchon constructs a multitude in *Vineland* that can serve as a model of resistance to Empire.

Compared to *Vineland*, Pynchon's earlier novels had bleak endings. In *The Crying of Lot 49*, protagonist Oedipa Maas watches her life unravel as she gets wrapped up in the mystery of the possibly fictitious Tristero system. Like the rocket bomb that he is indelibly tied to, *Gravity's Rainbow* protagonist Tyrone Slothrop ends the novel fragmented and dispersed. Likewise, Sidney Stencil is swallowed in a freak waterspout on the final page of *V.* In all three cases, an overarching, sometimes seemingly supernatural or legendary power structure guides and manipulates the characters. Power is abstract and haunting. It has mysterious names: V. or the Tristero. In the case of *Gravity's Rainbow*, it is only ominously referred to as They. These power structures are far less abstract or supernatural in *Vineland*, which makes them seem far more surmountable. As N. Katherine Hayles observes, "[T]here are also chances for recovery in *Vineland*. Precisely because it operates on a diminished scale, the problems seem more solvable, more as if they had a human face in contrast to the inhuman, looming presences that haunt *Gravity's Rainbow*" (25). As the supernatural They or the legendary Tristero, systems of power become a force greater than Tyrone Slothrop or Oedipa Maas can comprehend, much less oppose. Prairie Wheeler, on the other hand, can look her oppressor in the eye and make a joke about hemorrhoid cream. The human face of the oppressor makes possibilities for resistance palpable.

Of course, reactions to the endings of novels are typically emotional. To say that Pynchon's first three novels have bleak endings and *Vineland* is more hopeful is to have a subjective response, and subjectivities differ. In "*The Crying of Lot 49* and Other California Novels," Thomas Hill Schaub finds hope in the end of *Crying* and a dearth of revolutionary possibilities in *Vineland* and *Inherent Vice*. Schaub reads the Tristero as a real, revolutionary alternative to hegemonic power, stating, "[*The Crying of Lot 49*] at least leaves open the possibility that something unspoken but widely felt is afoot" (31). Oedipa Maas has found the Tristero in many corners, among far-right wingnuts and defense contractors and Jacobean plays and the bones at the bottom of a man-made lake. Together, those whom Oedipa encounters leave "open the prospect of an 'alternative' America—at the very least a way of remaining 'alien' yet 'relevant' to the nation" (32). Schaub describes the endings of *Vineland* and *Inherent Vice* as more fantastical: the Becker-Traverse family reunion that plays out as a mixture of space opera (with the Vader-like Vond) and myth (Vato and Blood carrying Brock into the underworld); Doc Sportello in *Inherent Vice* ends enshrouded in fog, seeking hope in one of the most hopeless places in the world—a Southern California freeway.

The primary distinction between Schaub's argument and mine resides in conceptions of revolutionary possibilities. During his interview in the documentary *The Examined Life*, Michael Hardt distinguishes two types of revolutions. The first "involves the replacement of a ruling elite with another better, in many ways, ruling elite." In a sense, this is what the Tristero seeks in *The*

Crying of Lot 49. It is revolution as regime change, whether they are aristocrats fighting aristocrats in medieval Italy or Yoyodyne employees passing notes under the noses of stockholders at a board meeting. Tristero is a more unified, hierarchical, vertical style of revolution. As Hardt notes, this type of revolution is largely discredited. There are few, if any, examples in history of a violent overthrow of one regime with a second regime that didn't utilize the means of their ascent to power to repress and control the population they came to rule. To use Althusserian terms, violent regime change requires the immediate implementation of Repressive State Apparatuses.

The second type of revolution Hardt suggests—one, he noted in 2008, that hadn't been tried—can be envisioned "as just the removal of all of those forms of authority—state power, the power of capital—that stop people from expressing their natural abilities to rule themselves." This type of revolution was attempted on large scales in Egypt and Tunisia during the Arab Spring and on smaller scales throughout southern Europe shortly afterward. In the United States, this type of revolution played out on a small scale during the Occupy movement. Finding hope at the end of both *Vineland* and *Inherent Vice* lies in understanding this second type of revolution.

In his reflection on Occupy, Bernard E. Harcourt develops the notion of "political disobedience" in opposition to civil disobedience. The latter, Harcourt explains, "aims not to displace the lawmaking institutions or the structure of legal governance, but rather to change the existing laws by demonstrating their injustice" (46–47). Inherent in civil disobedience is a respect for the existing dominant political and economic systems and the belief that either or both can be fixed by incremental changes to policy or practice. Occupy was characterized by its refusal to address specific policy changes for which they advocated. Much of the mainstream media attacked Occupy for this lack of civil disobedience, this lack of respect for the rule of law or existing institutions, this lack of a specific, quantifiable goal. Because of this lack, much of the mainstream media concluded that Occupy did not know what they wanted. This misinterpretation undermined the theoretical underpinnings of the movement.

Harcourt clarifies, "[N]o individual has the authorial voice to represent the movement or to make demands on its behalf" (53). Instead, Occupy is a horizontal, nonhierarchical movement. It exists to give voice to varied concerns, develop a consensus when possible, and develop the basic skills of democracy and self-rule. One of the essential points, according to Harcourt, is to make sure "there is a horizontal, nonhierarchical, and rhizomic quality to the leadership" (57). Many Occupy activists and writers acknowledge that, even in leaderless movements, there tend to be at least implicit leaders. Understanding this, Occupy strives to develop structural mechanisms to minimize this type of implicit leadership, to keep the movement as "leaderless" as possible. In *The Democracy Project*, David Graeber explains the rationale behind this. Graeber argues that "police will always try to identify leaders, and, if they can't find any, create a leadership structure by making arrangements directly with the negotiators and then insisting that the negotiators (and marshals) enforce them" (45). This is essentially a control tactic that robs movements of their agility. Pynchon demonstrates this in the People's Republic of Rock and Roll (PR³) sections of *Vineland*. Student protestors essentially occupied the College of the Surf. They began the work of developing a new society, yet their first move was to choose a leader. In this sense, they follow the more traditional of the two options Hardt outlines for a revolution: they sought to develop a new elite to displace the current elite. The members of the PR³ selected Weed Atman as their leader. This simplified matters for Brock Vond. With a leader in place, Brock could disable the movement by disabling Weed. Brock initiated several small-scale tactics to harass Weed. When these weren't enough, Brock conspired to murder Weed. The fall of the PR³ came at the moment of Weed's murder.

The civil disobedience and hierarchical structures of movements like PR³ represent the type of activism that many of the early Occupy planners sought to avoid. Graeber observes that activism during the first decade of the twenty-first century was characterized "by vast top-down antiwar coalitions for whom political action was largely a matter of marching around with signs" (7). Graeber and his fellow anarchists at the initial Occupy planning meetings sought to avoid this, to implement a horizontal, leaderless structure. They also sought to create a movement that was larger than a single issue. Reflecting on Occupy in *The Democracy Project*, Graeber concludes, "[I]t's precisely OWS's most revolutionary aspects—its refusal to recognize the legitimacy of existing political institutions, its willingness to challenge the fundamental premises of our economic system—that [are] at the heart of its appeal" (99).

For Harcourt, this "refusal to recognize the legitimacy of existing political institutions" is the key to political disobedience. According to Harcourt, "'Political disobedience' . . . resists the very way in which we are governed. It resists the structure of partisan politics, the demand for policy reforms, the call for party identification. It rejects the very idea of expressing or honoring 'the highest respect for law.' It refuses to willingly accept the sanctions meted out by our legal and political system. It challenges the conventional way in which political governance takes place and laws are enforced" (46). A large part of Occupy's legacy and revolutionary possibility lies in this notion of moving away from a system of either requesting policy changes while keeping the systems of power intact or replacing one ruling elite with another ruling elite.

It instead moves toward direct action in the form of creating spaces in which horizontal structures built on direct democracy can grow and flourish. In *Pynchon and the Political*, Samuel Thomas foresees this type of change in Prairie Wheeler, characterizing her revolutionary impulses as "doing it for yourself" (148). Building on Thomas's argument, I will examine the ways in which both the Becker-Traverse reunion and the Sisterhood of Kunoichi Attentives create spaces for more horizontal and democratic structures, and they retreat from the stultifying control of neoliberal power structures. My argument will not contradict Schaub's reading of hope in the end of the novels. It will simply move the paradigm of hope away from the type of revolution characterized by replacing one ruling elite with another and toward a revolution of political disobedience and a removal of or from state and capitalist power to spaces in which people are allowed to express their ability to rule themselves.

1984

It is ironic that Pynchon situates his hope for resistance in the year 1984. It is the year in which George Orwell set his fascist dystopia, after all.[1] Several critics have commented on Pynchon's irony. For example, Molly Hite describes the 1980s as "a time when the phrase 'American Left' sounds dangerously like an oxymoron" (140). Though Hite does not expand upon this notion, her point can be articulated fairly easily. In 1984 Ronald Reagan was reelected. That reelection signifies the heart of the neoliberal takeover. The eighties were a time when multinational corporations, governments, and supranational agencies conglomerated into the power system that Hardt and Negri refer to as Empire. In *A Brief History of Neoliberalism*, David Harvey specifically traces this eighties takeover as it occurred through the policies of former Federal Reserve chairman Paul Volcker, President Reagan, Prime Minister Margaret Thatcher, and Chinese Communist Party leader Deng Xiaoping. Harvey focuses on Reagan's policies in the early 1980s that attacked organized labor. According to Harvey, "It took less than six months in 1983 to reverse nearly 40 per cent of the decisions made during the 1970s that had been, in the view of business, too favourable to labour" (52). Reagan attacked labor unions through specific federal policies. He pushed to move industrialization from its union-controlled centers in the American Northeast and northern Midwest to so-called right-to-work states in the South and to foreign lands with lax labor oversight. Harvey further observes that, under Reagan, "public assets were freely passed over into private domain" (52). This private appropriation of public goods can be viewed as one of capitalism's final daggers into the preindustrial tradition of the Marxist commons.

While Reagan attacked unions ideologically for their role in regulating markets that, according to Reagan's neoliberal ideology, should remain unregulated, his secretary of the treasury, James Baker, "breathed new life" into the International Monetary Fund (IMF). Brady "used the IMF to impose structural adjustment on Mexico and protect New York bankers from default" (*Neoliberalism* 73). These policies, which regulate markets in favor of banks and multinational corporations while preaching in favor of unregulated markets, were mirrored globally by the neoliberal moves of Thatcher, Volcker, and Deng. This becomes the first historical context in which Pynchon situates *Vineland*: an America where labor unions are under attack, public wealth is being pirated by private enterprise, and supranational organizations are superseding the authority of representative democracies.

Additionally, 1984 represents a time of both increased law-enforcement funding and the acceleration of paramilitary forces fighting in the so-called War on Drugs. In "The Fourth Amendment and Other Inconveniences," David Thoreen elucidates the exponential growth of law enforcement and liberal forfeiture laws that characterized Reagan's domestic policy. The 1980s saw a dismantling of the Fourth Amendment and law enforcement agencies granted increased powers for surveillance and the seizure of property. Thoreen explores the role of the Federal Emergency Management Agency (FEMA) and the Department of Justice in expanding these surveillance and forfeiture practices. He even posits Louis Giuffrida, former head of FEMA under Reagan, as the real-life model for Pynchon's Brock Vond. Giuffrida, like Vond, propagated a sort of rehashed Cold War against certain groups of Americans, a war that greatly infringed on constitutionally protected civil rights, and a war against an abstract: the Drug War. Combining Harvey's and Thoreen's characterizations of 1984, *Vineland* is set against a backdrop of neoliberal takeover and authoritarian practices used to quell any resistance to this takeover. It becomes the perfect setting for the assembly of Wobblies, communists, sixties revolutionaries, and punk rockers who gather at the end of the novel.

Beyond the accumulation of neoliberal power, the 1980s represent a cultural void for some critics. In *Pynchon and History*, Shawn Smith addresses this cultural void. "Rather than the real values that make for a just society, such as charity, compassion, and responsibility to one's self and others," he states, "*Vineland* shows an America largely blinded by the illusory and empty values of the culture industry and the consumerist ethos of the mid-eighties" (106). These illusory and empty values are particularly salient with regard to television. Several critics have addressed the motif of television—the Tube, as Pynchon refers to it—in *Vineland*. Perhaps the most in-depth analysis of the Tube in *Vineland* comes in Brian McHale's *Constructing Postmodernism*. McHale describes "an ontology of television" in which "TV worlds insinuate themselves into the real world to pluralize the latter" (126, 129). As McHale argues, the Tube shifts the ways in which the characters develop their conception of reality. This is demonstrated several times throughout the novel. For example, Prairie's boyfriend, Isaiah Two Four, cheers up Prairie in a particularly stressful moment by assuring her that the worst is nearly over. He tells her, "Only a couple more commercials, just hold on, Prair" (105). DEA agent Hector Zuñiga is not only addicted to the Tube, he finds validation for his life in cop shows. The motif persists throughout the book. It works both to comment on and analyze the impact of the Tube on contemporary American culture and to establish a backdrop of a cultural void created from television's monological blue light.

This adds to the world and the context where Pynchon establishes a site of resistance against Empire: a society so hypnotized by television that its citizens barely notice the neoliberal revolution taking place around them. As David Thoreen explains, "Like Washington Irving's Rip Van Winkle, who slept through the political transition from monarchy to democracy, Zoyd Wheeler and the contemporary American voter have slept through a change in governments, this time from democracy to fascism" (217). This shift from a social safety net to a neoliberal state, from democracy to a new sovereignty, from the engaged citizenry of the sixties to the Thanatoids bathed in the blue light of the eighties, creates more than an ironic situation for a nascent multitude. It creates, as Molly Hite observed, a situation in which any sense of the American left seems like an oxymoron. However, no matter how dominant a power structure is, its power can never be complete. Empires inspire resistance movements. Exploitation breeds revolution. Economic historian Karl Polanyi explores this trend in *The Great Transformation*. He discusses double movements or countermovements that arise spontaneously within unregulated marketplaces. These countermovements typically lack a strong ideological or theoretical backing. Instead, they simply recognize the inevitable annihilation of land and labor inherent in a liberal economy and rise to protect both humans and the environment.

Hints of budding countermovements lacking a strong ideological or theoretical backing can be read in glancing passages throughout the novel. One example occurs when Prairie and Ché reminisce about the Great South Coast Plaza Eyeshadow Raid (327). South Coast Plaza is a large shopping mall in Orange County. Like many malls, it is freeway adjacent. Nearly a square mile of land was stripped of all vegetation to construct a giant parking lot and large, air-conditioned buildings dedicated to selling consumables, most of which were made in overseas sweatshops. At every stage, from the freeway to the parking lot to the air-conditioning, this environmentally destructive place exemplifies what Polanyi describes as treating land as a commodity. The minimum-wage employees inside and the sweatshop workers producing the consumables sold at the mall exemplify Polanyi's notion of treating labor as a commodity. On the surface, Prairie and Ché's raid may be a simple romp, kids having fun. However, the narrator describes security guards being overwhelmed by the sheer number of roller-skating adolescent shoplifters. The numbers are too great to contend with. This resistance through sheer numbers is reminiscent of Wobblie protestors who would flood a protest in a mass so great that local jails could not contain them all. Police had no recourse for the Wobblies, who outnumbered the available spaces in the local jails, other than to allow them to protest.[2] This somewhat symbolically links Prairie to her Wobblie great-grandparents. Of course, Ché, Prairie, and their compatriots were not outwardly staging a protest; they were shoplifting. Nonetheless, the girls' raid demonstrates the machinations of a countermovement. They rise spontaneously, without great theoretical or ideological grounding, to attack a system that exploits both land and labor.

Of course, this attack only provides an example of a countermovement. It is not a metaphor for or a guidebook to revolution, the most notable distinction being that the girls are simultaneously participating in and rising up against global commodity culture. This is an example of what Pynchon refers to in his foreword to *1984* as cognitive dissonance: "to be able to believe two contradictory truths at the same time" (xi). Pynchon goes on to acknowledge, "We all do it" (xi). Pynchon also explores this very human tendency throughout his subsequent work. His four most recent novels are populated by characters simultaneously resisting and complying with consumer corporate culture. The eponymous characters of *Mason & Dixon* frequently criticize burgeoning globalization built on the backs of slaves and exploited workers while sitting in coffeehouses, eating and drinking the very commodities produced by this unjust system. *Inherent Vice*'s Doc Sportello actively rejects the materialism of 1970 Los Angeles while driving the freeways in a Dodge Dart he loves as if it were sentient. This complexity is perhaps most directly confronted in *Against the Day*, when Reef Traverse and Flaco meet in a café in Nice.[3] Flaco notes that the café is a perfect target for anarchist bombers hoping to attack the bourgeoisie. Reef disagrees, stating, "I've got to where I like these cafés, all this to-and-fro of the city life—rather be out here enjoying it than worried all the time about some bomb going off" (850). When the bomb does go off, Pynchon describes the attack as horrific and largely senseless. The graphic language he uses to describe the carnage suggests Pynchon's own horror at this form of resistance. The entire scene also seems to advocate only a partial withdrawal from consumables or a marketplace. Indeed, even anarchist bombers Reef and

Flaco have come to enjoy some of consumer society's trappings. Pynchon seems to be arguing, instead, for an economy that prioritizes social relations over the marketplace—an ideology that stands in direct opposition to neoliberalism, which subverts all aspects of life to the marketplace. As this example demonstrates, Pynchon does not seem to wish to blow up the metaphorical café—in fact, he wants to get his coffee there. He simply rejects an ideology that privileges the café over humans. Examining the Great Eyeshadow Raid relative to Pynchon's subsequent works, the flashback can be read as a problematic rejection of (though not advancement against) neoliberalism. Pynchon's more articulated forms of resistance—which adhere more closely to Hardt and Negri's concept of the multitude and the notions of political disobedience articulated by Occupy theorists—are demonstrated in the examples of the Becker-Traverse reunion and the Sisterhood of Kunoichi Attentives, which I discuss below. The Great Eyeshadow Raid further highlights the notion that, though it is ironic and sometimes seemingly oxymoronic to situate hope for resistance to Empire in 1984, the height of the neoliberal takeover is the place where the countermovement begins to coalesce.

The Birth of Empire

Pynchon's examinations of both this neoliberal takeover and the nascent multitude mark the beginning of the stylistic and thematic shift that occurs in *Vineland*. Pynchon begins to drift away from a sixties radicalism concerned with authoritarian governments and characterized by paranoia. He drifts toward a more articulated concept of power that has much in common with Hardt and Negri's concept of Empire. Hardt and Negri contend "that sovereignty has taken a new form, composed of a series of national and supranational organisms united under a single logic of rule. This new global form of sovereignty is what we call Empire" (*Empire* xii). Hardt and Negri envision Empire as a networked structure without a single sovereign. Instead, government agencies, multinational corporations, and international financial institutions—which, at times, supersede the jurisdiction of national governments—act in concert to ensure that wealth and power remain in the hands of (to borrow an Occupy metaphor) a global 1 percent. Hardt and Negri's Empire is not the old model of a colonial empire exploiting the natural resources of regions with weaker military powers. It is a new form of sovereignty.

Hardt and Negri reject from the outset "the idea that order is dictated by a single power and a single center of rationality *transcendent* to global forces, guiding the various phases of historical development according to its conscious and all-seeing plan, something like a conspiracy theory of globalization"

(*Empire* 3). Indeed, Empire is neither an authoritarian individual ruling with an iron fist nor a conspiracy of the excessively wealthy. It is not "They" of *Gravity's Rainbow*. Instead, it is better understood as a horizontal network. Individual power among the humans composing the network shifts, with some humans rising relative to others, some profiting immensely, and some falling out of power, yet the structure—the single logic of rule—remains intact. This new paradigm of sovereignty, for Hardt and Negri, should not be defined "in purely negative terms." Specifically, one should avoid defining Empire "by the definitive decline of the sovereign nation-states, by the deregulation of international markets, by the end of antagonistic conflict among state subjects, and so forth" (*Empire* 13). These negative terms are too limiting. While Empire is characterized by the decline of sovereign nation-states, the leaders of those nation-states retain a certain amount of power in negotiating global trade during events like the G-20 summits. While an ideology of deregulation does characterize the neoliberal underpinnings of Empire, international markets are regulated by treaties such as the North American Free Trade Agreement and by organizations like the WTO. Antagonistic conflict continues among state subjects. These antagonisms create a permanent state of exception that lends authority to Empire. So while factors such as the declining power of nation-states, the notion of deregulation, and violent conflict add to the composition of Empire, the concept is far more complicated. Hardt and Negri maintain, "The new paradigm is both system and hierarchy, centralized construction of norms and far-reaching production of legitimacy, spread out over world space" (*Empire* 13). The structural logic of Empire can be viewed as "governance without government," an ideological consensus of rule (14).

The dialectic of Empire can be further understood in relation to its antithesis, the multitude. The multitude stands in opposition to Empire and is composed of, in a sense, the workers of the world. The contemporary workers of the world who construct the multitude differ from the early twentieth-century concept of the Industrial Workers of the World and Big Bill Haywood's notion of One Big Union. Instead, Hardt and Negri characterize twenty-first-century labor as "biopolitical production." Hardt and Negri use the term "'biopolitical production' to highlight that it not only involves the production of material goods in a strictly economic sense but also touches on and produces all facets of social life, economic, cultural, and political" (*Multitude* xvi). For Hardt and Negri, the industrial concept of eight hours for labor, eight hours for leisure, and eight hours for sleep have been replaced by the immaterial and affective labor of the twenty-first century. Immaterial labor is characterized by "immaterial products, such as knowledge, information, communication, a relationship, or an emotional response" (*Multitude* 108). The relationships and emotional responses of immaterial labor, in particular, compose "affective labor," that is, "labor that produces or manipulates affects such as a feeling of ease, well-being, satisfaction, excitement, or passion" (108). Thus, the global twenty-first-century workers who produce commodities, combined with those who produce knowledge, information, delivery systems, communication, and affects, who are all exploited in common by Empire's push for accumulation and the neoliberal ideology for which the logic of the marketplace saturates every aspect of life—cultural, economic, and political—compose the multitude.

While the multitude is bound by Empire's common exploitation of them, Hardt and Negri are careful to distinguish between a falsely unifying concept of "the people" and a multitude that allows its members to retain their singularities. For Hardt and Negri, the concept of "the people" robs humans of their individual concerns by imposing a homogeneity of concerns upon them. The multitude rejects this homogeneity. According to Hardt and Negri, "The multitude, in contrast, is many. The multitude is composed of innumerable internal differences that can never be reduced to a unity or a single identity—different cultures, races, ethnicities, genders, and sexual orientations; different forms of labor; different ways of living; different views of the world and different desires. The multitude is a multiplicity of all these singular differences" (*Multitude* xiv). By maintaining internal differences, the multitude need not choose between singularity and plurality. The multitude instead maintains its singularities but works in concert against the common exploitation of Empire.

These concepts articulated by Hardt and Negri provide both a vocabulary and a theoretical framework for understanding the shift that occurs in Pynchon's oeuvre beginning with *Vineland*. While Pynchon has wrestled with a new paradigm of global sovereignty at least since the time of his initial publication of "Under the Rose" in 1961, *Vineland* marks the more complex and fully theorized concept of a horizontal network of global sovereignty similar to that which Hardt and Negri define as Empire. While Pynchon has constructed a force of resistance to Empire from the Whole Sick Crew in *V.* to the Counterforce in *Gravity's Rainbow*, the motley cast of characters surrounding Prairie Wheeler in *Vineland* represents a more fully realized network of biopolitical laborers who work in concert against Empire while maintaining their singularities. Viewing labor as immaterial and affective further helps situate the sites for resistance Pynchon creates throughout *Vineland*.

Empire and the Permanent State of Exception

This definition of global sovereignty was first articulated by Hardt and Negri in their 1999 text *Empire*. Of course, *Vineland* precedes this definition by nearly a decade. Nonetheless, as Pynchon brings the systems of power he criticizes down to earth in *Vineland*, his description of these systems matches Hardt and Negri's description of Empire. A convenient example of Pynchon's Empire lies at the point where Pynchon moves the narrative of *Vineland* to Japan, places it in the perspective of Takeshi Fumimoto, and weaves Cold War–era monster movie tropes into his pastiche.

Takeshi, at this point, is called to investigate the destruction of a Chipco research laboratory. Little information is given about what type of corporation Chipco is, exactly, but the size of its laboratory, its fleet of passenger helicopters, its private railway station, and other signifiers of opulence suggest that it is a wealthy and powerful corporation. Takeshi is called in because, apparently, a Godzilla-type sea monster stepped out of the ocean and stomped on the research lab. Like so many Pynchon characters, Takeshi regards the official story with skepticism. He does not know how much Professor Wawazume—who recently wrote the floater for Chipco's insurance coverage—knows. Takeshi encounters Minoru in the monster's footprint. Minoru shows Takeshi the shrapnel from an Eastern bloc explosive with modifications made in South Africa. The device reminds both Takeshi and Minoru of time they spent together in the Himalayas dealing with a nuclear incident.

This particular moment elucidates Pynchon's construction of the system of power in the novel. First, Chipco has clearly hired an outside explosives expert to blow up its research laboratory and make the explosion look like a monster's footprint. Wawazume's insurance company was somehow complicit in Chipco's actions. This investigation brings together a seemingly freelance insurance investigator and a government bomb-squad expert. Takeshi acknowledges that his independence as an investigator is nominal. Despite his lack of a company pin, he is indelibly tied to the multinational corporate system. Minoru presents an interesting case as a government bomb-squad expert in a nation that not only has not been at war for over thirty years but that ostensibly has no standing army (though, of course, the Japanese Self-Defense Forces call that assertion into question). Minoru's work investigating explosions and defusing bombs keeps him so busy that his only moments of peace occur when he is in transit, typically by airplane. The mere fact that Minoru and Takeshi know each other so well suggests that corporate and national interests are often inseparable. The investigators' knowledge of Czech and South African explosives and bomb scares on the Indian/Tibetan border demonstrates the international scope of their interests. They are clearly tied to something much larger than a single insurance claim. They are operating as appendages of a system of power that exists as a network of corporate, national, and global interests. This network is extremely wealthy, powerful, and corrupt. The narrator observes, "Far above them some planetwide struggle has been going on for years, power accumulating, lives worth less, personnel changing, still governed by the rules of gang war and blood feud, though it had far outgrown them in scale" (146). Professor Wawazume's complicity with this system of power keeps him wealthy and powerful enough to have paparazzi following him. Minoru, who refuses to believe that a monster made the footprint, unaccountably disappears, much like Joseph Heller's Dunbar, who is disappeared in *Catch-22*.[4] Takeshi falls somewhere between Wawazume and Minoru. He neither profits from the Empire nor challenges it. He is simply swept along by it.

Takeshi's passivity in this scene could be familiar territory. Like Tyrone Slothrop in *Gravity's Rainbow* and Oedipa Maas in *The Crying of Lot 49*, Takeshi is paranoid and subject to the whims of gigantic power systems. However, Takeshi's paranoia is validated more by his affinity for amphetamines and their common side effects than as the result of a nefarious and incomprehensible They. The gigantic power systems, again, are brought down to earth. They are a network represented by a multinational technology corporation and the militaries of a few different nations. Pynchon further explores this network by following Takeshi and Minoru from the footprint of Empire to the most clear-cut representative of the machinations of Empire in the novel, Brock Vond.

Takeshi and Minoru, seeking clarification about the explosives debris they found under the footprint, go to a conference of federal prosecutors in search of an explosives expert. Takeshi encounters Brock Vond at this conference. The nature of the conference is not explored, but it is nonetheless curious. As a federal prosecutor for the Department of Justice, Brock's job would be more concerned with domestic laws and domestic affairs, not international laws and international affairs. Thus, his presence at an international conference would raise questions regarding what type of information the prosecutors might be sharing. Clearly, since Minoru knows he can find an expert at the conference who can identify on sight Eastern European and South African explosives by the debris they leave behind, the prosecutors' scope of competence expands beyond basic legal issues. The presence of explosives experts and prosecutors like Brock who specialize in quelling domestic resistance suggests that this conference is about sharing information regarding the maintenance of multinational corporate, national, and supranational interests. In other words, Brock is at a conference designed to perpetuate the power of Empire. The fact that the conference is in Japan may suggest that Pynchon is parodying the paranoid eighties notion that Japanese economic prowess would take over the United States. Perhaps, if Brock had survived, his next annual conference would be in Beijing. The humor behind the parody, of course, lies in Pynchon's demonstration of power stretching far beyond the notion of individual nation-states and expanding into a global network. Further, Brock's presence in Tokyo could seem out of character. Throughout the rest of the novel, he is concerned solely with domestic issues—quelling sixties rebellion and waging a drug war. At the conference, he is part of a global force as well as a national one, again reifying Pynchon's exploration of a power that is no longer characterized by simple authoritarianism.

Throughout the novel, Brock is constructed as a face of Empire. He is tied to international business concerns, domestic disputes, upper echelons of governmental powers, and to wars fought by Americans against Americans. These wars are particularly relevant to Hardt and Negri's conception of Empire. Hardt and Negri argue that "war has become a general condition: there may be a cessation of hostilities at times and in certain places, but lethal violence is present as a constant potentiality, ready always and everywhere to erupt" (*Multitude* 4). In other words, Empire maintains its power through a politics of perpetual warfare. Hardt and Negri explain that periods of war suspend democracy, subverting human rights by claiming that winning the war supersedes the rights of individuals, and if war can be perpetual, the suspension of human rights can be perpetual as well. *Vineland*'s Sasha Gates echoes this sentiment when she recalls that, prior to World War II, her life had been about fighting exploitative corporate powers by working with unions, participating in general strikes, advocating for the release of wrongfully imprisoned union leaders, and campaigning for the labor-friendly gubernatorial candidate Culbert Olson. However, Sasha says, "The war changed everything. The deal was, no strikes for the duration. Lot of us thought it was some last desperate capitalist maneuver, a way to get the Nation mobilized under a Leader, no different than Hitler or Stalin" (77). Sasha, like Hardt and Negri, observes that the resistance to Empire often takes a backseat to the ostensibly more important issue of winning a war. Thus, Empire makes war "the primary organizing principle of society" (Hardt and Negri, *Multitude* 12). Brock Vond becomes a figurative general of this perpetual warfare.

He fights first a war against sixties student activism and, second, the so-called War on Drugs. Of course, neither of these are wars according to the traditional usage of the term. As David Thoreen observes, "The War on Drugs is the fourth non-war war of the century, after the 'war' on the economic problems of the Great Depression, the Cold War, and President Johnson's War on Poverty" (224–25). Thoreen further argues that the War on Drugs is fought more like a traditional war than the previous "non-war wars." Brock demonstrates this. He organizes forces against the student activists of the PR[3] and then the residents of Vineland, who either passively condone marijuana cultivation and sales in their town or actively grow and sell marijuana. In the

War on Drugs, in particular, the narrative voice of *Vineland* takes on a martial tone. The narrator explains that

> most of Brock's troops had departed after terrorizing the neighborhood for weeks, running up and down the dirt lanes in formation chanting "War-on-drugs! War-on-drugs!" strip-searching folks in public, killing dogs, rabbits, cats, and chickens, pouring herbicide down wells that couldn't remotely be used to irrigate dope crops, and acting, indeed, as several neighbors observed, as if they had invaded some helpless land far away, instead of a short plane ride from San Francisco. (357)

Hardt and Negri claim, "High intensity police action, of course, is often indistinguishable from low-intensity warfare" (*Multitude* 39). The narrative description of Brock's war on Vineland supports this conflation. The police forces are described as "troops," they run in formation like soldiers, they engage in chemical warfare, and, as the neighbors observe, they act as if they are invading some land far away. Brock's version of the War on Drugs is described as an invasion of American soil by the troops of Empire. The language is similar when Brock organizes local police forces to invade the College of the Surf and dismantle the PR[3]. After the invasion, Brock brings several of the students to a facility that closely resembles a prisoner-of-war camp. The camp, which is named the Political Re-Education Program, or PREP, turns the prisoners of Brock's war on sixties activism into double agents for the Department of Justice. The ironic name, PREP, adds to the dark humor. Brock turns sixties hippies into eighties preppies. Most importantly, however, through his invasions and prison camps, Brock demonstrates that his work goes beyond the Department of Justice and engages in Empire's politics of perpetual war, specifically the permanent state of exception this perpetual war imposes upon civil rights.

Beyond his role in these domestic wars—which could perhaps be described as civil wars—Brock holds onto his role as an agent of Empire by a tenuous thread. Granted, Brock is incredibly powerful, particularly with regard to characters like Frenesi, Flash, and Zoyd. Even his partner Roscoe seems to be under Brock's sovereignty. Roscoe handles Brock the way an amateur snake handler deals with the cobra in his hand: keeping it an arm's length away, perpetually aware that it could strike at any second. Brock works throughout the novel to perpetuate the power of Empire. He seeks to be part of the upper echelons of power. Nonetheless, he himself is not a metonym for Empire. He is simply a part of the network.

As I mention above, Pynchon brings the power systems down to earth in *Vineland*. He mentions them by name, identifying them as "Hitler, Roosevelt, Kennedy, Nixon, Hoover, Mafia, CIA, Reagan, Kissinger, that collection of names and their tragic interweaving that stood not constellated above in any nightwide remoteness of light, but below, diminished to the last unfaceable American secret" (372). Thus, for Pynchon, the once-supernatural They becomes the earthly leaders who consolidated neoliberal power: the fascist Adolf Hitler; the antilabor, corporate-friendly presidents Ronald Reagan and Richard Nixon; criminal organizations like the Mafia and federal organizations like the CIA that both strive to maintain a multinational, consumer-driven corporate culture; leaders of antidemocratic military coups like Henry Kissinger; and perpetuators of a politics of perpetual warfare like Franklin (or even Theodore) Roosevelt and John F. Kennedy.

The systems of power, as they are named here, represent the more powerful members of Empire. Hardt and Negri invite readers to view Empire "as a tree structure that subordinates all of the branches to a central root" (*Empire* 300). Hitler, Roosevelt, and that "connection of names" are perhaps higher branches. Utilizing other metaphors, Hardt and Negri refer to Empire as both a horizontal network and a hierarchy. Empire's power is spread out among various competing interests who hold various amounts of power, yet power is not expanded beyond this network. Thus, to return to the metaphor of the tree, Brock aspires to climb to a higher branch. After all, "He'd caught a fatal glimpse of that level where everybody knew everybody else, where however political fortunes below might bloom and die, the same people, the Real Ones, remained year in and year out, keeping what was desirable flowing their way" (276). Brock feels limited in his ability to rise within the hierarchy of Empire. He believes that the more powerful individuals would forever view him as little more than a hired thug whose services benefited them and, further, who became expendable once his services were no longer needed. Like the Darth Vader Brock alludes to in his final scene with Prairie Wheeler, Brock has only limited power. He is manipulated by the Real Ones who hold a greater amount of power within Empire.

This represents a divide in the way in which Pynchon deals with power. Unlike the more supernatural power structure of *Gravity's Rainbow*, where They held dominion over a preterite population that would ostensibly represent Us, *Vineland* brings power relations into a discursive area where They, to some extent, become Us. Or, at least, We are indelibly, perhaps even inevitably, complicit in perpetuating Them. While Brock Vond is complicit in perpetuating the power of Empire, he is also excluded from it at its highest levels. His attempts to rise in the hierarchy of Empire are viewed as threatening to those who hold more power than him. After Brock has invaded Vineland, secured the area, confiscated land, and directed operations, his power is stripped away when, "Suddenly, some white male far away must have wakened from a dream, and just like that, the clambake was over" (376). Brock's funding is pulled away from him. He is forced to retaliate on the verge of his greatest authoritarian victory. This pulling of Brock's funding and his power illustrates that power is constantly being negotiated within Empire. Some individuals fall from the tree.

Brock's expulsion from Empire casts him into a space inhabited by characters who are neither wholly of Empire nor of the multitude. This space is occupied by characters like Frenesi and Flash, who start the novel as federal snitches but, after becoming victims of budget cuts that end their careers, must find a new way to survive. It is also occupied by Ralph Wayvone. Though he is a mafioso figure and the Mafia are among the names Pynchon's narrator lists as the Real Ones—the ones with the real power within Empire—Ralph recognizes that, regardless of his underworld power, he will remain a "wholly-owned subsidiary" (93). Ralph is a subsidiary of a multinational corporation while Frenesi and Flash are subsidiaries of the American government. They are all complicit in perpetuating the power of Empire while, at the same time, being exploited by it. This blurred space between Empire and the multitude invites the reader to go beyond concepts of two sides competing for global sovereignty and to view power structures in a more complex fashion.

A Counterculture Complicated by Complicity

In general, most of the characters in the novel are simultaneously complicit in perpetuating the power of Empire and exploited by it. What seems to matter, however, are the details of the complicity and exploitation, specifically, how complicit one is and in what ways one is exploited. As Molly Hite observes, "In *Vineland*, complicity is a fact of life, but it ... is not by definition total and does not by definition rule out resistance" (147). Instead, characters must ask themselves in what ways they are complicit in perpetuating systems of power, and they must examine sites for resistance. These issues of complicity, which lie at the heart of *Vineland*, echo one of the arguments Linda Hutcheon makes in *The Politics of Postmodernism*. Hutcheon asserts, "[T]he postmodern we know has to acknowledge its own complicity with the very values upon which it seeks to comment" (10). In other words, resistance can only begin once the characters (and, by extension, the readers) recognize the ways in which they perpetuate the system they criticize. The character of Zoyd Wheeler provides a convenient illustration of this concept.

Throughout the novel, Zoyd and his nemesis Hector make much of Zoyd's "virginity" with regard to his noninformant status. When seemingly everyone in the novel is selling, trading, or bargaining for information to take down sixties rebellion, Zoyd refuses to become an informant. His virgin status in this regard validates, for him at least, his identity as a countercultural figure. His resistance takes a negative status—that he was never an informant—rather than a positive status as one who has advanced any sort of cause. He is presented as someone who operates outside the boundaries of consumerist culture and government oppression, yet his very livelihood is underwritten by the federal government in the form of Supplemental Security Income (SSI) provided for his annual acts of public insanity. Should he fail to perform one of these acts annually, he stands to lose not only his income but custody of his daughter, Prairie. In this way Zoyd—like Frenesi, Flash, and Brock—is in the employ of the federal government. Further, because the SSI checks are not enough to fully support Zoyd, he works a variety of odd jobs in and around Vineland. Most of these jobs are piecemeal. None of them are union. His willingness to take this work undermines the power of the unions that once organized in Vineland, the very unions for which Prairie's grandmother Sasha worked, the unions Prairie's great-grandfather Jess Traverse fought for and, during the fight, lost the ability to walk. Zoyd's scab status in a sense validates Reagan's antilabor, neoliberal policies. Zoyd has sidestepped the long-fought gains of nineteenth- and twentieth-century labor battles; the unions they created; the social safety net of health insurance, eight-hour days, and retirement plans they advocated for; and the basic human dignity associated with being a professional laborer. He has accepted the neoliberal notion that his labor is a commodity (though, as Polanyi observes, commodities are products created for resale and human labor, by definition, is not a commodity) and therefore subject to the laws of supply and demand. This uncritical acceptance ignores the long history of destruction of civil rights and social relations caused by viewing labor or land as a commodity.[5] Zoyd gets little in return for his dismissal of labor rights other than the vulnerability of a paycheck-to-paycheck existence. Thus, Zoyd's self-identification as a countercultural figure is complicated by his complicity. The first thing he must do to engage in viable resistance is recognize this complicity. He is dependent on the federal government for his livelihood. His scab status helps perpetuate the ever-widening divide between the those who control the wealth and those who create it. His complicity undermines his resistance. Nonetheless, as I argue below, his complicity does not completely eliminate his power to resist.

In order to discover the site where Zoyd and, by extension, Pynchon's audience can resist Empire despite our complicity in perpetuating it, I turn to the opposing sites of resistance created by Pynchon in *Vineland:* the failed student movement of the sixties and the emerging multitude of the eighties.[6] Like Pynchon, I will begin with an analysis of the failed rebellion and end with an exploration into new possibilities. Because *Vineland* views sixties rebellion through the retrospective eyes of Prairie Wheeler, I will do the same.

At its core, *Vineland* is a novel about Prairie Wheeler searching for her deadbeat mother. Entwined in Prairie's search for her mother is a search for ways in which to create an identity. This identity relies upon a family and cultural history to which Prairie has limited access. In this regard, Prairie's search for her mother is also a search for herself, her future, and her role in an America that Pynchon presents as at war with itself. Prairie's search is most poignant when she investigates her mother's role in 24 fps. Prairie experiences the sixties through files stored on the Kunoichi archive computers and the film archives kept by Ditzah in her house in the San Fernando Valley. The counternarrative to sixties rebellion told through these archives serve as a synecdoche of student rebellion. Pynchon's historiography matches that of his former Cornell classmate and collaborator Kirkpatrick Sale's description of real-life activists Students for Democratic Society in his book *SDS*.[7] According to Sale, the story of the SDS is "a story which above all tries to explain how in ten years an organization could transform itself from an insignificant band of alienated intellectuals into a major national force; what that force meant to the universities, the society, and the individuals it touched; what happened to undo it just as it appeared to reach the height of its power; and what legacy it left behind" (6). Likewise, Prairie watches 24 fps from its inception as an insignificant band of alienated activists to its confrontation with the Justice Department at the College of the Surf, where student activism has gained in power, arrogance, and naïveté enough to commandeer private property and secede from the United States. Prairie traces this evolution down to its failure, just as Sale does with the SDS.

In both cases, the failure is coupled with a turn toward violent resistance. Sale begins his historiography of the SDS with the explosive end of the group. The explosion was both literal—several members of the SDS were killed when the bombs they were making exploded—and figurative—the explosion effectively ended the SDS; nothing was left of the movement but metaphoric fragments.[8] The stylistic decision of Sale to begin his story of the SDS with its violent ending reminds his readers that, regardless of what happens throughout the rest of his history, it will end in failure. This structure serves to use the history of the SDS as a warning against the futility of violent resistance. In *There's Something Happening Here*, David Cunningham's history of COINTELPRO, Cunningham seconds Sale's interpretation, stating, "The emergence of the Weather Underground signaled the end of SDS as a viable mass movement" (65). In other words, when the members of the SDS transformed into the Weather Underground and employed violence as their primary tool of resistance, the entire movement crumbled.

Likewise, Pynchon uses the violence at the College of the Surf to explode 24 fps. Prior to their engagement in the College of the Surf, 24 fps is not exactly pacifistic. DL has a violent role in the organization. She serves as "security," which means violent engagement to her. What is significant about her role, however, is its scale and its scope of practice. She uses violence only as a resistance, never as an advancement. She defends. She does not attack. In almost every case when, as a member of 24 fps, she engages violently with her opposition, the engagement is tailored to transport herself and other members of 24 fps away from danger and to a safe place. Once 24 fps enters the College of the Surf, however, the actions of their rebellion mirror those of civil war. The members of PR^3 secede from the United States. The members of PR^3 must know that the act of commandeering American soil for foreign purposes will be seen as an act of aggression or invasion by the United States. Thus, this secession is a direct confrontation. The members had to know that it would—as it did—provoke a hostile response from the federal government. Further, the PR^3 ultimately fails as soon as a gun is introduced into the equation. Brock gives the gun to Frenesi, who passes it on to Rex Snuvvle, who uses it to kill Weed Atman. Following the shooting, federal forces invade the PR^3 and violently take it back. The members of 24 fps disperse, never to reassemble as an activist group. The student resistance is quelled.

Prairie witnesses these events in the novel's 1984, in the context of Brock's pursuit of her and her mother. She contemplates the methods of ridding herself of Brock. DL tells her, "[U]nless you can call on troops in regimental strength, and the hardware that goes with 'em, best not even think about messing with Brock" (266). For DL, who has already tried to kill Brock once and who has witnessed Brock's ability to wage war against the American people in both the sixties at the College of the Surf and in the eighties in Vineland, violent resistance to Brock is futile. Implicit in her comment, though, is the notion that, unless a resistance group can assemble the military might of Empire, violent resistance is futile. The College of the Surf incident demonstrates exactly how undermanned the PR^3 is to deal with the forces assembled by the Justice Department. After all, Brock's troops decimate the entire movement in a matter of hours. Likewise, the SDS demonstrated the futility of bomb making against the world's largest military power.

Part of the impetus behind violent resistance in *Vineland* is presented as naïveté. While discussing the PR^3's secession, the narrator comments, "In those days it was still unthinkable that any North American agency would kill its own civilians and then lie about it" (248). From Prairie's 1984 perspective and the reader's 1990s (and beyond) perspective, this disbelief in the U.S. government's willingness to wage war against its citizens is naïve. Prairie is witnessing

Brock's martial activities under the banner of the War on Drugs. For Prairie and for readers who remember the War on Drugs' no-knock warrants; the violent battles waged largely in poor rural or inner-city areas; the massive stockpile of weapons obtained by the Drug Enforcement Administration (DEA) and other antidrug units; and the forfeiture laws that allowed antidrug wings of police departments to enrich their coffers through the cars, boats, houses, and various other properties confiscated and subsequently auctioned for the profit of these departments, the notion of any North American agency killing its own civilians is easy to believe. After all, the War on Drugs was the most militaristic of America's twentieth-century nonwar wars. Even from Sasha Gates's perspective as the daughter and granddaughter of labor activists familiar with the wrongful convictions and executions of the Haymarket martyrs in Chicago in 1887; the wrongful conviction and execution of Joe Hill; the battle between striking steel workers and Andrew Carnegie's mercenaries (who were backed by the state militia) in Homestead, Pennsylvania, in 1892; the massacre of striking miners and their families by the National Guard in Ludlow, Colorado, in 1914; and various other incidents in this vein, an American war on American people is far from unthinkable.[9] By showing this violent strain of sixties rebellion both through the perspective of Prairie and by following explorations into Sasha's activism in the thirties, forties, and fifties, *Vineland* presents violent resistance to Empire as futile and lacking in both historical knowledge and critical thought.[10]

Occupy Vineland

Thus far in the novel, Pynchon—like Hardt and Negri—defines Empire not as a faceless or supernatural enemy but as a network of humans and a single logic of rule dedicated to neoliberal ideology; he presents Empire as engaged in a series of civil wars as a means of restricting civil rights; he considers the role of complicity with Empire among those who resist it; and he analyzes the failure of violent revolution. His final step, then, is to provide a positive site for resistance. He does this most saliently in two places: first, with regard to the family at the Becker-Traverse family reunion; second, in the social and economic alternatives suggested by the Sisterhood of Kunoichi Attentives.

Vineland ends with most of the major characters gathered at the Becker-Traverse family reunion. The narrator introduces the reunion in idyllic tones, describing dawn gracefully emerging in the great north woods of California. The Beckers, Traverses, and other guests arise to this almost mythical morning. Even woodland creatures arise among them. This is followed by a bustle of pleasant activity that denotes families enjoying quality time with one another.

The land upon which they gather is also intriguing. The reunion is held, apparently, not in a state or national park nor on a campground or any other type of private property. No one has paid a fee to camp there. The land lies off the beaten path, away from county or state roads, in a place that, strictly speaking, may not exist in Northern California. It is clear that no one in the Becker-Traverse clan owns the land. No one profits from the land. It seems to be an old-growth forest that the Beckers, Traverses, and whoever else attends the reunion use gently, then leave for the next creatures who should pass by. Because the land is not turned into a commodity (a campground, timberland for a logging company) or a public property (a park, a preserve), because it lies off the network of public and private roads and is instead accessible through paths worn by vehicles accessing the land, because it is not policed by federal, state, or county employees or by private security, the land is relatively autonomous from capital and Empire. It therefore exemplifies the Marxist notion of the commons. This is where Pynchon begins to develop his site for resistance to Empire.

The notion of family at the family reunion is greatly expanded in the narrative. Significantly, very few of the characters assembled at the Becker-Traverse family reunion are named Becker or Traverse. Several, strictly speaking, cannot be considered related to the Beckers or the Traverses. This is particularly true once characters like DL, Takeshi, and a handful of Thanatoids join characters like Zoyd at the reunion. While all are taken to be family, none are related. Instead, those who gather at the reunion constitute a familial community that has been drawn together by their resistance to (and, to some extent, complicity in) Empire. The metaphor of family is important because the characters seem to be together less by choice and more as a circumstance of their births, their socioeconomic status, and their place in a system of power. This is a far cry—perhaps even a polemical one—from the "family values" that George H. W. Bush campaigned to reinstate in the late eighties (which, in all likelihood, was happening at the exact time Pynchon was finishing his composition of *Vineland*). For Bush's campaign, family values signified a nostalgic return to the fifties notion of "family" as a controlling patriarch and his submissive wife and children. Ostensibly, this family would also be white (or perhaps black like the family in *The Cosby Show*). There is nothing nuclear, nothing genuinely patriarchal about the Becker-Traverse clan gathered at the end of the novel. Hardt and Negri, like Pynchon, warn against a "nostalgia for past social formations" (*Multitude* 190). For Hardt and Negri, nostalgic cries for family values are dangerous. They argue that "the ultimate object is the reconstruction of the unified social body and thus the recreation of the people" (*Multitude* 191). In other words, the danger lies in using family to create homogeneous concerns—and typically the concerns of the patriarch—instead of honoring the singularities of individual family members. Pynchon seems to share this concern.

Like most families outside the novel and outside the nostalgic longing for "family values," the guests at the Becker-Traverse reunion are not a unified group. Pynchon has constructed them, instead, as a motley assemblage. They cannot be lumped together into a false concept like "the people." Instead, they mirror Hardt and Negri's definition of the multitude, which is, in short, "an irreducible multiplicity; . . . singularities that act in common" (*Multitude* 105). In accordance with this definition, those who gather at the reunion come from various walks of life. They are Wobblies, pot growers, victims of the fifties red scare, socialists, labor activists, veterans of the sixties student movement, and others living on what is often conveniently and erroneously referred to as the fringes of society. In many ways—their intergenerational makeup, their diverse backgrounds, their leaderless structure, their attempt to remove themselves from state power and the power of capital, their expression of self-rule, their situation in opposition to the powers of Empire or the 1 percent, their political disobedience—they foreshadow Occupy encampments.

Several critics have interpreted this assembly at the Becker-Traverse family reunion as a site of resistance. Among them, Shawn Smith notes, "Families, surrogate families, and communal social structures oppose the text's fascist collective" (129). Smith's simple passage highlights the importance of a sense of nonpatriarchal family and community as the specific resistance to fascism. His statement echoes N. Katherine Hayles's argument in "'Who Was Saved?'," where Hayles convincingly argues that Pynchon develops a dichotomy in *Vineland*, positing the antifamily agents of suppression such as Brock against the more family-oriented activists such as Sasha and Zoyd. Pynchon further articulates the nature of the resistance when Jess Traverse reads a passage from Ralph Waldo Emerson, which Jess first encountered in William James's *The Varieties of Religious Experience*: "Jess reminded them, 'Secret retributions are always restoring the level, when disturbed, of the divine justice. It is impossible to tilt the beam. All the tyrants and proprietors and monopolists of the world in vain set their shoulders to heave the bar. Settles forever more the ponderous equator to its line, and man and mote, and star and sun, must range to its line, or be pulverized by the recoil'" (*Vineland* 369). This is a complex citation. The fact that it comes from Jess Traverse, who is less a patriarch in the family—after all, he has hardly appeared in the pages of the novel until this moment, and he is presented as someone who neither seeks nor wants control of the lives of his family members—and more simply the family elder, suggests that Pynchon is connecting the wisdom of this citation not with patriarchy but with a wisdom drawn from shared history. That shared history is passed on not only from family elders but from intellectuals who have come to represent a certain freedom of thought and questioning of authority. Because Jess originally read the passage in a "jailhouse copy" (369) of James's book, the wisdom also comes from some anonymous, community-oriented individual who saw fit to donate this book—through one means or another—to a jail library. Finally, this citation comes to the reader from Thomas Pynchon as a way of highlighting the importance of creating a counternarrative to Empire's narrative of resistance. Thus, while Pynchon does investigate the failure of turning to violence in sixties rebellion, he also argues, through this passage, that sixties rebellion, like the rebellion of communists and labor activists that preceded it, like the punk rockers of Prairie's generation that follow it, all aid in "restoring the level . . . of the divine justice." This counternarrative echoes Polanyi's notion of a countermovement. By situating this movement on the Marxist commons of the Becker-Traverse reunion (the very type of commons attacked by Reagan's neoliberal appropriations), with its polemical family values, the countermovement becomes one that actually does contain both theory and ideology.

Jess's validation of resistance movements at the end of Pynchon's novel, which, to some extent, explores the failures of those movements, demonstrates what Stefan Mattessich refers to as Pynchon's "refus[al] to surrender the myth of the American promise" (9). The American left, with its desire for a more democratic society, with its embrace of the commons, with its focus on reconstructed families and communities, is not an oxymoron, and it has not been destroyed by the Reagan years. It is, in fact, gathered to resist the corporate takeover of the American promise. As Molly Hite observes, "This return is not a restoration; it does not bring back the sixties—or the thirties, or the teens. But it does reconstitute a community of resistance in a widened historical context" (148). The Becker-Traverse reunion groups together resistance movements that have previously been historicized as separate: the Wobblies, fifties communists, sixties student activists, and eighties punk rockers. In his history of the SDS, David Cunningham notes, "The SDSers . . . clearly separated themselves from many Old Leftists by asserting that such reforms did not require the working class as the driving agent of change" (44). In *Vineland*, Pynchon heals this separation—an act that takes on even greater significance when read in light of the Occupy movement. In *Power Systems*, Noam Chomsky warns, "Unless the labor movement is revitalized and becomes a core part of the movement, I don't think [Occupy is] going to get very far" (67). The Becker-Traverse reunion seems to brandish the same warning.

Pynchon does not present the Old Leftists and the New Left as a unified whole. They are instead part of the multitude, "groups we had previously assumed to have different and even contradictory interests manag[ing] to act in common" (Hardt and Negri, *Multitude* 86). Zoyd, despite his scab activities, aligns himself with a family of labor activists. Frenesi, the federal snitch, jitterbugs with her mother, Sasha, whose career in Hollywood was destroyed by federal snitches through the House Un-American Activities Committee. The multitude at the reunion resist the Empire that exploits them by gathering on land in the public commons and turning to nonpatriarchal, nonunified families and communities for support. As Eric Solomon argues, "[A]ll the characters and themes of the novel will coalesce at the end as surreal forces will combine to sustain family and defeat the government" (163). The text supports Solomon's argument. Brock, the agent of Empire, the Darth Vader, is destroyed. Prairie, the hope for a new generation, stands up to him. The reunion demonstrates Hardt and Negri's notion: "Dominance, no matter how multidimensional, can never be complete and is always contradicted by resistance" (*Multitude* 54). The Becker-Traverse family reunion is the site of resistance against Empire's dominance.

The reunion as Pynchon's site of resistance, however, is incomplete. The multitude assembles at the reunion. The assembly serves to demonstrate the power of the commons and community. Prairie's arrival at the reunion is preceded by her flashback to the Great Eyeshadow Raid, which allows the reunion to also be cast as a rejection of consumerism. Pynchon's construction of the reunion further serves as a counternarrative to the typical historiography of sixties rebellion. This idyllic moment in mythical Vineland even has a moral like any other fable. N. Katherine Hayles summarizes the moral: "If salvation comes, it will arrive by cherishing the small everyday acts of kindness that flourish in networks of kinship and friendship" (28). However, the multitude, the commons, the reconstructed family and community, the rejection of consumerism, and the counternarrative are not enough to defeat Brock. He instead suffers his real defeat when his funding is pulled by a nameless white man who has climbed higher on the tree of Empire than Brock. Further, his defeat may symbolize a temporary respite for the multitude from the tyranny of Empire, but Empire has not suffered any real defeat. They have simply moved their perpetual war to another front.

The reunion alone as the site of resistance is problematic. The first problem lies in its lack of efficacy. Again, the reunion does not defeat Brock. The second problem lies in the reunion's lack of acknowledgment of its own complicity. On this public commons, among this reconstructed community, the Beckers, Traverses, and guests watch televisions, they camp in recreational vehicles that are notorious gas guzzlers, they cook breakfast in RV microwaves or on propane stoves, they drink coffee, and they generally consume their consumables. Appearances to the contrary, they have not completely escaped

Empire. Their gasoline and propane purchases support multinational oil corporations. Their recreational vehicles support the automobile industry. The coffee they drink is emblematic of globalized trade and Americans' addiction to it (a point Pynchon extensively articulates in *Mason & Dixon*). Perhaps most importantly, television, as Isaiah Two Four points out, at least partially led to the failure of sixties rebellion. All this money spent on the reunion helps perpetuate Empire.

The third problem resides in the moment after Prairie rejects Brock, his funding is pulled, and he disappears. At this moment, Prairie seems to pull an about-face. She searches for Brock; she yearns for him. This seems to reveal that Prairie has inherited the same genetic strand that Frenesi suffers from while she masturbates to a *CHiPs* episode. Frenesi muses, "[It's] as if some Cosmic Fascist had spliced in a DNA sequence requiring this form of seduction and initiation into the dark joys of social control" (83). She worries that her love of fascism is somehow encoded within her. In his chapter on *Vineland* in *Pynchon and the Political*, Samuel Thomas begins with an epigraph from Deleuze and Guattari warning that fascism exists within us on a molecular level. In order to counter this fascism, we must first be constantly aware of its presence. With this in mind, perhaps Prairie's yearning for Brock is not so much an about-face as a reminder that our molecular fascism requires constant vigilance, lest it overtake our more revolutionary impulses.

Nonetheless, all three of these problems entwined in the Becker-Traverse reunion suggest that, if Pynchon's hope for resistance is to expand beyond what Hayles refers to as "a few moments of grace" (28), the reader must look elsewhere in the text.

The Sisterhood

The expansion of Pynchon's site of resistance lies in the Sisterhood of Kunoichi Attentives.[11] Unlike the Becker-Traverse family reunion, which is an annual respite from the power of Empire, the Sisterhood serves as a perpetual safe harbor for the multitude. When DL becomes too entwined in the interests of Empire, she flees to the Sisterhood, knowing it is the only safe place for her to untangle herself. Likewise, when Brock begins sniffing around Vineland and posing a threat to Prairie, DL brings her to the Sisterhood's mountainside retreat, where Prairie is able to hide out long enough to make sense of her dilemma. As Samuel Thomas observes, the retreat is a "deliberate escape from something . . . a refuge from a bigger, badder, more powerful world" (135). Even Takeshi seeks his resurrection through the Sisterhood. Because it exists in the novel as a safe harbor, a hideout, and a place of rebirth, the mountainside retreat of the Sisterhood of Kunoichi Attentives deserves further examination as a site of resistance.

In all likelihood, the mountainside retreat strays from Hardt and Negri's vision of the multitude. While Hardt and Negri come from a Marxist tradition and demonstrate an inherent mistrust of private property, the mountainside retreat of the Sisterhood exists within the logic of late capitalism. The retreat is on private property. They protect this property with a gate. Thus, it is even a gated community. Further, they are funded through the lucrative "self-improvement business" (107). They advertise in mass-market magazines. They market themselves to children. They rely on a mixture of nostalgia and orientalism to sell their self-improvement platform. Through all these elements, they demonstrate their complicity with Empire.

Recognizing this complicity is the first step in the Sisterhood's resistance. They understand the logic of the market and work within it. Despite their somewhat deceptive marketing attempts, however, their program of spiritual rebirth is not presented as a façade. All the characters in the novel who turn to the Sisterhood in a time of need find what they need at the retreat. DL is untangled from Empire there. Prairie does begin to find her mother and, through that act, begins to find herself and her role in society while she is at the retreat. Takeshi is reborn there (annually, in fact). Even the Sisterhood's advertising campaign's soft promises of "some chorus line of Asian dewdrops" (107) are destroyed when visitors arrive to find the Sisterhood a multiethnic group. Further, though they exist on private property, that property is open to members of the multitude who can, as Prairie explains it, "earn what you eat, secure what you shit" (109). Even the gates function in the book to prevent Empire's invasion rather than to prevent the arrival of the multitude. Through these methods, the Sisterhood's complicity becomes conscious. This consciousness allows them to manipulate Empire in their favor.

Further, the Sisterhood does overlap with Hardt and Negri in several ways. First, the Sisterhood's work is essentially biopolitical. They create immaterial products: the information Prairie needs to find her mother; the pseudospiritual martial arts knowledge that DL pursues; and the feelings of ease, of well-being, of safety, of personal growth that characterize affective labor. Hardt and Negri further maintain, "[B]iopolitical production shifts the economic center of gravity from the production of material commodities to that of social relations" (*Commonwealth* 135). The biopolitical production inherent in the Sisterhood's business model does drift away from the strictly material, strictly industrial production that a Marxist bourgeoisie inextricably entangles itself in. The knowledge, communication, and feelings of ease and safety produced by the Sisterhood are more difficult to commodify. Hardt and Negri contend,

"Biopolitical products . . . tend to *exceed* all quantitative measurement and take *common* forms, which are easily shared and difficult to corral as private property" (*Commonwealth* 136). In other words, because the biopolitical production of the Sisterhood is so difficult to measure quantitatively, because it is so difficult to translate into a simple commodity, it becomes a power with more autonomy than industrial production. Capital can hover over it parasitically, but the biopolitical production ruptures traditional relationships between capital and industry.

This, again, echoes aspects of Occupy. In their study on women in the Occupy movement, Megan Boler, Averie Macdonald, Christina Nistou, and Anne Harris examine the exact types of labor women tend to do within Occupy. They find that women in the movement tend to fall into three categories of connective labor, which they define as "a body of un(der)-acknowledged, often immaterial work being carried out by women to support and sustain contemporary social movements" (450). These roles—as administrators, documentarians, connectors—serve to foster the horizontal structure in complicated ways. The women whom Boler and her colleagues interview tend to work autonomously, in charge of various websites, Facebook pages, or other social media campaigns, but being in charge of this small aspect of a much larger movement should not be mistaken for usurping the "leaderless" aspect of Occupy. They organize, they support, they generate ideas, but they reject power and control on any larger scale.

Similarly, when Hardt and Negri discuss the specifics of resistance from the multitude, they observe, "The most important organizational characteristic of these various movements is their insistence on autonomy and their refusal of any centralized hierarchy, leaders, or spokespeople" (*Multitude* 86). Resistance movements are organized more like networks that do have leaders and spokespeople, just not centralized ones. For example, many of the Occupy theorists I cite in this work and many of the women whom Boler, Macdonald, Nistou, and Harris interviewed in their study can exist as voices contributing to Occupy, but none can exist as *the* voice for the resistance movement. All are free to speak provided each clarifies that she speaks for herself. Likewise, the Sisterhood does have leaders, just not centralized leaders. For example, Prairie, in her effort to earn her place at the retreat, becomes the head of the kitchen. She takes charge over the menu and the use of resources. She manages the others in the kitchen. She is not, however, part of a hierarchal chain of command. Like the women of the Occupy movement whom Boler, Macdonald, Nistou, and Harris interview, Prairie simply fills a need. Sister Rochelle, who is described as "Senior Attentive, or mother superior of the place" (108), does fill a leadership role. She outlines conditions for DL, Prairie, and Takeshi's stay at the Kunoichi, but her role rejects the logic of late capitalism in two significant ways. First, as I mention above, all these characters find what they need at the retreat. Sister Rochelle facilitates this process. Her role is one of nurturing and assistance. She does not seek to profit off DL, Prairie, or Takeshi. She does not exploit their labor. She instead ensures that their time at the retreat is communally profitable. Second, Sister Rochelle rejects standard notions of competition associated with capitalism. Though the Sisterhood is in the business of spiritual readjustment, Sister Rochelle tacitly supports DL and Takeshi's enterprise into what they refer to as karmic readjustment. DL and Takeshi labor in biopolitical production similar to the Sisterhood's. The Sisterhood rejects the capitalist impulse to profit parasitically off DL and Takeshi's karmic readjustment business. Instead, the two groups cooperate for their mutual benefit rather than attempting to destroy each other through profit-driven competition.

Ultimately, the Sisterhood stands in opposition to Empire. Pynchon makes this clear from the very introduction of the mountainside retreat. The narrator introduces the retreat through the eyes of Prairie: "As they got closer, Prairie saw archways, a bell tower, an interpenetration with the tall lime surfaces of cypresses, pepper trees, a fruit orchard . . . nothing looked especially creepy to her. She was a California kid, and she trusted in vegetation. What was creepy, the heart of creep-out, lay back down the road behind her, in, but not limited to, the person, hard and nearly invisible, like quartz, of her pursuer, Brock Vond" (108). This description first envisions the retreat through an ecological perspective. The lushness of the vegetation is welcoming, a sense of home for Prairie (as, perhaps, her name itself would suggest). Second, it presents a dichotomy: Prairie's very identity is reinforced by the retreat while the Empire that lies behind her threatens to destroy her. In this way, Pynchon signals to the reader his site of resistance to Empire. It resides in a social business engaging in biopolitical production: one that is complicit with corporate society but recognizes that complicity and moves beyond it; one that rejects consumerism by refusing to sell consumables and by rejecting the notion of spirituality as a commodity; one that accepts payments beyond the typical system of cash currency; one that exists for mutual profit instead of exploitative profit; one that reconstructs notions of family and community to provide a safe harbor; and one that rejects competition in favor of cooperation. The Sisterhood is not perfect. As Thomas observes, "Both 'dystopia and utopia' are contained within its boundaries" (146). Nor is the Sisterhood alone enough to take down the Empire in the novel. It exists only as a respite from Brock and the other forces that are "the heart of creep-out." But the Sisterhood of Kunoichi Attentives' mountainside retreat coupled with the Becker-Traverse family reunion serve to introduce Pynchon's conceptions of a world that can exist in opposition to Empire.

These two examples serve only as the beginning of Pynchon's investigation into new sites of resistance. His four subsequent novels expand and articulate these notions. *Mason & Dixon* travels back to the revolutionary atmosphere that preceded the new republic of the United States to construct a coherent vision of the multitude as the true founders of the American promise. *Against the Day* both further explores the futility of violence in resistance to Empire and expands the counternarrative of resistance movements, specifically the anarchist and socialist movements of the late nineteenth and early twentieth centuries. *Inherent Vice* further develops the socially conscious alternative economic structure hinted at by the Sisterhood of Kunoichi Attentives. *Bleeding Edge* investigates the possibilities of an electronic commons. All four of these novels enlarge the notions of a multitude, an Occupation, and their underlying revolutionary potential.

While these novels more clearly articulate Pynchon's sites for resistance, they all rely on the framework established in *Vineland*. After all, *Vineland* serves to bring systems of power down to earth, to give these powers human faces, and present them as surmountable. *Vineland* introduces and explores the destructive elements of Empire's perpetual civil war and highlights the importance of recognizing how these nonwar wars are really attacks on both the American people and the American promise. *Vineland* explores complicity as a gray area wherein people can recognize the ways in which they perpetuate the systems they oppose yet use this recognition as a starting point for a new path of resistance. *Vineland* demonstrates the futility of violent resistance to Empire while simultaneously proposing new methods of peaceful attack. For all these reasons, *Vineland* serves as the thematic foundation for *Mason & Dixon*, *Against the Day*, *Inherent Vice*, and *Bleeding Edge*. Pynchon's new approach to the American promise begins here.

CHAPTER 3

Mason & Dixon and the Ghastly Fop

MASON & DIXON (1997) continues the shift in Thomas Pynchon's oeuvre initiated by *Vineland*. The novel's narrator, the Reverend Wicks Cherrycoke, tells the story of astronomer Charles Mason and land surveyor Jeremiah Dixon constructing the border between Pennsylvania and Maryland, the border that would bear their names and go on to become the infamous dividing line between the North and South or, as Dixon phrases it in the novel, the "Line between their Slave-Keepers, and their Wage-Payers" (692). The story begins with Mason and Dixon's time in South Africa, recording the first transit of Venus in 1761 for the British Royal Society.[1] The story continues through their years on the line (1763–68), their separate recordings of the second transit of Venus in 1769, Dixon's death in 1779, and the death of Charles Mason in 1786, a week prior to Cherrycoke embarking upon his nearly monthlong storytelling session. As a postmodern reprisal of Walter Benjamin's storyteller,[2] Cherrycoke narrates the construction of the concept of America and how it was born in conjunction with global trade. He bears witness to the nascent Empire (as Michael Hardt and Antonio Negri define the term) built of national governments and the sovereignty they share with global trade companies like the British and Dutch East India Companies, which were referred to as "chartered companies" in the eighteenth century though today would be called multinational corporations. By following Mason and Dixon through the slave colonies of Dutch South Africa, Pennsylvania, and Maryland, Cherrycoke confronts the interrelationship between empire and slavery at the same time he examines the depth of injustice and exploitation inherent in a system of global commodity culture. Finally, through this self-reflexive historiography in which Cherrycoke is given free rein to wander into the subjunctive, or the imagined as true,[3] Pynchon explores the possibilities of creating a more just America, one that changes the shape of the borderlines carved from a legacy of slavery, genocide, and class and gender oppression.

Before Cherrycoke is able to begin his tale, he and his listeners are situated in a context of conspicuous consumption. Just as *Gravity's Rainbow* begins with "A screaming comes across the sky" (3), which serves notice to the reader—she is about to embark upon a breakneck journey through the birth of rocket

{49}

science and into humanity's perhaps sexual love of death—*Mason & Dixon* begins with a loaded projectile. In the latter case, the screaming across the sky is softened to the lob of a snowball: "Snow-Balls have flown their Arcs" (5). The flight is followed by a scene of wealth, privilege, and abundance. The children put away their toys and enter into a rich scene of consumables "punctuated by the ringing Lids of Boilers and Stewing-Pots, fragrant with Pie-Spices, peel'd Fruits, Suet, heated Sugar" (5), decorated by expensive (and not-so-expensive) furniture either purchased from or constructed from materials found in various spots around the globe. All these representatives of global commodity culture have been paid for by the ethically dubious weapons dealer and family patriarch Wade LeSpark. The reader learns in a subsequent chapter that "Mr. LeSpark made his Fortune years before the War, selling weapons to French and British, Settlers and Indians alike,— Knives, Tomahawks, Rifles, Hand-Cannons in the old Dutch Style, Grenades, small Bombs" (27). Further, LeSpark's brother-in-law and the novel's storyteller, Wicks Cherrycoke, begins his tale by explaining that he has been banned from England but continues to live on a stipend that his father "has ever kept his promise to remit to me, by way of certain Charter'd Companies" (9). In this way, Cherrycoke establishes his complicity in the chartered companies, their global trade, and the subsequent wars and slavery inherent in this system of Empire. Further, when his nephews ask for a story of America, the story opens following the precedent Pynchon set in *Gravity's Rainbow*, that is, major themes are established in the first sentences. The story is told, and therefore understood, through the context and the lens of a society built on consumables, global trade, dubious ethics, war, and slavery. Moreover, Cherrycoke's complicity in these injustices that he will criticize is established at the onset of his tale.

Just as Cherrycoke must live under the umbrella of chartered companies, Mason and Dixon's trajectory is established by them. The power of these chartered companies is first presented to Mason by the future royal astronomer, Nevil Maskelyne, with whom Mason is stationed at St. Helena. Maskelyne says:

> "We are quite the Pair, then,— that is, I presume," peering at Mason, "both subjects of the same Invisible Power? No? What is it, think ye? Something richer than many a Nation, yet with no Boundaries,— which, tho' never part of any Coalition, yet maintains its own great Army and Navy,— able to pay for the last War, as the next, with no more bother than finding the Key to a certain iron Box,— yet which allows the Britannick Governance that gave it Charter, to sink beneath oceanick Waves of Ink incarnadine." (140)

Though the power of which Maskelyne speaks is "invisible," he sees its workings quite clearly. He speaks specifically of the East India Company, which has the power to wage and fund a series of colonial wars in the Indian subcontinent. Perhaps Maskelyne's direct connection to the East India Company through his brother-in-law and the administrator of the EIC, Clive of India, allows Maskelyne to recognize the power this chartered company holds, the wealth it is capable of amassing, and the political power it wields. Long before Mason or Dixon connects their work for the Royal Society to these chartered companies, Maskelyne—whose connections to Clive will perhaps be the deciding factor in his ascension to astronomer royal—outlines the power for Mason. Maskelyne's explanation serves to articulate for Mason and Dixon "the connections between the [East India] Company and their Royal Society employers, portrayed in terms of marriages no less dynastic than those between royal families" (Olster 112). Mason is not yet prepared to confront the overwhelming power of Empire, so he dismisses Maskelyne's explanation with a joke.

The invisibility that Maskelyne "sees" reinforces Samuel Thomas's argument in *Pynchon and the Political*. Thomas observes, "Systems of economic power and social control, on a large and small scale, rely on invisibility" (59). This is an inherent characteristic of ideological rule. As Louis Althusser asserts in "Ideology and Ideological State Apparatuses," "one of the effects of ideology is the practical denegation of the ideological character of ideology by ideology: ideology never says, 'I am ideological'" (49). Instead, ideology presents itself as the natural order of things, the default setting, so to speak. Thus, Mason's dismissal of Maskelyne's analysis is not entirely denial on Mason's end. Instead, he is operating as an interpellated subject in the ideological rule of economic liberalism.

On the verge of their voyage to America to create the line that will bear their name, Mason and Dixon finally do acknowledge their complicity with Empire. Dixon asks Mason, "[W]hy has ev'ry Observation site propos'd by the Royal Society prov'd to be a Factory, or Consulate, or other Agency of some royally Charter'd Company?" Mason responds, "Charter'd Companies may indeed be the form the World has now increasingly begun to take" (252). Dixon, like Mason in the earlier conversation with Maskelyne, dismisses this revelation with a joke. Nonetheless, the repetition of revelations helps to build the seriousness of this theme within *Mason & Dixon*. Similar to what he did with Empire in *Vineland*, Pynchon establishes a genuine larger force that is controlling the characters. Mason and Dixon are not paranoid. They are pawns in a game played beyond them. In Pynchon's first three novels, these larger forces were vague; their very existence was questionable. Pynchon gave them nebulous-sounding names like V., the Tristero, or simply They. In *Vineland*, he begins naming these larger forces, making them less mythical, casting them in human terms and therefore creating a force that a counterforce can confront.

The names these forces are given in *Vineland* are "Hitler, Roosevelt, Kennedy, Nixon, Hoover, Mafia, CIA, Reagan, Kissinger, that collection of names and their tragic interweaving that stood not constellated above in any nightwide remoteness of light, but below, diminished to the last unfaceable American secret" (372). In *Mason & Dixon*, the larger forces are the British and Dutch East India Companies, the Royal Society, and, to a lesser extent, the British government. Mason and Dixon find themselves engulfed by what critic Stacey Olster describes as "a world in which a shift from imperialist to imperial sovereignty has resulted in the decentered and deterritorialized apparatus that Michael Hardt and Antonio Negri call 'Empire'" (108). Historical parallels between European empires and Hardt and Negri's concept of Empire make sense. Most historians situate the contemporary notion of nationhood with the American and French Revolutions. Both of these events occurred after the majority of the events in the novel, so it is no surprise that Mason and Dixon's travels occur in a place and a time when individual nations have less sovereignty over the protagonists' lives than international commerce does. Whether they are in the Dutch colony of South Africa, England, or the British colonies of Pennsylvania and Maryland, Mason and Dixon seem to be more subjects of chartered companies than subjects of any nation. The chartered companies dictate the political and cultural events that surround the novel. Their impact is widespread enough to steer the very scientific inquiries that Mason and Dixon pursue.

From a scientific standpoint, the work pursued by Mason, Dixon, Maskelyne, and the other astronomers in the novel is primarily concerned with facilitating global trade. Mason and Maskelyne are both "Lunarians," that is, they subscribe to a system of determining longitude at sea through the careful observation and calculation of lunar distances. Maskelyne, in particular, must confront his beliefs regarding the determination of longitude when a watchmaker named John Harrison produces a chronometer that keeps perfect time at sea, thereby making lunar calculations obsolete. While the events surrounding Lunarians and chronometers make for dramatic and at times hilarious passages in the book, the passages are underscored by the fact that longitude at sea is not so much a pursuit inspired by scientific curiosity as it is a pursuit to facilitate navigation for navies and freighters. Further, Mason and Dixon's very legacy lasting into the twenty-first century is the boundary they created. This boundary was an impressive scientific achievement. For eighty years prior to 1763, surveyors and astronomers tried and failed to draw the boundary that Mason and Dixon marked. However, all this is underscored by the fact that the boundary is fundamentally a property enclosure, a means for wealthy politicians to levy taxes, a way of separating private property from that which would belong to the public (or, in the case of the Native Americans encroached upon by the line, that which would belong in the commons). All of Mason and Dixon's endeavors throughout the novel facilitate the acquisition and retention of wealth that is not shared with Mason or Dixon or redistributed in any way that could be described as just.

Mason and Dixon's enterprises for the benefit of chartered companies and national governments follow the same pattern that continued through the twentieth century and into today. During the two World Wars and the Cold War that defined much of the twentieth century, physics became the prominent science. This rise is indelibly tied to national governments and their desire to wage war from as far away as possible—a service that the study of physics can accommodate through rockets, bombs, and the combination resulting in intercontinental ballistic missiles—and with wartime profiteers building an industry out of the construction (and destruction, frequently at the cost of many human lives) of these rockets and bombs. Not incidentally, Pynchon traces this entanglement in *Gravity's Rainbow*. Currently, the wealthiest industry in the United States is the pharmaceutical industry. This coincides (more through causation than correlation) with the current rise and advancements in the field of biology. Likewise, at the birth of global trade, which was contingent upon navigation at sea, astronomy became the science of the British empire.

Though I mentioned earlier that Mason and Dixon seem to be more subjects of chartered companies than subjects of any nation, it is important to note that Hardt and Negri's notion of Empire also articulates the deep links between national governments and multinational corporations. In fact, they define Empire as sovereignty that has taken a new form "composed of a series of national and supranational organisms [like multinational corporations] united under a single logic of rule" (*Empire* xii). Thus, Mason and Dixon's pursuit of astronomy does not simply fall under the auspices of chartered companies. In an early flashback, Mason explains to his wife, Rebekah, "Astronomy is as soil'd at the hands of the Pelhamites as ev'ry other Business in this Kingdom" (209). The Pelhamites to whom Mason refers are the followers of then–prime minister Henry Pelham. In this passage, Mason is asserting that the British government stands to gain both power and wealth similar to that of the companies to which they grant a charter.

By demonstrating the interrelationship between astronomy and Empire, *Mason & Dixon* highlights the ontological ramifications behind Empire's control of intellectual inquiry. Under the umbrella of Empire, scientific inquiry is typically steered by the funding or defunding of the power structures in control. For this reason, not only is scientific inquiry limited to or by the whims of the marketplace, our cultural imagination and curiosity face similar limitations. The significance of this will become more clear below, where I discuss Pynchon's use of the subjunctive and his discussions of what, exactly, was lost in the Age of Reason.

Mason most poignantly confronts the ways in which his scientific inquiry is complicit in perpetuating the unjust machinations of Empire when he and Dixon are on the verge of sailing to America. In a conversation with Dixon, Mason laments "Foolishly seeking in the Alignment of Sun, Venus, and Earth, a moment redeem'd from the Impurity in which I must ever practice in life" (247). Mason's lamentation diffuses the typical perspective astronomers (and casual eyewitnesses) frequently experience when witnessing a major astronomical event like the transit of Venus: the sense that our human lives seem so small compared to the grandeur of the universe. Instead, that moment when Earth, Venus, and the sun align is brought down to material concerns. Instead of a moment of epiphany, the conclusion Mason draws from his experience comes in the form of an internal voice announcing to him, "The Business of the World is Trade and Death, and you must engage with that unpleasantness, as the price of your not-at-all-assur'd Moment of Purity.— Fool" (247). In this fashion, Mason's experience of the transit of Venus within the context of slavery in South Africa forces him to acknowledge his complicity just as Cherrycoke's complicity is acknowledged in the setting of his storytelling. Hopefully, this acknowledgment expands beyond the pages of the book and into the reader's world, encouraging her to examine her own complicity.

Debunking the Founding Fathers

Beyond the entanglements of science and global trade, *Mason & Dixon* continues its examination of the burgeoning Empire by historicizing the protagonists' encounters with the so-called Founding Fathers as inextricably linked to the shadier sides of commerce. In "General Wolfe and the Weavers," Frank Palmeri observes, "Pynchon's narrative is very interested in debunking conventional and strongly entrenched heroes" (194). Palmeri refers specifically to Pynchon's portrayal of General James Wolfe, but the sentiment can be expanded to include Pynchon's characterization of Thomas Jefferson, Benjamin Franklin, and George Washington.

Thomas Jefferson makes a cameo appearance in the novel. Dixon encounters Jefferson in a Virginia tavern. At a loss to produce a revolutionary sentiment when it is his turn to propose a toast, Dixon raises his glass "To the pursuit of Happiness" (395). Jefferson is taken by the phrase and expresses his plans to use it himself. This innocuous, largely humorous scene divests Jefferson of any authorship of his famous phrase regarding the natural rights of men, those being "life, liberty, and the pursuit of happiness." John Locke is the original author of the natural rights of man, specifically life, liberty, and property. If Jefferson gets the phrase "pursuit of happiness" from Dixon (in a toast at a tavern, no less), he can take credit for none of the originality of the opening sentence of the Declaration of Independence. It is a subtle poke at Jefferson. It works mostly as a joke, very much in line with Jefferson's declaration, "Virginia. This Land of Sensual Beasts" (396). In other words, Virginia is for lovers—a sentiment to be found on T-shirts currently for sale throughout the state. The sophistry attached to Dixon and Jefferson's phrase "the pursuit of happiness" also suggests that many of the values of the American Revolution may have been rhetoric picked up willy-nilly more than the genuine belief system of the leaders of the revolution.

Benjamin Franklin has a much larger role in the novel. He first encounters Mason and Dixon in a backstreet drugstore. Dixon is plotting to purchase "an hundred Cases" (267) of Daffy's Elixir, a blended concoction of alcohol and opium. Franklin instructs Mason and Dixon, in line with the pithy phrases he produces in *Poor Richard's Almanack*, "Strangers, heed my wise advice,— Never pay the Retail Price" (267). This adage demonstrates Franklin's trademark frugality. More significantly, Franklin's presence in a shady drugstore on a "mission of chemical Necessity" (266) also exposes the connection between global trade and addictive substances. This connection is reinforced when the three reconvene at a coffee house. The opium that Dixon seeks to purchase by the case; the wine, whiskey, and ale that spur the debates between grape and grain and follow every adventure of Mason and Dixon; and the ubiquitous coffee houses and overindulgences in caffeine all serve to complicate the characters' complicity with systems of global trade. Not only metaphorically, the characters tend to be literally addicted to the products of a global consumer culture. Franklin's first appearance in the novel shows him as a man well versed in these addictive substances.

Further, Franklin is taken off his pedestal as an American hero and a Founding Father through his actions in the novel. He is presented originally as an entertainer (Mason and Dixon watch him perform on the glass harmonica), a paranoid double agent (he suspects that Dixon is a Jesuit spy and that Mason is an agent for the East India Company), and a philanderer (he attracts the lovely Dolly and Molly to his side). In this way, Franklin becomes more of the human he represents himself as in his autobiography, in which he frequently engages in questionable, if not abhorrent, behavior toward women, or his essays, in which he frequently expresses views that are horrifyingly racist to a twenty-first-century audience. Franklin is divested of the role of the idealized hero that he has played in American folklore.

George Washington provides the most conflicting example of a Founding Father debunked. He is certainly constructed as an affable character. He sends a preternatural carriage to pick up Mason and Dixon in Philadelphia. Somehow, this horse-drawn carriage is able to travel the 150 or so miles from Philadelphia to Mount Vernon in a single night. Washington is generous enough to stock the carriage with porter and sandwiches. And, upon Mason and Dixon's arrival, Washington invites them to sit on his porch and engage in a relaxing conversation. He even offers them marijuana, a pipe to smoke it out of, and snacks to cure any subsequent munchies. He is a fun character. The conversation that follows Mason and Dixon's wild ride to Mount Vernon, however, takes on an air of seriousness.

First, Washington betrays his personal greed. He outlines for Mason and Dixon his desire to establish an Ohio company, that is, a chartered company profiting off the natural resources of what, at the time, was land occupied by Native Americans, land that the British government prohibited American colonists from settling upon. Washington is daunted by neither law nor ethics. He tells Mason and Dixon, "Americans will fight Indians whenever they please, which is whenever they can,— and the Brits wherever they must, for we will be no more contain'd, than tax'd" (277). The Americans of whom Washington speaks are specifically any army Washington can raise—which will later become factions of the Revolutionary Army. His desire to kill Native Americans may be lightly expressed, but it gains depth in retrospect when the reader compares Washington's flippant attitude toward Native Americans with the atrocity committed by the Paxton Boys in Lancaster later in the novel. Separately, both Mason and Dixon visit the site where the Paxton Boys slaughtered a tribe of Native Americans. Both characters confront their separate disgust at the act. Nonetheless, the act serves as a concrete explication of what Washington means when he says, "Americans will fight Indians whenever they please." Specifically, Washington is expressing his willingness to commit genocide in order to form a chartered company. This version of Washington is a far cry from the honest lad of folklore who confesses to cutting down his father's cherry tree because he cannot tell a lie.

Beyond Washington's genocidal ideations, his sexism is inescapable. The sweets that he, Mason, and Dixon munch on are provided by his wife, Martha. Martha is so pressed upon, so overworked that she is described as seeming "to bustle even when standing still" (280). Nonetheless, she produces for the men "Tarts, Pop-overs, Gingerbread Figures, fried Pies, stuff'd Doughnuts, and other Units of Refreshment" (280). Baking all these sweets would have taken a tremendous amount of free labor on the part of Martha. Clearly, it is having a negative impact on her well-being.

In addition, Pynchon presents Washington as a slaveholder. This is a complex presentation. On the one hand, Washington's slave, Gershom, seems so happy that Washington claims to be Gershom's master in name only. Nonetheless, Washington still views himself as a master and still orders Gershom around. Gershom's happiness is tied to his outlet as a stand-up comedian. This role is, of course, one more of Pynchon's clever anachronisms. In all likelihood, colonial Virginia boasted no slave stand-up comics in the style of Gershom. He is, instead, a sort of pre-Revolutionary Redd Foxx. He tells "King Joaks," which he describes as "Slave-and-Master Joaks, re-tailor'd" (284). The jokes he tells are superficially pleasant, making light of the imbalance of power. Like Redd Foxx himself, and Foxx's joke about getting fired upon in World War II and running so far back away from the line of fire that he bumped into a general, Gershom's jokes reveal a deep-seated sense of injustice. Gershom reflects Tony Tanner's assessment of Pynchon's tone in *Mason & Dixon*: "What Pynchon realises, beyond any other contemporary writer, is that the best way to be deadly serious is to be whimsically unserious" (234). Gershom, and by extension Pynchon, is deadly serious in portraying the foundation of America as motivated less by an ideology of freedom and equality and more by wealthy landowners seeking to expand their wealth at the expense of women, slaves, Native Americans, and contract employees like Mason and Dixon.

Gershom further presses the issue of slavery in the novel. The issue is inescapable. Any discussion of American literature—or America as a construct—sooner or later must confront this legacy. The specter of slavery haunts Mason and Dixon. As their time in America draws to a close, Dixon processes his experiences not only on the line but in traveling throughout the empire. He concludes that one common element follows him and Mason everywhere. Dixon tells Mason:

> Slaves. Ev'ry day at the Cape, we lived with Slavery in our faces,— more of it at St. Helena,— and now here we are again, in another Colony, this time having drawn them a Line between their Slave-Keepers and their Wage-Payers, as if doom'd to re-encounter thro' the World this public Secret, this shameful Core. . . . Pretending it to be ever somewhere else, with the Turks, the Russians, the Companies, down there, down where it smells like warm Brine and Gunpowder fumes, they're murdering and dispossessing thousands untallied, the innocent of the World, passing daily in to the Hands of Slave-owners and Torturers, but oh, never in Holland, nor in England, that Garden of Fools . . . ? Christ, Mason. (692–93)

Dixon recognizes just how entangled he, his actions, and his culture are with slavery. He sees the concept that Hardt and Negri summarize: "slave labor in the colonies made capitalism in Europe possible" (*Empire* 122). Dixon meditates on his complicity in the system. And he, in particular, has been bothered by slavery throughout the novel. His discomfort with the institution made him suspicious to the whites in South Africa; it made him dangerous among the slaveholders in America. Pynchon seems to revel in the irony that the historical Jeremiah Dixon was a Quaker who, according to Dixon family legend at least, confronted a slave driver in Baltimore and took his whip,[4] yet this same Dixon's name would be adapted and come to serve as a nickname for the slaveholding states: Dixie.

Much has been written about Dixon's abhorrence of the institution of slavery and about Pynchon's treatment of slavery in the novel. Most critics point to the aforementioned specific moment when Dixon confronts the slave driver. The incident occurs late in the novel, shortly before Mason and Dixon are to return to England. Both are in Baltimore when they witness a slave driver beating slaves unmercifully. Dixon intervenes, takes the whip from the slave driver, punches him in the face, takes his keys, and unlocks the chains that hold the slaves. This is, in a sense, a moment of catharsis in the novel. Dixon has opposed slavery throughout the novel, but this is his most dramatic moment of action against it. T. C. Boyle, in his review of *Mason & Dixon*, refers to the scene as Dixon's moment of "true heroism" (9). Barry Lewis, in his essay "Teaching Pynchon's *Mason & Dixon*," refers to this as the "moment of final suspense" (156) in the novel, that is, the moment at which the author's major theme is revealed. Lewis goes so far as to suggest teaching the novel as a way of unpacking the meaning of Dixon's action with the slave driver. Lewis claims, "This episode, and the novel as a whole, therefore illustrates the insight that all that is necessary for evil to triumph is for good men to do nothing" (156–57). While Lewis does provide a well-meaning adage, I strongly disagree with his suggestion that the novel should be simplified in this way. *Mason & Dixon* is a gigantic novel. It is a rich vein that scholars can mine for entire careers. In this chapter, I am doing no more than digging in one part of the thematic caverns that Pynchon has created in *Mason & Dixon*. Beyond the empire, slavery, and subjunctive that I discuss in this chapter, there is rich work that has been done and is yet to be done with Pynchon's historiography, his notions of time in the novel, his gendered reading of the new republic, and various other topics. To minimize the novel to a slogan that fits on a bumper sticker, as Lewis has done, does a disservice to a novel with the breadth, depth, and insight of *Mason & Dixon*. The other problem with Lewis's reading lies in the events that immediately follow Dixon's unchaining of the slaves.[5]

In his essay "The Sweetness of Immorality," Brian Thill revisits Dixon's confrontation with the slave driver. Thill investigates the complexity of this moment. He observes the problems with situating heroism in this moment of violence. First, Thill argues that Dixon's attack can be read as one more reification of the "suffering black body" (51) and violence privileged with a sense of paternalism. Further, Thill points out that nothing is accomplished by this confrontation. While punching the slave driver may have been cathartic for Dixon and may even be cathartic for the reader, it does nothing to hinder the progress of slavery. The institution will be unmarred by Dixon's actions. The uselessness of escape is immediately noted after Dixon unchains the slaves. A slave tells Dixon, "Sheriff's men'll be here any moment,— don't worry about us,— some will stay, some'll get away" (699). This statement by the slave highlights the futility of the situation. While Dixon has unchained them, the slaves still stand in the middle of a slaveholding city in the middle of a slaveholding state. The very hue of their skin makes them conspicuous. Their chances of escape are slim. And even if they do escape, their options for a peaceful, just life are severely limited. In other words, the slaves may be temporarily unchained because of Dixon's actions, but they are far from free.

Thill also suggests, "Part of the problem for characters like Dixon is that their actions are tainted by complicity with the system that they seem to oppose" (55). As Dixon himself has noted throughout the text, he benefits greatly from the system of global commodity culture and its attendant slavery. He benefits directly when slaves serve him food (as they do both in the Vroom household in South Africa and in various inns in Pennsylvania) or when, as in the case with Gershom, they entertain him. He benefits less directly from the institution when he relishes sugar and coffee that is imported from slave colonies. Dixon's very employment derives from his superior ability as a surveyor to create a border between the wage payers and the slaveholders (though it should be noted that slavery was legal in both Pennsylvania and Maryland during the time when Mason and Dixon worked in the two colonies, the primary difference being that slavery was generally practiced on a larger scale in Maryland).

Dixon reveals his frustration with his own complicity when, instead of fleeing the scene where he has assaulted a slave driver and where a hostile crowd is closing in on him, he pauses to wonder, "What's a man of Conscience to do?" (699). In other words, how can one person like Dixon, who is simultaneously disgusted by the injustice of slavery yet addicted to the spoils of it, work toward a more just world? Brian Thill raises the same issue, stating: "[W]hat is much less clear is what should be done about it" (68). The answer Thill arrives at is bleak. He concludes, "If there are choices to be made in the world of *Mason & Dixon*, . . . they would seem to be between the doomed ineffective heroism of the small act of kindness and violence, the radical reorganization of economic power based on the mass awakening of the socially conscious consumer class, or the retreat into any of a number of attractive, albeit temporary, fantasies"

(74). Thus, Thill suggests that little can be done about the injustices that Dixon confronts. Reading Pynchon's subjunctive, in which the "attractive, albeit temporary fantasies" become a pathway into envisioning a more just world, a way of inspiring a "mass awakening of the socially conscious consumer class," provides a more hopeful approach than suggested by Thill. I discuss this with more depth and connect it to the Occupy movement later in this chapter.

"Commerce without Slavery Is Unthinkable"

As I mention above, there is a danger in placing too much weight on Dixon's act of violent resistance to slavery. It can be oversimplified. Along similar lines, Tony Tanner argues that it does Pynchon a disservice to read the novel as "a sort of politically correct disguised tract concerning the treatment of Indians and Blacks by white settlers" (232). Indeed, little new information can be gained from the insight that chattel slavery is unethical. Instead, as Christy L. Burns suggests in "Postmodern Historiography," readers of *Mason & Dixon* "interpret history as a dialogue between the differences and the uncanny similarities of that time's 'angle' and their own." Following the lead of both Tanner and Burns, it is important to question what, exactly, Pynchon's exploration into eighteenth-century slavery says about twenty-first-century society.

Contemporary protest movements elucidate these connections. Specifically, the 2003 documentary *The Yes Men* features two American antiglobalization activists, Jacques Servin and Igor Vamos, who have succeeded in masquerading as representatives of the World Trade Organization. At one point, the documentary follows the pair to Finland, where they pose as lecturers from the WTO. As such, they give a presentation at an international trade conference. The presentation focuses on slavery and its adaptation to market forces. Servin argues that the invisible hand of the marketplace would have altered slavery had the American Civil War not ended the institution of chattel slavery. According to Servin, it would be much cheaper for multinational corporations to move their factories to the location where the workers already reside than to kidnap, enslave, house, and feed the slaves. He compares the costs of maintaining a slave in Finland to the benefits of instead keeping slaves in overseas sweatshops, where, Servin ironically notes, the slave is free. Servin's conflation of the terms *slave* (referring to chattel slavery of the eighteenth and nineteenth century) and *employee* (referring to laborers in overseas factories who are paid wages below a basic subsistence level) makes a powerful statement about the exploitation of workers in the twenty-first century. Injustices are frequently incommensurable, and a ranking system of injustices is counterproductive. With this in mind, Servin's presentation in *The Yes Men* demonstrates that, while chattel slavery may be mostly relegated to history books, exploitation and injustice continue to be inextricable from global commodity culture. As Hardt and Negri observe, "[S]lavery and wage labor engaged each other as dance partners in the coordinated steps of capitalist development" (*Empire* 122). As Reverend Cherrycoke reflects, "Commerce without Slavery is unthinkable" (108). For a twenty-first-century audience, it becomes important to understand that the requisite exploitation and injustice bred from those same systems which created chattel slavery continue to exist.

Mason & Dixon is largely concerned with understanding this injustice and exploitation. Pynchon broadens his examination beyond the issue of chattel slavery. Like Servin, he conflates the term *slave* with other terms for workers. One notable early example of this occurs when Mason and Dixon are still in South Africa. Dixon immediately shows an abhorrence for slavery, so the white South Africans avoid him. Mason's views are not as readily transparent. Because of this, the family with whom Mason and Dixon typically dine, the Vrooms, ensnare Mason into their dubious plot. The family matriarch, Johanna Vroom, wishes to couple Mason with her slave, Austra, the result of the coupling being to produce a slave child. As Austra explains to Mason, Johanna desires Mason's "Whiteness" (65) because slaves with a lighter tint to their skin sell for more on the slave market. The Vrooms' plot is unsettling for most contemporary readers of the novel. Mason is likewise troubled when Austra approaches him with Johanna's plan. He says it is unthinkable in England for one person to feel entitled to bid another person to have a child. Austra shrugs off Mason's assertion, saying, "Poh. White Wives are much alike, and all their Secrets are common knowledge at the Market. Many have there been, oblig'd to go on bearing children,— for no reason but the man's pride." Mason responds, "Our Women are free" (65). As Austra observes, Mason's professed belief in freedom is compromised by his use of the possessive pronoun "our." Pynchon thus subtly reminds his reader that marriage laws in eighteenth-century England still considered wives to be the property of their husbands, perhaps not chattel slaves, exactly, but humans who were legally the property of other humans.

This reminder becomes more poignant when Mason and Dixon meet Martha Washington, who is George's property and is worked until so frazzled that she seems to bustle while standing still. The gendered exploitation of the entire Vroom plot is telling. First, all three Vroom daughters are drawn into the intrigue. Though all three are adolescents less than half the age of Mason (the youngest daughter is twelve, the oldest sixteen), Johanna sets them loose to sexually titillate Mason into a state of priapism. They chase after Mason, wiggle on his lap, rip their bodices (which are cleverly designed to allow a young Vroom to both rip open her bodice and refasten it quickly), and otherwise tease him in hopes that his desires will be transferred onto Austra in a profitable way. Nor does Johanna leave the teasing solely to her daughters. Finding herself alone in a room with Mason, she takes the opportunity to rip her own bodice. Pynchon presents these exploits in a madcap fashion, but the serious undertones are not ignored. Austra's seemingly willful participation in the plan does not lessen the fact that she remains a slave and the Vrooms' ownership of her extends to her womb. The limited opportunities for all the Vroom women are suggested by their complicity in such an unsavory plan. Mason is similarly highlighted as the subject of a different type of exploitation, this time at the hands of the disenfranchised women. The family's patriarch, Cornelius Vroom, seems to be intentionally oblivious to the entire intrigue. He turns a blind eye to the girls' dinnertime flirtation; he consistently avoids the rooms of ripped bodices. Nonetheless, should Austra provide the Vrooms with a light-skinned baby to sell in the slave market, it is Cornelius who would become the custodian of the wealth produced. Untangling this complex web of exploitation presents a situation in which chattel slavery is merely one symptom of the larger disease of exploitation in the marketplace.

Mason confronts the conflation of the term *slavery* again in America. During the first break in their work on the line, Dixon travels south into Virginia while Mason goes north into New York. While in Brooklyn, Mason falls in with a group of American revolutionaries led by the mysterious Captain Volcanoe. The revolutionaries and Mason discuss the concept of virtual representation—the name the British government used to describe the representation that American colonists had in Parliament. During the conversation, Mason admits that he has never owned land, that the rooms he has inhabited have all been part of his contract for employment. One of the revolutionaries responds, "Then you're a Serf. As they call it here, a Slave" (406).[6] Pynchon's ironic employment of the Marxist concept of a wage slave by an American revolutionary is amusing. Nonetheless, Pynchon's point is complicated when Mason dismisses this notion of slavery as "shallow Sophistry" (407). The conversation among the revolutionaries continues to address the exploitation of contract employees and other laborers. Specifically, because Mason is from the Stroud, the revolutionaries discuss the deplorable working conditions of the weavers there. This discussion again solidifies the connection both Pynchon and Yes Man Jacques Servin make between the exploitation and injustice of chattel slavery and the further exploitation and injustice inherent in a system of global commodity capitalism. As critic Stacey Olster observes, this conflation does not "suggest that Pynchon is preaching equivalency among the various forms of bondage—whether denoted in terms of hirelings, indentured servants, contractual agents, or slaves—the novel depicts" (109). Instead of suggesting equivalency, Pynchon complicates labor and exploitation. He goes beyond the simple notion that chattel slavery is unethical. Instead, he links the exploitation of divorcing labor from the wealth it produces with the injustice of global economic systems. In all these cases, the workers are alienated from their labor. In the purest Marxist sense, their value is equated with the marketplace. They are only valuable in regard to what they produce. They become a commodity—labor to be bought and sold—and thereby sacrifice some of their individuality and humanity. This notion of labor as a commodity becomes more poignant in *Against the Day* when Pynchon engages with the fatal flaw of economic liberalism: treating labor and land as commodities when, by definition, neither are.

Reflecting on both Captain Volcanoe's usage of the term *serf* and Stacey Olster's inclusion of "indentured servants" takes on a richer significance when considering contemporary economics and resistance movements. As Maurizio Lazzarato observes in *The Making of the Indebted Man*, neoliberal capitalism is dependent on a debtor-creditor dynamic. Social safety nets, education, and much of the work of governments in Europe and the United States are filtered through the financial industry. Money is borrowed for everything from wars to roads to universities to food stamps. Nearly all major purchases in the United States—houses, cars, and the like—are financed through bank loans. Smaller consumer goods are financed through credit cards. This creates a situation in which workers owe capital a growing percentage of their paychecks prior to earning the money. This situation is exacerbated in times of financial crises, during which times taxpayers bail out the very financiers to whom they are indebted. This frustration found a voice in the Occupy movement. In "Scenes from an Occupation," Astra Taylor describes an experience she had in Zuccotti Park during the occupation. She encountered a young man who called out for all activists to write down the total of their debt on giant sheets of paper. He shouted, "Come and tell us how valuable you really are to the one percent" (52). Taylor, experiencing a sense of shame, wrote down her mid-five-figures student loan debt. The shame, perhaps, was associated with the acknowledgment—amid a backdrop of freedom and participatory democracy—that once she left the occupation, she resumed her life in an economic relationship very similar to that of a medieval serf or colonial indentured servant. As Lazzarato observes, "The debtor-creditor relationship . . . intensifies mechanisms of exploitation and domination at every level of society, for within it no distinction exists between workers and the unemployed, consumers and producers, working and non-working populations, retirees and welfare recipients. Everyone is a 'debtor,' accountable to and guilty before capital" (*The Making* 7). Like Mason in a room of revolutionaries, our economic bind in relation to chartered companies and more contemporary supranational economic institutions calls into question very basic questions of our freedom and enfranchisement in a system of global capitalism.

Additionally, the dangers inherent in simplifying the issue of chattel slavery have been explored by theorist Megan Boler. In her book *Feeling Power: Emotions and Education*, Boler warns against what she refers to as empathetic readings of texts. She uses the example of Art Spiegelman's *Maus* and her introductory multicultural literature course. She finds that her students tend to empathize with the character of Art, who is listening to his father tell stories of the Holocaust. Through their empathy with Art, the students are divested from the experience of the Holocaust itself and any feelings of complicity. They are able, in fact, to dismiss issues of injustice in the text. According to Boler, additional problems with empathetic readings occur when a reader tries to imagine herself as a character in a book about a disenfranchised culture of which she is not a part, and when she imagines how she would react as a member of that culture. Boler demonstrates the impossibility of this type of genuine empathy. She further suggests that this attempt to empathize more often than not leads to readers judging the characters. It is this judgment that Boler wishes to avoid.

Boler's warnings can instruct a reader's approach to *Mason & Dixon*. When confronted with slaveholding societies such as those Mason and Dixon reside in, the temptation to separate oneself from feelings of complicity is powerful. A reader cannot be blamed for seeking refuge in the knowledge that chattel slavery was outlawed before she was born, or for imagining herself in Dixon's shoes and feeling the cathartic release when Dixon assaults the slave driver. Both of these reactions, however, separate the reader from the injustice in the text (in the same way that empathy with Art separates readers from the injustices in *Maus*). Boler suggests that readers perform what she calls testimonial readings, readings that bear witness to the injustices the characters face, that refrain from judgment, that investigate the systems of power that create these injustices, and that explore the reader's complicity in these systems. Pynchon's connections with Empire and slavery afford the reader the opportunity to bear witness to the injustices upon which the wealth in America was built and to recognize our own role in this system of injustice. Finally, with the use of the subjunctive in the text, Pynchon allows us to imagine possible worlds in which we confront this injustice in meaningful ways.

Subjunctive America

The ways in which Reverend Cherrycoke narrates the story provide an entry point into Pynchon's use of the subjunctive as a tool for envisioning social justice. As the primary storyteller in the novel, Cherrycoke relates information that he could not possibly possess firsthand. He narrates Mason and Dixon's innermost thoughts, though neither character chooses to share those thoughts with him. In fact, Mason and Dixon seem to view Cherrycoke as something between a tolerable nuisance and an intolerable one. Beyond this, Cherrycoke narrates events that occurred continents away from him, in worlds and time periods to which he has no firsthand access. The audience that listens to Cherrycoke's story in the LeSpark parlor frequently accosts Cherrycoke for his storytelling liberties. Cherrycoke's response is more complex than contradictory. He both seeks shelter in the subjunctive, that is, his prerogative to present the imagined as true, and self-reflexively admits his unreliability. In this way, he is a prototypically postmodern storyteller. He rejects what Jean-François Lyotard terms "grand narratives." Instead, he acknowledges that our conceptions of the world are built upon narrative knowledge and therefore contain all the dubious elements attendant to reframing experiences into narrative formats. Cherrycoke articulates this most clearly when he writes:

> Facts are but the Play-things of lawyers,— Tops and Hoops, forever a-spin. . . . Alas, the Historian may indulge no such idle Rotating. History is not Chronology, for that is left to Lawyers,— nor is it Remembrance, for Remembrance belongs to the People. History can as little pretend to the Veracity of the one, as claim the Power of the other,— her Practitioners, to survive, must soon learn the arts of the quidnunc, spy, and Taproom Wit,— that there may ever continue more than one life-line back into a Past we risk, each day, losing our forebears in forever,— not a Chain of single Links, for one broken Link could lose us All,— rather, a great disorderly Tangle of Lines, long and short, weak and strong, vanishing into the Mnemonick Deep, with only their Destination in common. (349)

This passage reflects the postmodern condition suggested by Brian McHale in *Constructing Postmodernism*, where McHale clarifies "that we need not abandon metanarratives—which may, after all, do useful work for us—so long as we 'turn them down' from metanarratives to 'little narratives'" (24). In other words, Cherrycoke self-reflexively abandons a search for epistemological truth. Instead, he seeks narratives as we understand them, full of the gossip of the quidnunc, the hidden intelligence of the spy, and the humor of the taproom wit. While Cherrycoke cannot be relied on to spin facts or to wield history as a weapon, he can be relied on to recognize discursive voices from which we can draw meaning, provided we turn that meaning down from a grand narrative into a little narrative.

It is further notable that this selection of Cherrycoke's comes not during his story but as a passage that he cites from his subjunctive book *Christ and*

History. This citation adds to the discursive voices a spiritual one. Entwining a spiritual element into a postmodern history about the Age of Reason proves to be a significant move on Cherrycoke's part. Several critics point to Cherrycoke's—and, by extension, Pynchon's—lament that a certain amount of spirituality and magic are lost in the Age of Reason.[7] Christy L. Burns succinctly summarizes this when she observes that Pynchon, mostly through the character of Mason, "struggles to hold onto the magical, even as Enlightenment thought was calling for its extinction." Thus, the astronomer royal Nevil Maskelyne is caught casting clandestine horoscopes, and his fellow astronomer Charles Mason—who, let us not forget, is one of the premier scientists of his day—converses with ghosts and narrates tales of pygmies living in a mythical time perpetually relegated to eleven days ago. As Mason and Dixon clear their borderline into the depths of the Maryland and Pennsylvania woodlands, they cast a pallor of Enlightenment, with its rigid scientific proofs and mathematical precision, over the myths, legends, and folklores that bring meaning to the lives of the cultures bisected by the line. Magic and spirituality get lost in the Age of Reason.

Beyond the subjunctive as a space to critique Enlightenment philosophy, *Mason & Dixon* juxtaposes the subjunctive with the burgeoning global marketplace. This presents itself from the time when Mason and Dixon first arrive in America. Mason and Dixon barely have the time to disembark from their transatlantic voyage before they are besieged with advertisements in America. They step off the ship to be greeted by various hawkers selling aphrodisiacs, flasks, the services of a prostitute, and even salvation. This concept of religion-as-commodity greeting Mason and Dixon upon their arrival in America is significant. It introduces another conflation Pynchon plays with in *Mason & Dixon*: the conflation of business and religion. This conflation gains significance later in the novel. Cherrycoke's narrative is interrupted by his benefactor, Wade LeSpark. LeSpark narrates his adventures dealing weapons. It is dangerous work. He sells to all sides of the conflicts, raising the possibility that two warring factions could both be armed by LeSpark. Nonetheless, LeSpark characterizes his experience as "safe inside the belief as unquestioning as in any form of Pietism you could find out there that he, yes little JWL [J. Wade LeSpark], goeth likewise under the protection of a superior Power,— not, in this case, God, but rather Business. What turn of earthly history, however perverse, would dare interfere with the workings of the Invisible Hand?" (411). In other words, the higher power that LeSpark recognizes is capitalism, attended by Adam Smith's concept of the "invisible hand" of the economy. For LeSpark, this invisible hand does more than Adam Smith's original concept, which was expected to self-regulate excesses in the marketplace, and protects him amid the wilderness of violence and war that he both fosters and profits from. In both cases, a genuine age of reason would have to recognize the invisible hand as something based more in magic or spirituality than in logic.[8] LeSpark's vision of the invisible hand, though, is downright religious. It is a higher power—indeed, a superior one. It is a benevolent protector. Like Pynchon's conflation of slavery and wage labor, this conflation of religion and business does not suggest an equivalency. Instead, Pynchon blends these terms together as a means of better understanding the impact of Empire on contemporary society. Specifically, the conflation highlights the illogical, quasireligious belief in a self-regulating marketplace that is a foundational ideology of neoliberalism.

Returning to Mason and Dixon's arrival in America, the barrage of hawkers is significant because they draw attention to the fact that, while the Age of Reason sought to eliminate magic, Empire simultaneously created what Raymond Williams famously termed "the magic system": the contemporary advertising industry.

Building on Williams's notion of the magic system, Sut Jhally examines the value system implicit in advertising. Jhally argues that, if an alien anthropologist were to study contemporary American culture by examining the primary stories that are promulgated throughout our society (which is how he characterizes advertising), the anthropologist would likely conclude that we are a society obsessed with magic. We believe that commodities are bestowed with the supernatural powers necessary to transform ourselves and our lives into the realm of perfection. This equates to Mason and Dixon's voyage deeper into the depths of the American continent. The further they sally from Philadelphia, the more mythical the land becomes. Mason and Dixon encounter perfectly symmetrical mounds beyond the capacity of human construction, coaches and taverns with interiors vastly larger than their exteriors, a sentient mechanical duck that can fly at speeds faster than the human eye can detect, ghost visions, memories of mythical worms, tall tales of mythical astronomers, a cameo by Popeye in a western Pennsylvania tavern, even a werebeaver. Among the preternatural elements Mason and Dixon encounter are a golem whose footsteps can be heard from miles away, who is essentially a giant, and a field of vegetables so large that a family can carve a house out of a single beet and live inside, eating the walls as it deems necessary. Combining these last two elements—a giant and magical vegetables—a contemporary reader can make connections to this magic system of advertising: among the mythical elements Mason and Dixon encounter is, essentially, the Jolly Green Giant of General Mills' long-standing advertising campaign. The giant in Pynchon's world is a golem. He follows a poet. The vegetables are the property of a distant race of beings. The Native Americans who oversee the vegetables assume this race of beings is from another planet. A contemporary reader saturated in images of the Jolly Green Giant and the magic system can read the size of the vegetables as a metaphor for the size of late twentieth-century factory farming. The role of the Native Americans as mere custodians of land until it can be repurposed for the profit of a multinational corporation is problematic. The Jolly Green Giant is constructed out of, well, that material from which golems are constructed. Christy L. Burns observes, "Re-imagining, in Pynchon, may often be a way of progressive revisioning, but it can alternately be co-opted for exploitative forms of entrepreneurship." In the case of the golem and the giant vegetables, the myths of early America can be seen as not lost to the Age of Reason but co-opted by the age of neoliberalism.

Nonetheless, a reader should not ignore the first half of Burns's observation above. The subjunctive in Pynchon does work as a form of "progressive revisioning." Jhally asserts that, while advertising does produce a magic system wherein the stories transmit the value system that perpetuates neoliberal culture, it is a fragile system. Jhally recommends dismantling this system by producing new stories that are more attractive than, say, a giant selling vegetables. Pynchon's use of the subjunctive does exactly that. He creates his own magic system, one that is far more attractive and that transmits very different values than the one produced by multinational corporations and national governments.

In "Bordering the Subjunctive in Thomas Pynchon's *Mason & Dixon*," Adam Lifshey asserts, "Subjunctive America, the antithesis of declarative imperialism, is that unmapped and atemporal space where alternative possibilities yet abound, where plural local realities exist side by side, a culturally creative place that is distinct from, and therefore resistant to, the imperial cartography imposed upon the New World" (6). In other words, Pynchon creates not just one rebuttal to the "declarative imperialism" of an Age of Reason, not just one counternarrative to the doxa of Empire. Instead, he creates multiple spaces, stories, and worlds that call into question any sense of the "normal" or "natural" in the hegemony of global commodity culture. Just as Pynchon's prose itself is complex, discursive, and open to various approaches and avenues for meaning, the stories in Cherrycoke's subjunctive chapters afford freedom to readers. As Tony Tanner claims, "Pynchon does not care for single authorised versions" (233). Instead, Pynchon provides multiple possibilities for meaning.

This discursive approach is in line with Brian McHale's explorations of the usefulness of postmodernism. McHale states, "Above all, we choose one story or variant over another for its superior *interest*. Minimally, we strive to tell stories that are at least *relevant* to our audience; optimally, we hope to make our stories compelling, if possible even gripping" (*Constructing* 26). McHale, like

Reverend Cherrycoke, aborts the search for a grand narrative, replacing it with a series of little narratives that can be useful. When applying this to *Mason & Dixon*, the question remains, useful in what ways?

One place to seek answers to this question is the scene in the novel featuring a Quaker in a Philadelphia coffee house. Amid the revolutionary discussion in the coffee house, the Quaker points out the abundance of sugar everyone is consuming. He observes that the sugar is produced from the slavery south of Philadelphia. The Quaker asks, "If we may refuse to write upon stamped paper, and for the tea of the East India Company find a tolerable *Succedaneum* in New-Jersey red root, might Philosophy not as well discover some Patriotic alternative to these vile crystals that eat into our souls as horribly as our teeth?" (329–30). In broader terms, the Quaker is asking what other stories we could tell to replace the magic system's narrative of consumption, specifically the self-destructive, addictive consumption in that coffee house. True to his form of providing discursive testimonials without judgment, Cherrycoke gives the Quaker time to speak without affording a commentary or rebuttal.

One answer to the Quaker's question may be: protesting sugar is too specific. Just as, above, I discuss the problem of attacking chattel slavery without acknowledging that even its abolition leaves intact the destructive and exploitative practices of Empire, attacking sugar without acknowledging its role in the greater system of global consumer capitalism is simply a means of metaphorically punching a slave driver in the face. Instead of creating a direct substitute for sugar while leaving Empire intact, perhaps a more effective approach would be to tell stories of a better world existing independent of Empire's exploitation.

A New Historical Novel of America

The challenge to tell more liberating stories harks back to a literary discussion surrounding the novel of the early American republic. Notably, critic W. Channing in 1815 called for a new type of American literature,[9] one built of historical novels that did similar work in the service of constructing an American identity as that which Walter Scott's novels had done in constructing an identity for the British empire. These historical novels would then help determine the idealized values of American culture and transmit what that cultural value system was. The most canonized novels that answered Channing's call were the Leatherstocking Tales of James Fenimore Cooper. In these novels, Cooper promotes the values of white supremacy, particularly in relation to Native Americans, and narrates the genocide of Native Americans as inevitable. Perhaps, as Carolyn L. Karcher argues, these values led to the survival and canonization of

Cooper's novels. After all, regardless of its professed values, much of the wealth in the United States was built on the backs of exploited populations and justified through policies of genocide and institutionalized racism, sexism, classism, and heterosexism.

At the same time, other novelists who promoted different value systems answered Channing's call and wrote novels that rivaled Cooper's in popularity. Specifically, Lydia Maria Child's *Hobomok* and Catharine Maria Sedgwick's *Hope Leslie* produced counternarratives to the Leatherstocking Tales. Both Child and Sedgwick endeavored to write women and Native Americans back into the history of the early republic. From a twenty-first-century perspective, there are problems with both of these novels. *Hobomok* ends with the eponymous Native American character willfully vanishing to make room for European settlers and thereby seeming to portray the genocide of Native Americans as part of the natural course of events.[10] *Hope Leslie*, while inviting the possibility of interracial marriage through two minor characters who live among the Native Americans, leaves no room for interracial marriage within European American society. Nonetheless, both Child's and Sedgwick's novels serve as important—perhaps vital—counternarratives to those of Cooper. Instead of judging the troubling elements of *Hobomok* and *Hope Leslie*, a reader would be better served to remember Megan Boler's argument in *Feeling Power* and read the novels as testimonials. Doing so allows the reader to investigate issues of gender and race in the new republic, to raise questions about the systems that created these injustices, to recognize complicity in those systems, and to seek possible avenues leading toward a more just world. Child's and Sedgwick's novels provide that first, necessary step.

Likewise, *Mason & Dixon* can be read as an attempt to answer Channing's call to write the new historical novel of America (albeit nearly two centuries after Cooper, Child, and Sedgwick). Like Child and Sedgwick, Pynchon writes diverse voices back into the narrative of colonial times. Like Child and Sedgwick, Pynchon addresses systems of injustice. Like its predecessors, Pynchon's novel has troubling aspects. Specifically, Pynchon's representation of George Washington and Benjamin Franklin as philandering slaveholders embarking upon genocide can be upsetting for an American audience schooled from a very young age to idealize—perhaps even idolize—these historical figures. Pynchon even goes so far as to attack the Founding Fathers more or less directly. At one point in the novel, a west Pennsylvania tavern patron states, "The coming Rebellion is theirs,— Franklin, and that Lot,— and Heaven help the rest of us, if they prevail" (488). For a twenty-first-century reader reading this statement with a balanced sense of American history, this line echoes with the resonance of a revolution fought in the name of liberty and justice that produced instead a legacy of slavery, genocide, economic exploitation, institutionalized sexism and heterosexism, and various other injustices. This, in fact, is the fundamental problem that all American authors have faced when historicizing the American project: the contradiction inherent in a racist, sexist, classist, heterosexist society founded in the name of justice. Nonetheless, American fiction has been and continues to be one battlefield upon which these injustices are confronted.

Pynchon seems to recognize this. Fiction and other types of literature factor heavily within Cherrycoke's storytelling. Cherrycoke's narrative is a bricolage of texts that have drifted in and out of American literary canons. He directly alludes to Laurence Sterne's *Tristram Shandy* and Jonathan Swift's *Tale of the Tub*. British novelist Samuel Johnson makes more than a cameo appearance. Although subjunctively, Johnson is a major character in one chapter. Another minor character, Timothy Tox—the poet responsible for the oft-quoted poem "The Pennsylvaniad," though only existing within the pages of *Mason & Dixon*—seems to be a fictionalized version of Joel Barlow, the real-life poet who wrote the poem *The Columbiad*, which has more than a few similarities to Tox's poem. Mason's dream of the North Cape and the exploitation of the Native population bears an eerie resemblance to a chapter of Bartolomé de las Casas's *A Brief History of the Devastation of the Indies* in which Casas describes Spaniards working Arawak pearl divers literally to death. Even Mason's final memory of Dixon relates a story in which a Benjamin Franklin, bearing an unmistakable resemblance to Dr. Frankenstein, electrocutes Dixon. The tone of the stories at times drifts into a recognizable form of American gothic storytelling reminiscent of Washington Irving and Nathaniel Hawthorne.

This bricolage is most notable through its incorporation not only of gothic elements but of a fictional gothic serial that invades *Mason & Dixon*. Throughout the novel, characters both in the 1760s tale of Mason and Dixon and in the 1786 Christmastide when Cherrycoke narrates the story read magazine and book installments of *The Ghastly Fop*. At one point, *The Ghastly Fop* actually takes over the narration of the tale. The story is no longer told entirely in Cherrycoke's voice. It is read from the pages that his niece and nephew share. The installment of *The Ghastly Fop* that is incorporated into the narrative borrows much from early American captivity narratives. It traces a European American settler named Eliza who is kidnapped from her Pennsylvania farm by Native Americans and taken into the wilderness northward. Eliza's kidnapping and voyage to Montreal follows closely Ann Eliza Bleecker's 1790–91 serial "The History of Maria Kittle." This may be an intentional allusion; perhaps Pynchon names the captive "Eliza" as a nod to Bleecker. Regardless, the narrative manages to further write the discursive experiences of French and Spanish Jesuits and one Chinese feng shui master into a colonial narrative. Perhaps more importantly, Eliza is a lesbian.[11] Upon her return to Pennsylvania, she engages in a loving relationship with Zsuzsa Szabó, a Prussian cavalrywoman. They continue to work on the line with Mason and Dixon's crew. Their presence and their open sexuality seem to cause no problems beyond a few broken hearts of axmen who had a crush on Zsuzsa. *The Ghastly Fop*'s intrusion into the novel, then, provides one more fiction transmitting values that are then incorporated into the "real world." It is one more testimony among the many discursive voices from which readers can seek to recognize systems of injustice, complicity, and subjunctive ways for a more just world.

Pynchon, of course, does not provide a single clear proposal for a more just world. He does not even provide a few clear proposals from which the reader can choose. Instead, *Mason & Dixon* narrates a series of subjunctive testimonies that serve to trigger the reader's imagination regarding what a world beyond Empire could look like. Two subjunctive testimonies in particular strike me as narratives that are useful. First, after Mason and Dixon leave America, Cherrycoke lingers behind to tell one more story. The final chapter in the section entitled "America" follows a subjunctive Mason and Dixon who do not stop nearly forty miles short of the Ohio territory the way the historical Mason and Dixon did. Instead, the subjunctive Mason and Dixon continue the line deep into the continent, moving through lands that would become Ohio, Indiana, Illinois, and on into the Great Plains. Their progress is not halted until their nightly astronomical sessions allow them to discover the new planet Uranus. Upon this discovery, the subjunctive Mason and Dixon decide to turn around and head back to England. As they are making this decision, Dixon asks, basically, what people will do without their line. Mason responds, "They will have to live their lives without any Line amongst 'em, unseparated, daily doing Business together, World's Business and Heart's alike, repriev'd from the Tyranny of residing either North or South of it. Nothing worse than that" (709). Mason's choice of words is intriguing. He states that, without the line, people will have to find a way to live "unseparated." More common terms for unseparated would be "together" or "unified." But Mason is not suggesting togetherness or unity. He is suggesting simply a lack of separation, the absence of a dividing line. It calls to mind Michael Hardt and Antonio Negri's definition of the multitude: "The multitude is composed of innumerable internal differences that can never be reduced to a unity or a single identity—different cultures, races, ethnicities, genders, and sexual orientations; different forms of labor; different ways of living; different views of the world; and different desires" (*Multitude* xiv). In fact, the diverse voices Cherrycoke represents throughout the novel, with their different cultures, races, ethnicities, genders, and sexual orientations, are a representation of the multitude. Without the boundaries born of an age so ostentatious as to call itself the Age of Reason, without the tyranny of Empire and the divisions and exploitations that accompany it, without the co-opted magic system, the multitude may envision a new way to live, one in which the "World's Business and Heart's alike" are the same thing.

Finally, on the last page of the novel, Mason's sons, William and Doctor Isaac, envision their new life in America. It is a subjunctive America, not the America they found when they traveled there with Mason in his dying days, but the one they imagined when they were children and Mason was carving his line through the wilderness. It is the America that lives up to its promises of freedom and equality. William and Doctor Isaac imagine "Stars so close you won't need a Telescope" and "Fish jump into your Arms" (773). This vision conjures the image of a relationship with the land and the people on the land that Mason and the Native Americans envisioned at the end of the Mason-Dixon line, when they discussed "Sky-fishing" (651). Sky-fishing referred initially to stars that attend astronomers while astronomers attend the stars. This sense of reciprocity can be expanded. Within the context of the original conversation, sky-fishing is about Mason and Dixon attending Native Americans while Native Americans attend Mason and Dixon. Beyond that, sky-fishing reciprocity can mean an activity in which discursive voices attend one another and the various subsequent testimonies, in which what the multitude fishes for in the sky is a magic system that envisions a more inclusive, more just world. All this is summed up by Mason's youngest son, Doctor Isaac: "We'll fish there. And you too" (773).

This discussion of the subjunctive, when taken as a whole, does come with a caveat. Just as Tony Tanner warned against reading *Mason & Dixon* as "a sort of politically correct disguised tract" (232), I am careful to avoid reading the subjunctive in *Mason & Dixon* as nothing more than an example of a postmodern discussion of difference and hybridity. In *Empire*, Michael Hardt and Antonio Negri criticize the transformative potential of postmodernism. They assert, "When we begin to consider the ideologies of corporate capital and the world market, it certainly appears that the postmodernist . . . theorists who advocate a politics of difference, fluidity, and hybridity in order to challenge the binaries and essentialism of modern sovereignty have been outflanked by the strategies of power" (138). In other words, Hardt and Negri view postmodernism—specifically, postmodernism's play with difference, its attacks on Enlightenment grand narratives, and its push to include diverse voices—as a means of supporting Empire's drive to break down national borders and to encourage difference and hybridity as concepts that justify global commodity trade.

To a certain extent, the discourse of Empire, particularly with its adherence to the magic system, embraces the discourse of postmodernism. When postmodern theorists envision a world that is more inclusive across the lines of race, gender, class, and sexuality, they provide a dream that the magic system can sell back to them. Empire can take these notions of diversity and present them through an advertising campaign that represents diversity, yet it is important to recognize that this representation of diversity does not promote the concept. It instead promotes the commodity that the advertisement features. If a more diverse world accompanies it, that is fine from the perspective of the marketplace. But that is not the goal of the advertisement. This is also the point where Pynchon's discussion of slavery and exploitation becomes most significant. From Empire's perspective, this discussion of diversity can accompany an advertisement, but a celebration of difference cannot go so far as to suggest that the workers in overseas factories are equally human and have a right to just working conditions.

In short, Empire—particularly through its magic system—has learned to tell postmodern stories. Nonetheless, there is a difference between telling a story that adheres to the characteristics of a theory and actually subscribing to the ideology. While the marketplace of global commodity capitalism can repackage ideas of difference and hybridity and sell those ideas back to potential customers, corporate culture is still dependent on mass production, which, by definition, is neither difference nor hybridity. It is a repetition of the same. Most postmodern stories told through Empire's magic system are merely stories told to mask the similarities of fungible commodities. Likewise, any talk of inclusion for diverse voices on the part of the magic system ignores the racism and ignorance necessary to perpetuate the abhorrent labor conditions of many of the factories producing the goods.

Pynchon's stories, on the other hand, seek to genuinely include discursive voices. Particularly through his discussions of storytelling, nation-building, madness in the Age of Reason, slavery, exploitation, and the subjunctive, his novel seeks to understand the systems that cause injustice, the ways in which we are complicit in these systems, and the possible avenues for resistance to or advancement beyond these systems of injustice. This is a far cry from simply representing difference as a means of selling mass-produced, fungible commodities. Nonetheless, the conclusions drawn from both Hardt and Negri and Pynchon seem very similar. Hardt and Negri conclude, "Difference, hybridity, and mobility are not liberatory in themselves, but neither are truth, purity, and stasis. The real revolutionary practice refers to the level of *production*. Truth will not make us free, but taking control of the production of truth will" (*Empire* 156). For Hardt and Negri, the truth is not the liberating element. Liberation instead comes from the ability to promulgate the truth. In context, the truth that Hardt and Negri seek to tell regards the activities of death squads in Central America or similar incidents. In *Mason & Dixon*, Pynchon tells the "truth" of the injustices that Hardt and Negri wish to promulgate. His representation of, for example, the Paxton Boys massacre of Native Americans at Lancaster is based very much in the historical record. Pynchon goes even one step further and uses actual words that the historical Charles Mason wrote in his journal in 1764 to describe the fictional Mason's reaction to the massacre. Pynchon's meticulous research throughout his historical novels allows him to tell these types of truths. Yet Pynchon takes the project of liberation beyond Hardt and Negri's conclusion. He does not seek to take control of the production of truth; he instead controls—to a certain extent—the production of stories. This is why his use of the subjunctive is so significant in *Mason & Dixon*.

Pynchon lets facts remain as the playthings of lawyers (as Cherrycoke describes them) or of ineffective historians. He recognizes, instead, that cultural values are created and empowered through stories. The real liberation becomes the ability to create a counternarrative that is more attractive than the narrative promoted by Empire and its magic system. Through the subjunctive, Pynchon creates a narrative that includes difference and hybridity, but it also incorporates community, family, and autonomy. In his subjunctive storytelling, Pynchon creates worlds that the marketplace, by definition, cannot deliver. Because the marketplace of Empire is based on gain, because profit is the overriding value, the marketplace is antithetical to an economy of social relations. As Karl Polanyi argues in *The Great Transformation*, for a self-regulating marketplace to work, the economy must take precedence over land and labor. Land and labor, humans and the nature surrounding them, are the essential elements to social relations, to community, family, and autonomy. Thus, Pynchon's subjunctive stories can (and do) deliver something that is ultimately more attractive than the stories of Empire, of the marketplace. Pynchon's subjunctive stories narrate a world where social relations seize priority back from the annihilation of the marketplace.

Occupy Colonial America

The subjunctive becomes real when these conclusions are read in the light of the Occupy movement. Like Eliza and Zsuzsa, Pynchon's subjunctive couple who cross over from the pages of *The Ghastly Fop* into Mason and Dixon's reality, the Occupy protestors in Zuccotti Park provide a subjunctive world to overlay onto our contemporary situation. The significance of their world was highlighted during a speech Slavoj Žižek gave in Zuccotti Park and later published in *Occupy: Scenes from an Occupation*. During the speech, Žižek observes, "[T]he ruling system has even oppressed our capacity to dream. . . . It's easy to imagine the end of the world. An asteroid destroying all life and so on. But you cannot imagine the end of capitalism" (67). Žižek goes on to argue for the need of this imaginative, subjunctive, fantasy space as a first step in the march toward a more just world. The occupation itself created a microcosm of an alternative to global capitalism. Protestors created an autonomous space constructed with free radical libraries, a makeshift health-care system, breakout groups charged with exploring issues as diverse as sanitation and sexism, and forums in which the disenfranchised gained enfranchisement. A general assembly was formed. A horizontal space characterized by self-government and run by consensus followed. To some extent, this alternative demonstrated by the Occupy protestors addressed concerns shared by the characters in *Mason & Dixon*. They demonstrated the possibilities of an economic system that moves beyond the wage slavery and debtor-creditor dynamic that Captain Volcanoe detests, that rejects the chattel slavery (and the contemporary similarities addressed by the Yes Men) which Jeremiah Dixon struggled with, and that acknowledges the unacknowledged and unpaid domestic labors practiced by Martha Washington and so many women across the globe. The positioning of the occupation in the heart of Manhattan's financial district further makes visible the "invisible" that Maskelyne sees. Activist Sarah Leonard, while describing the events of October 4 in Zuccotti Park, concludes, "It's starting to look like there is a critical mass of people ready to make headlines out of taxpayer-funded cops keeping New Yorkers from directly protesting the banks they bailed out" ("Scenes" 45). That critical mass of people suddenly makes the ideology of neoliberalism visible as an ideology. Samuel Thomas argues that much of this ideology "must remain *invisible* in order for the system to survive" (59). Thus, the very presence of the occupation threatens the sense of neoliberal capitalism as "natural."

Obviously, Occupy Wall Street was an imperfect demonstration. Its significance shouldn't be diminished by its imperfections, though. As Žižek told the crowd at Zuccotti Park, "Remember that our basic message is, 'We are allowed to think about alternatives'" ("Don't Fall" 68). We need the subjunctive. We need the imagined seen as real, even if it is only a demonstration of alternatives in a park. We need room beyond the confines of the Enlightenment's pseudo-religious worship of Reason, beyond Locke's "life, liberty, and property," and beyond neoliberalism's ideology of accumulation to explore a world like our own, only more just, more egalitarian.

Žižek raises questions of the protestors: "What social organization can replace capitalism? What type of new leaders do we want?" (68). Possible answers for the first question have been explored throughout this book. The second question raises new issues. Several critics have observed Pynchon's anarchist leanings. Also, one of the original occupiers, David Graeber, has examined the anarchist roots of Occupy in his book *The Democracy Project*. With this in mind, Žižek's second question reveals the irony (or possibly just the oxymoronic nature) of an anarchist leader. Ostensibly, anarchism would have no leader. A merging of reality and theory presents a different situation. As Astra Taylor notes in her "Scenes from an Occupation," "From what I can tell, decisions are being made by various committees and working groups and by a wide variety of autonomous actors, not just through publicly deliberated group consensus" (65). In other words, individuals were arising as leaders in Zuccotti Park (though this happened subtly and behind the scenes). This is not necessarily a contradiction of terms, as one more peek into *Mason & Dixon* will demonstrate.

In some ways, Occupy Wall Street replicates Pynchon's representation of Mason and Dixon's construction of the line. On that project, Mason and Dixon were the leaders. Presumably, Mason outranked Dixon, but at no point in the book does Mason pull rank. Dixon feels free to disagree and express his disagreement. Mason and Dixon argue. On small issues like the superiority of wine over beer or coffee over tea, they maintain their differences. However, on all issues of the line, Mason and Dixon proceed by consensus. Additionally, because they are determining the placement of the line through astronomical calculations, most of their work must be done at night, when the stars are visible. The actual construction of the line would be done during the day, when Mason and/or Dixon is sleeping. This means that the crew leaders (surveyors, axmen, etc.) work somewhat autonomously of Mason and Dixon's "rule."

This marginally hierarchical organization mirrors many contemporary small businesses and small-scale enterprises. Mason and Dixon's undertaking, however, is a large-scale enterprise that Pynchon represents as fairly egalitarian. There are still leaders, but the leaders have very restricted and specific authority. They are, by and large, unconcerned with power. The lack of concern Pynchon's representation of Mason has is very much in line with how Mason represents himself in the journal he kept while working on the line. Mason's journal is full of astronomical observations, descriptions of skies, landscapes, and weather. It even veers toward the political when he describes the Paxton Boys. Yet Mason never addresses his power as the leader of the mission and never hints at any desire to be in charge. The crew—perhaps in real life and certainly in Pynchon's fictional universe—works mostly autonomously.

This representation of leadership in mostly egalitarian organizations calls to mind Michael Hardt's observation of Thomas Jefferson's politics. Hardt asserts, "The revolutionary process requires a remaking of human nature that destroys the habits of servitude and develops the capacity for self-rule. Along with these capacities grow the political imagination and desires, which can press continually far beyond the present situation" (xxiii). In other words, participatory democracy cannot occur instantly. It is not enough to pitch a tent in a park or to fight a revolution. Especially when one considers our roles in an economic system that casts at least 99 percent of us as debtors, wage slaves, serfs, indentured servants, or whatever descriptive term we put on our exploitation by Empire, the "habits of servitude" are difficult to break. Instead, democracy must be deliberated upon. It must be learned. It must be practiced and developed as a skill.

Mason and Dixon's mostly egalitarian team also aligns with David Graeber's discussion of the foregrounding of democracy in colonial America. Graeber observes, "Most of all, historians have noted the endless fears among the leaders of colonial communities and military units that their subordinates were . . . beginning to absorb Indian attitudes of equality and individual liberty" (*Democracy* 180). The character of George Washington in *Mason & Dixon* reflects this concern. He discusses fighting the Native Americans at every chance he can muster, not only so he can obtain their land or become more wealthy, but because that land and wealth supply Washington with the exact type of economic power that he wields over those who live closest to him, notably his slave Gershom and his wife, Martha.

Washington's desire for domination over all who are near him contrasts with Mason and Dixon, who largely eschew power. Their work building the line matches Graeber's description of eighteenth-century pirate ships (which Graeber argues were institutions of participatory democracy by necessity). Graeber claims, "Captains . . . usually functioned much like Native American war chiefs: granted total power during chase or combat, but otherwise treated like ordinary crewmen" (178). Mason and Dixon's power is similar to that of the captains and war chiefs. They were granted authority when determining the direction and placement of the line. Without that power, the enterprise would have been pointless. After all, we often follow leaders because they provide knowledge, skills, or insight we lack. Situations frequently call for leaders on very pragmatic levels. Once Mason and Dixon determine where to run the line, they revert to being ordinary crewmen.

Graeber also points out that early American colonists were "a collection of people in which there was likely to be at least some firsthand knowledge of a very wide range of directly democratic institutions, ranging from Swedish *things* (councils) to African village assemblies to Native American federal structures, suddenly finding themselves forced to improvise some mode of self-government in the complete absence of any state" (178). This characterization matches the cast of characters Pynchon uses to construct the line. They are a multicultural bunch specifically inclusive of the veterans Graeber names:

Swedes, Africans, and Native Americans. The crew also welcomes all comers, including Eliza and Zsuzsa (who challenge the heteronormativity of the crew), Dr. Zhang (who challenges the basic religious makeup of the crew), an automaton duck, a French chef, and a whole host of other outcasts. Their inclusiveness allows for General Assembly–type discussions in which the crew get together around a campfire to express concerns, tell stories, or otherwise share worldviews. Mason and Dixon's crew lack a human microphone, but, like Occupy Wall Street, they are built on the principles of participatory democracy.

After describing a day spent in Zuccotti Park, Astra Taylor concludes, "All things considered, I'm most sympathetic, and impressed, when I think of the general assemblies as a kind of political theater" (65). The power of Occupy lies in this theater, this subjunctive, this imagined alternative. Likewise, *Mason & Dixon* finds its political urgency in its magic, its subjunctive. Therein lies the power to envision a world beyond the slavery, the exploitation, the chartered companies, the new versions of serfdom, and the global capital that define Mason and Dixon's time and mirror our own. A decade and a half before the first activists pitched tents in Zuccotti Park, Pynchon borrowed an astronomer and a surveyor from history and rewrote them to Occupy colonial America.

CHAPTER 4

Against the Day and a World Like Ours, with One or Two Adjustments

IN *MASON & DIXON*, Thomas Pynchon infuses his historical novel with clever anachronisms—not limited to but mostly comprising technologies or allusions that would not have been available for his eighteenth-century characters. These anachronisms serve as a means of tying the historical text to the time when the novel was written. They signal to the reader that *Mason & Dixon* is as much a text about America in the late twentieth century as it is about an astronomer and a surveyor traveling through the empires of the Enlightenment. It is simultaneously a text about America's past, present, and future. These anachronisms are frequently humorous. The Reverend Wicks Cherrycoke is warned that, should he smoke any of the hemp in the colonies, he should not inhale—a joke that would be meaningless in the eighteenth century but resonates for a twentieth-century reader who remembers President Bill Clinton's notorious claim to have once smoked marijuana but not inhaled. Perhaps the most humorous anachronism is the character of Gershom. Gershom is George Washington's slave but also a stand-up comedian with a sense of humor that would slide seamlessly into a contemporary comedy night in the Apollo Theater in Harlem. The humor of Pynchon's anachronisms—and of his novel in general—make more palatable his explorations into the chattel slavery, exploitation, and injustice that constructed America.

Pynchon continues this project of writing a historical novel to expose and criticize past injustices and tie them into contemporary economic and political systems in *Against the Day* (2006). *Against the Day* expands the scope from *Mason & Dixon*. *Mason & Dixon* explores the construction of the American republic through Enlightenment justifications of traditional imperialism to foster global trade. *Against the Day* moves the exploration into an era of more fully realized globalization. *Mason & Dixon* does have a somewhat global perspective. The protagonists are Englishmen who travel from England to South Africa to America and back to England, yet the focus of the novel, as well as the bulk of the action in the novel, centers on the burgeoning United States and is told from a postrevolutionary perspective. *Against the Day* starts in the

United States, but the focus of the novel is less specific to any nation-state. Characters roam across the States, into Europe, deep into Asia (sometimes literally underground Asia), to points antipodal to Colorado and even to Counter Earth, a place that mirrors the Earth itself, only at a 180-degree orbital remove. These travels further illustrate not only the impact of the exploitation and injustice that is a legacy of eighteenth- and nineteenth-century imperialism but also the larger projects of economic liberalism that emerged from this age of Enlightenment and imperialism. Rather than clever anachronisms as a signal of a historical novel exploring contemporary situations, Pynchon introduces the concept of bilocation in *Against the Day*: the ability to be in two places in one time. Pynchon's use of bilocation is more nuanced than that, however. Beginning with a crystal of Iceland spar—a transparent stone that has the ability to split a ray of light and generate a double-refracted image of anything viewed through it—Pynchon develops an extended metaphor for viewing the past as a double-refracted image that demonstrates not only contemporary society but multiple possible worlds that can construct our future.

As we will see later in the chapter, Pynchon's project of examining possible alternatives to neoliberal capitalism aligns with the primary goals of Occupy. One of the ideological foundations of capitalism, stretching back to Adam Smith's *Wealth of Nations*, has been the notion that marketplaces are simply a condition of human existence. Capitalism is the natural state of affairs. After the neoliberal revolution of the 1980s, this idea shifted to present neoliberalism as the only foreseeable alternative. One of the most powerful aspects of both *Against the Day* and Occupy is their shared invitation to explore alternatives. By setting up in Zuccotti Park, Occupy presents an alternative space of participatory democracy in the heart of the financial district. Through the trope of bilocation, *Against the Day* places that counternarrative in turn-of-the-century historiographical fiction.

Against the Day's bilocation is illustrated in less humorous ways than the anachronisms in *Mason & Dixon*. For example, the character of Lew Basnight emerges in the novel from an indistinct past. He is aware of committing some type of horrible act that triggers a scandal familiar to everyone in his life but himself, a scandal so horrible no one will speak of it to Lew because the mere act of describing it would cause them to relive it. So Lew emerges as if from another life or, more specifically, from a life that has been split in two. For the rest of the novel, the reader gets the sense that the Lew about whom they are reading is the second Lew, the double-refracted one, the one who is viewed through Iceland spar. It is as if Lew somehow had the ability to be in two places at once—to bilocate—and the novel follows the second Lew while the original Lew, aware of his scandalous behavior, continues in the world he created.

Bilocation is not limited to characters in the novel. The characters Kit Traverse and Dally Rideout travel to Europe on the cruise ship S.S. *Stupendica*. The ship is the site of their first encounters and their budding love affair. Several hints have been given throughout the novel that Kit and Dally are destined to become a couple. Yet their love affair is torn asunder almost immediately when the *Stupendica* splits into two ships. The second *Stupendica*, a warship in the Austrian navy known as the *Emperor Maximilian*, heads to Africa with Kit involuntarily working in its hull. The original *Stupendica* continues to Trieste with Dally and her family. The split of the *Stupendica* illustrates the split between the leisure products of the capitalist class and the violence at the core of capitalism. The bilocations in the novel—as evidenced by Lew Basnight—are not limited to a commentary on capitalism and violence. Nonetheless, the split of the *Stupendica* does introduce the theme that this chapter is most concerned with. I will focus specifically on the bilocation of nineteenth-century economic liberalism and anarchic resistance and its split ray of contemporary neoliberalism and Pynchon's vision of a better future.[1] In several places, Pynchon's vision will mirror aspects of the Occupy movement. Seemingly, these topics could be split even further into (1) the economics of liberalism and neoliberalism and (2) the politics of anarchism and Pynchon's vision of a better future. As I will argue below, even Iceland spar cannot separate economics and politics in a "free" market society. Exploring this bilocation will give form to the project Pynchon has been undergoing since *Vineland:* envisioning a future that wrests wealth and power from the opulent few who steer at the helm of national governments, multinational corporations, and supranational organizations; a future that moves the contemporary ideology away from the free-market/neoliberal utopian ideal of accumulation of wealth; a future that replaces this power system and ideology with a life based on social relations constructed out of reconstituted family systems and communities. Specifically, I will explore Pynchon's transformative use of fiction as a pathway to this better future.

Treating Land and Labor as Commodities

Against the Day begins with a self-reflexive engagement with fiction. The first characters introduced are the Chums of Chance, five aeronauts who are semi-fictional even within the context of the novel. The Chums of Chance exist as storybook heroes in the novel—at one point later in the novel, one of the "real" characters, Reef Traverse, reads a Chums of Chance novel. Their fictional status is further highlighted by the fact that the Chums seem to age only a few years over the thirty-year course of the novel. The Chums are also part of the reality of the novel. They engage with characters who are taken to be real (i.e., not self-reflexively fictional but largely constrained to the rules of a nonfiction world). In the opening scene, they approach the World's Fair in Chicago in 1893. The fair is described "as the great national celebration [that] possessed the exact degree of fictitiousness to permit the boys access and agency. The harsh nonfictional world waited outside the White City's limits" (36). Through the Chums of Chance, Pynchon conflates nonfiction and fiction, the real and the imaginary. He does this perhaps to further his use of the subjunctive in *Mason & Dixon* or perhaps to show that no genuine distinction can be made between fiction and nonfiction in the sense that postmodern ontology develops from the real and imaginary with commensurate seriousness.

The Chums of Chance are an important force in this conflation. The sections of the novel that feature the Chums are a pastiche—perhaps even a parody—of boys' adventure novels similar to but not limited to *Tom Swift* novels. The reader of *Against the Day* is dropped into the Chums' fictional world. Other novels in the Chums' series are mentioned. The reader is advised to "see *The Chums of Chance and the Evil Halfwit*" (5). Other adventures, specifically "*The Chums of Chance at Krakatoa*" and "*The Chums of Chance Search for Atlantis*" (6), are referenced. In his essay "Genre as History," Brian McHale observes that Pynchon tends to align his pastiche with the time period he historicizes. For example, *Gravity's Rainbow*—which is set during the years of World War II—employs the elements of 1940s spy novels; *Mason & Dixon* reconstructs captivity narratives and gothic novels popular during the eighteenth century. *Against the Day* begins with the most popular fiction of 1893: boys' adventure novels. McHale further explains, "To map an era's genre system is to map its popular *self-representations*. Every popular genre, for all its obvious limitations, distortions, and suppressions, captures the way a historical epoch represented itself *to* itself" ("Genre" 25). In other words, Pynchon's pastiche of popular entertainments from the time period that he historicizes allows the reader to see culture represented in ways similar to the ways the culture constructed itself. The postmodern technique of pastiche further alerts readers to what was left out in popular entertainments.

While boys' adventure novels of the late nineteenth century would focus on the hegemonic values of the time period—economic liberalism, patriotism, and patriarchy being chief among them—Pynchon immediately confronts this hegemony. Jeffrey Severs observes that, from nearly the opening pages, "*Against the Day* constantly undermines an abstracted version of capitalism with its material underpinnings—the harsh smells of mining camps, the sounds made by cattle going to slaughter" (224). Severs's point is reinforced by the Chums' first view of Chicago: "As they came in low over the Stockyards, the smell found them, the smell and the uproar of flesh learning its mortality—like the dark conjugate of some daylit fiction they had flown here, as appeared increasingly likely, to help promote" (10). This scene not only juxtaposes the utopian liberal vision of a perfect world (that "daylit fiction" the Chums "help promote") with the material effects of capitalism (the sounds and smells of a slaughterhouse), as Severs argues. Pynchon also connects this vision self-reflexively to fiction and ominously to death.

In *The Great Transformation*, Karl Polanyi explores the history of economic liberalism, covering specifically the nineteenth century. Polanyi's primary thesis is that economic liberalism—and specifically its reliance on the gold standard—led to the economic collapse and conditions of injustice that sparked both World War I and World War II. Polanyi's history can also serve as a backdrop to the economic situation that permeates *Against the Day*. Polanyi observes, "While in imagination the nineteenth century was engaged in constructing the liberal utopia, in reality it was handing over things to a definite number of concrete institutions the mechanisms of which ruled the day" (220). For Polanyi, the vision of economic liberalism is largely a fiction. It resides only in the imaginary. Adam Smith's notion of an invisible hand guiding the markets is a quasispiritual notion lacking empirical support. Markets have never regulated themselves. If society ever genuinely attempted to create a self-regulating market, the result would be annihilation.[2] Nonetheless, the ideology of economic liberalism—its utopic imaginary and the concept of freedom that attends its free markets—results in real, material suffering. Pynchon illustrates Polanyi's aforementioned statement through the Chums of Chance. The Chums begin the novel with a belief in a vision of economic liberalism's utopia. The first political view any Chum espouses is Lindsey Noseworth's expressed displeasure with anarchy as a virus afflicting the otherwise healthy body of capitalism. Nonetheless, "the concrete institutions . . . which ruled the day" obscure this vision. The Chums venture into the White City that is the Chicago World's Fair. Before they can view any of the European attractions that advertise this liberal utopia, they must travel through the "signs of cultural darkness and savagery" (22). The "cultural darkness and savagery" are embodied in the exhibits of the colonized nations, the exhibits of the half-hidden populations exploited and oppressed by global economic liberalism: Zulu dancers, Indian swamis, Pygmies, and Brazilian Indians. "To the boys it seemed that they were making their way through a separate, lampless world, out beyond some obscure threshold, with its own economic life, social habits, and codes, aware of itself as having little if anything to do with the official Fair" (22). The outskirts of the fair rip the Chums out of their comfortable fiction. They can no longer be protected by the conventions of boys' adventure novels and all that those conventions ignore. Instead, they are confronted by the material impact of economic liberalism, the cultures torn asunder or wiped away, the economies based on social relations devastated by one that privileges gain and accumulation over humans. The Chums equate the scene with darkness—that which they cannot see. And there is no way that the Chums would have been able to see this before, trapped as they were in the conventions of a series of popular novels, the purpose of which was to promote a very specific, hegemonic view that ignores the material effects of economic liberalism. Through this passage, Pynchon seems to be asking his readers to follow the same journey as the Chums, to look beyond the cultural fictions of a society sold on (or at least being sold) a free-market ideology and instead examine the long-standing effects of this economic system.

In *Against the Day*, the political perspective is clear. Before the Chums explore much of the fair, Pynchon introduces the novel's antagonist, Scarsdale Vibe. Vibe is a robber baron modeled on the tradition of industrialists like John D. Rockefeller, Andrew Carnegie, and J. P. Morgan. Unlike Pynchon's earlier industrialist, Pierce Inverarity from *The Crying of Lot 49*, who was known to wake up old lovers in the middle of the night with comic impersonations and who, not incidentally, was killed by a falling bust of robber baron Jay Gould, Vibe is no laughing matter. Before Vibe appears in the pages of *Against the Day*, the narrator describes him and plutocrats of Vibe's ilk as "forces that might be described, with little risk of overstatement, as evil" (30). Vibe's evil is illustrated in his first actual presence in the novel. He walks into an upscale Chicago hotel carrying a silver cane that is also outfitted as an air gun capable of shooting a small-caliber bullet. Vibe is confronted by an elderly woman who recognizes him as a robber baron and tells him that his mother should have strangled him in the crib. Vibe responds by shooting the woman in the leg. This is a very telling scene.

First, the fact that the elderly woman accosted Vibe demonstrates the depth of hatred for plutocrats that will permeate the novel. Nearly every character who encounters Vibe wishes, in some way, for his death. Pynchon's decision to make the first person who expresses this wish a woman is significant. Women in particular bear the weight of economic liberalism's oppression in the novel. In a scene that quickly follows Vibe's presence in the novel, the reader witnesses a labor meeting where the narrator describes "Women in surprising numbers, bearing the marks of their trades, scars from the blades of the meatpacking floors, squints from needlework carried past the borderlands of sleep in clockless bad light, women in head-scarves, crocheted fascinators, extravagantly flowered hats, no hats at all, women just looking to put their feet up after too many hours lifting, fetching, walking the jobless avenues, bearing the insults of the day" (49). Subsequently, the novel explores these characters: women whose labor is exploited, women who have few economic opportunities and almost no possibilities for autonomy, and women who become autonomous yet must travel a path through Hell to get there.[3] With this in mind, the elderly woman accosting Vibe becomes a gendered representation of discontent with the economic system that the novel historicizes as particularly brutal to women. She becomes, in a sense, an embodiment of what Candace Falk describes as "The Destroying Mothers": anarchists, feminists, suffragettes, and revolutionaries like Emma Goldman, Elizabeth Gurley Flynn, Voltairine de Cleyre, and Margaret Sanger who fought against the injustices of economic liberalism (Carswell, "Destroying Mothers" 52).

Vibe's overreaction to the elderly woman's harangue is equally significant. It not only stands to represent plutocracy metaphorically shooting down nineteenth-century women activists; it also demonstrates Vibe's unequivocal viciousness. He puts a bullet into the body of an unarmed human who poses no physical threat to him. Pynchon gives the reader no reason to view this scene with any complexity. Vibe demonstrates no redeeming characteristics, here or anywhere in the novel. Pynchon bestows on him nothing likeable or even human. He is, with no risk of overstatement, evil. It is odd that Pynchon, who demonstrates the complexity in every situation, who resists notions of purity at every chance, should write a character as purely antagonistic as Vibe. Even the villain in *Vineland*, Brock Vond, was given a past filled with scars that could make his actions, if not justifiable, at least complicated by very human motivations. Vibe has no such complications. Throughout the novel he continues to be the character (perhaps even caricature) presented in this opening scene: a robber baron with a complete disregard for humanity.

Pynchon's two-dimensional portrayal of Vibe in a novel that frequently goes beyond the third dimension is curious. A reader must ask what purpose is served by this characterization of Vibe. One possible answer to this question has to do with Vibe as a representation of a doxa—a belief or ideology that has become naturalized in a society though it is anything but natural. A contemporary reader of *Against the Day*, most likely living in a neoliberal society, would be indoctrinated with neoliberalism's ideology of accumulation, summarized nicely by Wendy Brown as a belief system in which "all dimensions of human life are cast in terms of market rationality." Attendant to subsuming all dimensions of life to market rationality is a sense that the wealthy are inherently superior to the masses. In *A Brief History of Neoliberalism*, David Harvey outlines exactly how this ideology has become the hegemonic belief in the United States, Europe, Japan, and China. Supposing the reader of *Against the Day* is in one of these regions of the world, she is likely more than simply exposed to this neoliberal ideology; it would be the prevailing view of her culture. Because this belief has become the doxa, questioning this belief becomes difficult. Pynchon would have to de-doxify the reader's inclination to view Scarsdale Vibe as her superior.[4] By characterizing Vibe as evil instead of just bad, Pynchon dismantles the doxa surrounding his text.

Pynchon's bilocation of nineteenth-century economic liberalism and contemporary neoliberalism helps demonstrate that this neoliberal doxa is a fairly recent phenomenon. As Karl Polanyi observes in *The Great Transformation*, "Nineteenth-century civilization alone was economic in a different and distinctive sense, for it chose to base itself on a motive only rarely acknowledged as valid in the history of human societies, and certainly never before raised to the level of a justification of action and behavior in everyday life, namely, gain" (31). While a neoliberal hegemony depicts the desire for accumulation or gain as an inherent human trait, Polanyi's economic history demonstrates that the desire for gain is not inherent. It is, instead, a culturally constructed belief system, and a fairly recent one at that. Further, it is a dubious belief system. An economy or marketplace focused primarily on gain or accumulation is unable to deliver the most basic human needs or desires to most of humanity. By definition, the market cannot produce social relations. It does not bring people together in ways that afford emotional connections or deep and loving relationships. It does not promote genuine artistic expression. It does not promote autonomy. It does not provide leisure time that is genuinely free of responsibilities for anyone except a small percentage of extremely wealthy people. It does not provide any of these very basic human desires. In fact, by dismissing social relations in favor of an economy of accumulation, liberalism actively works against those aspects of life that humans have traditionally valued the most. Instead, economic liberalism results in fractured societies and fractured human relations. It then offers to remedy the situation through the sale of commodities that cannot repair the fracture. A society based on accumulation creates economic and ethnic Others, legions of oppressed, exploited, and starving humans who serve an opulent few. This society is built on, as Occupy activist Jodi Dean describes it, "capitalism's reliance on fundamental inequality" (88). Dean goes on to argue that the real resonance of Occupy comes in the division between the 1 percent and the 99 percent because "it asserts [identity] as the 'we' of a divided people, the people divided between expropriators and expropriated" (88). While systems like this have roots digging down at least to eras of feudalism, this system is anything but natural.

As Polanyi further observes, "The outstanding discovery of recent historical and anthropological research is that man's economy, as a rule, is submerged in his social relationships. He does not act so as to safeguard his individual interest in the possession of material goods; he acts so as to safeguard his social standing, his social claims, his social assets" (48). According to Polanyi, while individual traits varied, human societies traded under the principles of reciprocity, redistribution, householding, or some combination of the three. Polanyi discusses Trobriand Islanders as an example of reciprocity. According to the culture of the islands, each inland village traded with a coastal village to create a symmetry. Each village traded what geography granted them in abundance for that which their geography lacked. In short, a coastal village would trade fish for vegetables grown inland. Reciprocity can also be exemplified in tribes of hunter-gatherers, where the hunters shared the spoils of their activities with gatherers who did likewise. Redistribution denoted societies in which grains and other consumables were gathered in storehouses and spread among both producers of consumables and the nonproducing parts of the population who accounted for the military and leisure classes. While redistribution did lead to class stratification and exploitation in many cases, Polanyi suggests that, because land and labor were never treated as commodities, stratification and exploitation were held somewhat in check. Householding societies, like those of ancient Greece, produced cash crops such as cattle and grains for the household first, then sold only the excess of production. In householding societies, "markets and money were mere accessories to an otherwise self-sufficient household" (56).

In relation to Polanyi's view of economic history, a character like Scarsdale Vibe represents a heretofore unknown level of opulence. Because land and labor were not treated as commodities and because social relations took precedence over economies of gain, Vibe's wealth could not have existed. It would have been broken up by some form of reciprocity or redistribution. Classic liberalism, particularly with respect to Adam Smith's argument that, because human societies have always traded and bartered, capitalism has always existed, provides a narrative that normalizes Vibe's opulence. This narrative—when accepted by twenty-first-century neoliberals—ignores the specifics of previous human economies. It ignores the evidence presented by Polanyi that, while previous societies did trade and barter, they tended to trade and barter only the excess of their production. They never sacrificed their own necessities to serve the opulence of an "elite" few. Therefore, at least according to Polanyi's historiography of economic liberalism, nineteenth-century industrialists like Vibe who accumulated inordinate wealth at the expense of so many were not natural. They were the fairly recent product of a European society transitioning into advanced stages of economic liberalism.

Pynchon explores Europe's transition into advanced stages of economic liberalism through the adventures of the Traverses in Venice. Kit Traverse notices the transition first. He has traveled to Venice with his brother, Reef. The brothers plan to assassinate Scarsdale Vibe because Vibe hired the killers who assassinated Kit and Reef's father, Webb. During the planning stages, Kit sits at a café in Venice and meditates on the city:

> The town was supposed to've been built on trade, but the Basilica San Marco was too insanely everything that trade, in its strenuous irrelevance to dream, could never admit. The numbers of commerce were "rational"—ratios of profit to loss, rates of exchange—but among the set of real numbers, those that remained in the spaces between—the "irrationals"—outnumbered those simple quotients overwhelmingly. Something like that was going on here—it even showed up in this strange, patternless subset of Venetian address numbers, which had already got him lost more than once. He felt like a person familiar with only real numbers watching a complex variable converge. (732)

Of course, Venice has long been an outpost for a form of globalization, dating back centuries to the time when Venice was instrumental in the spice trade from Asia into Europe, and later on to North America. The key difference between the simple trade that existed historically in Venice and the trade that surrounds Kit resides in its scope. As Polanyi contends, prior to economic liberalism becoming hegemonic, trade was not about accumulation. Merchants and producers first took care of their local needs, then sold the excess. Everything was not a commodity; only the excess was. Nineteenth-century economic liberalism, however, demanded that the marketplace supersede everything.

Obvious examples call into question Polanyi's historicizing of European economic history. For example, it would be difficult to argue that the House of Medici was primarily one of social relations and not of accumulation. However, looking beyond these specific examples and examining general trends, as Polanyi does, supports three points. First, when one views the economic history of humanity, the overwhelming trend is one of economies of social relations—be they through the reciprocity of hunter-gatherers or small farming villages; the redistribution of ancient Egyptians, Babylonians, Chinese, and Incans; or the householding of ancient Greeks. Second, that the economy of Europe in the late nineteenth and early twentieth centuries was increasingly becoming an economy of gain. Third, economies of gain tend to lead to unrest, war, famine, and institutionalized injustice. It is this institutionalized injustice that Pynchon confronts through the Traverses in Venice.

The Venice Kit meditates on has not fully converted to the ideology of economic liberalism. The town does not privilege "ratios of profit to loss, rates of exchange." It does not share the "strenuous irrelevance to dream" that is liberalism. Instead, the "'irrationals'—outnumbered those simple quotients overwhelmingly." The people around Kit refuse to buy into the myth that the unregulated marketplace will bring with it freedom and wealth. Or, if not a complete refusal, they at least seem to resist the definitions of freedom and wealth that liberalism employs. Perhaps this is why Kit, who earlier in the novel refused Vibe's offer to make Kit Vibe's principal heir, feels so at home here.

Instead of propagating the myth of a liberal utopia, Venice cultivates its identity in its art history: the architecture and paintings, the human expressions that constitute an organic culture. Vibe's arrival in Venice threatens this. Vibe visits Venice to accumulate some of the art that the city is known for. His purpose winds up tensions within the art and anarchist communities. The first piece that Vibe examines is a fictional painting entitled *The Sack of Rome*. The painting depicts a class war in which the plutocracy are losers. Horses ridden by nobility turn to bite their riders. Peasants urinate on their superiors. "Scarsdale . . . could see right away without the help of hired expertise that this was what you'd call a true masterpiece, and he'd be very surprised indeed if somebody hadn't already sold reproductions of it to some Italian beer company to use in local saloons over here" (726). Vibe's response to this artwork is telling. He is unable to judge the art as anything but a commodity. The value he recognizes in the painting is entwined with the marketplace. From Vibe's perspective, the painting is a masterpiece precisely because he can envision it as an advertisement. Art's worth is connected to its commodification. Vibe further demonstrates his ignorance of the human expression behind the painting. Clearly, the artist wishes to illustrate a discontent with class inequality and the market system by metaphorically stringing up merchants and attacking masters. Vibe's ignorance of this message seems to be tied to the root of the word *ignorance*: to ignore. Vibe willfully strips the art of its humanity—or at least its human expression—as a way of shifting art into the sphere of commodity.

Vibe's response to this painting, and to artwork in general, is exactly what infuriates his would-be assassin, Andrea Tancredi. Tancredi describes Vibe's invasion of the Venetian art world as "a campaign of extermination against art itself" (738). Tancredi is not bothered by the act of purchasing art. His views are not that pure. As he further explains, "It's not the price tag . . . it's what comes after—investment, reselling, killing something born in the living delirium of paint meeting canvas, turning it into a dead object, to be traded, on and on, for whatever the market will bear. A market whose forces are always exerted against creation, in the direction of death" (738). As I mentioned above, part of the problem lies in Vibe's willful ignorance, in his stripping art of its capability to express raw human emotion—killing the art, so to speak—and turning it into a commodity. Tancredi expands beyond this by pointing out that the marketplace leads forever in the direction of death (or, to use Polanyi's term, annihilation). This is a core problem of economic liberalism, as explored by Polanyi and others. For an unregulated marketplace to work, things that are not commodities must act as commodities. Humans and land are not commodities because they are not items produced to be sold, and commodities, by definition, are items produced to be sold.

The inevitable destruction caused by treating labor and land as commodities can be bilocated to contemporary, neoliberal societies. As Jodi Dean observes in her essay exploring the ideological roots of Occupy, there are inherent "contradictions that are demolishing capitalism from within (global debt crises, unsustainable patterns of consumption, climate change, the impossibility of continued accumulation at the rate necessary for capitalist growth, mass unemployment and unrest)" (90). All the contradictions Dean lists are direct results of treating land as a commodity ("unsustainable patterns of consumption, climate change, the impossibility of continued accumulation at the rate necessary for capitalist growth") and labor as a commodity ("global debt crises, mass unemployment and unrest"). In the essay built from a speech she gave at Zuccotti Park, Naomi Klein expands on the destruction wrought by treating land and labor as commodities, arguing,

> [T]oday everyone can see that the system is deeply unjust and careening out of control. Unfettered greed has trashed the global economy. And it is trashing the natural world as well. We are overfishing our oceans, polluting our water with fracking and deepwater drilling, and turning to the dirtiest forms of energy on the planet, like the Alberta tar sands. And the atmosphere cannot absorb the amount of carbon we are putting into it, creating dangerous atmosphere warming. The new normal is serial disasters, economic and ecological. (47)

Because humans and land are not commodities, they cannot be expected to act as such. Humans cannot be expected to wait out market fluctuations between supply and demand. We need to eat in the intervening time; we seek a stability that an unregulated marketplace cannot provide. Land, likewise, requires more time to replenish itself than the unregulated marketplace affords. Polanyi provides the example of Spanish sheep pastures that were annihilated when the marketplace insisted on producing more wool than the land could sustain. Overgrazing created a wasteland out of the pastures. The core principle that leads the unregulated marketplace forever toward death can be simplified by the understanding that humans cannot be expected to live on sub-subsistence wages simply because labor's supply outweighs its demand; land cannot be expected to produce more than is physically possible simply because the demand for its production outweighs its supply. Art, in the Venice of *Against the Day*, becomes the metaphor for this problematic of liberalism expecting that which is not a commodity to act like a commodity.

For Tancredi, art is alive. It is created to express human emotions. More than that, it is a means by which the disenfranchised can gain a voice in larger society. *The Sack of Rome* exemplifies this. The painting is an expression of the injustice that a vision of a liberal utopia ignores. The artist's frustration lives within the painting and is conveyed to someone who views it on a prerational level. While art has always been sold, and it is probable that even this painting had been in the marketplace, it has never been just a commodity. Vibe kills it by robbing it of its ability to speak for the disenfranchised, by turning it into nothing more than a commodity, by forcing it into a hegemonic belief that everything must be subject to the laws of the marketplace. Tancredi seeks to rescue art and all it stands for—the Venice of "irrationals"; the spaces between ratios of profit and loss, rates of exchange—by killing economic liberalism's inevitable bastard offspring, the plutocrat.

Because Vibe is willfully ignorant of any worldview beyond his own, he would be unable to understand Tancredi's argument. Vibe is completely invested in the doxa. More than that, his belief system borders on the religious. Karl Polanyi, throughout his history of economic liberalism, depicts the belief in unregulated markets as somewhat religious. Liberalism replaces the concept of a benevolent god with that of a benevolent market. Instead of God working in mysterious ways, the Invisible Hand does. This is unequivocally faith based. Vibe is devout, a convert to this market-based pseudoreligion. From his perspective, art must be robbed of its expression so it can become a commodity; people and land must be exploited; everything must fall under the logic of the marketplace.

By the time Vibe arrives in Venice, the reader is well aware of Vibe's belief system. Much earlier in the novel, Vibe depicts his own role in economic liberalism as that of a soldier in a class war. Vibe characterizes anyone espousing rights for workers as "abscesses suppurating in the body of our Republic" (332). He casts off any type of negotiation with labor or discussions of a more egalitarian society as "such a cruel farce, cruel to both sides" (333). Vibe paints himself as a crusader at the altar of economic liberalism, hell-bent on satiating "this strange fury I feel in my heart, this desire to kill off every damned socialist and so on leftward, without any more mercy than I'd show a deadly microbe" (332). In his own words, Vibe is a religious soldier fighting a class war against everyone on whom his wealth is based.

Perhaps because he envisions himself in a class war, he recognizes that people want to kill him. Vibe is constantly protected by his main bodyguard, Foley Walker. He carries the aforementioned walking cane that can double as a small-caliber rifle. He even employs a small army to protect him in Venice. Yet Vibe is too devout to recognize why people want to kill him, to understand that people's homicidal impulses toward him are one logical reaction to the system of gross injustice that he perpetuates. Vibe gains no insight from Tancredi's assassination attempt.

Tancredi approaches Vibe outside an opulent ball in Venice. That much is certain. The narrator presents events in an intentionally vague manner. If Tancredi has a weapon—which the reader assumes he does because Kit and Reef Traverse, witnesses to the event, assume he does—the reader cannot see it. He may have a gun, though friends of Tancredi's later declare that no gun was found on the scene. He may have a small bomb, though again it is unclear. Nonetheless, Vibe's private army wastes no time descending on Tancredi. When he does not halt his approach, the private army opens fire, first shooting him until he falls into a pool of his own blood, then attacking his corpse. While the private army kicks Tancredi's lifeless body, "Scarsdale Vibe all but danced up and down in delighted approval, loudly offering procedural advice. . . . When his voice was too hoarse to go on, he approached and looked down for a while on the torn corpse in its bath of public light, feeling blessed at having witnessed firsthand this victory over Anarchist terror" (743). Vibe retreats into the solace of the word *terror*, of classifying this attack as a terrorist act. In the act of naming and classifying, he absolves himself of the responsibility of asking difficult questions. He does not examine what about his life fosters such a hatred in the masses as to necessitate his hiring of a small private army and to compel the army to act in such an unhesitating and extreme manner to every perceived threat. He cannot imagine that his belief system and consequent actions are a crime against labor and art, perhaps even against humanity. He does not recognize that he is unique in human history for being the recipient of all the favors that an economy based solely on gain produces. He does not see the inevitable annihilation assured by a hegemony that values accumulation over social relations. He cannot understand that his opulence comes at the price of the well-being of most of humanity. Most of all, he does not question how natural his doxa really is. When Pynchon sets up the scene in this way, however, with a fully reprehensible character—jumping mad and exempt, pardoned from all his crimes—the reader must question the doxa.

Beyond the question of doxa, the reader must investigate the motivation behind these assassination attempts. On a surface level, each would-be assassin (or would-be attacker) of Vibe has her own personal reasons. For Kit and Reef Traverse, they wish to kill the man who paid to have their father killed. It is a matter of family vendetta. For Tancredi, it is an attempted assassination of the man killing the art Tancredi holds dear. For the elderly woman who accosted Vibe early in the novel, her attack was in the name of economic equality. When these motivations are added together, the sum becomes what Karl Polanyi describes as a double movement or a countermovement.

Countermovements and *Jacqueries*

Polanyi suggests that, whenever a government approaches laissez-faire or an insufficiently regulated market, resistance forms to counter it. It is this spontaneous resistance that defines the double movement or countermovement. Polanyi argues that liberal ideology interprets this resistance as conspiracy or the planned actions of some type of oppositional ideology. Or the double movement may be characterized as some type of abscess or disease, as Scarsdale Vibe characterizes it. Polanyi's investigation reveals something different. According to Polanyi, "While laissez-faire economy was the product of deliberate State action, subsequent restrictions on laissez-faire started in a spontaneous way. Laissez-faire was planned; planning was not" (147). He further articulates, "The countermove against economic liberalism and laissez-faire possessed all the unmistakable characteristics of spontaneous reaction" (156). In other words, if there really were an invisible hand guiding the unregulated marketplace, history shows that it would push the marketplace toward regulation and toward resistance movements that oppose the unregulated marketplace. Polanyi understands the motivations behind this resistance, also. He explains, "Indeed, that a community would remain indifferent to the scourge of unemployment, the shifting of industries and occupations and to the moral and psychological torture accompanying them, merely because economic effects, in the long run, might be negligible, was to assume an absurdity" (224). While Scarsdale may expect labor to act as a commodity—he may even wage war against humans who refuse to act as commodities—the humans who comprise the labor understand the absurdity and resist spontaneously.

The most salient example of a double movement in *Against the Day* resides in the character of Webb Traverse. Webb is a miner and an anarchist bomber. His exploits with dynamite are legendary. He is dubbed by storytellers prone to embellishment as the Kieselguhr Kid. Unlike Scarsdale Vibe, who is a caricature of a plutocrat, Webb's characterization as an anarchist bomber is complex. He is part legend and part fiction, certainly. Yet the majority of his portrayal is speckled with the very material motivations of a father, a husband, and a working man. It is important to notice, too, that before he was an anarchist bomber, he was just a miner who used dynamite in the service of capital. He blew up pieces of Colorado, creating what he viewed as "poisoned mountains" (89) of slag. He turned the dynamite against the mining company not because of any preconceived anarchist belief. Instead, he recognized the injustices against land and labor that the mining company perpetrated and lashed out with the weapon that was at hand. Examining his words throughout the novel, Webb's allegiances were with the miners' union, with workers' rights.

When Webb is first introduced in the novel, he has a conversation with Merle Rideout. Webb's theory, at this point, is largely unarticulated, yet he is well along the path of his career as a dynamite revolutionary. In a discussion on alchemy with Merle, Webb asks why capital would bother with alchemy. He explains that capital "[h]ad their own magic, doin just fine, thanks, instead of turning lead into gold, they could take poor people's sweat and turn it into greenbacks, and save that lead for enforcement purposes" (79). With this statement, Webb demonstrates his recognition of the exploitation of labor by capital. His presence in Merle's shed, where Webb thinks he smells homemade explosives cooking, suggests Webb's desire for action. Nonetheless, he holds no fully realized theory. Webb even laments his inability to theorize. "If there'd only been the simple luxury of time," he thinks, "maybe to do nothing but put his feet up on some wood porchrail, roll a cigarette, gaze at the hills, let the breezes slide over him—sure—but as it was, he never saw a minute that didn't belong to somebody else. Any discussion of deeper topics such as what to keep hammering at, what to let go, how much he owed who, had to be done on the run, with people he hoped were not going to fink him out" (91). For Webb—who is the one working-class male in the novel who engages in a lifetime of traditional industrial labor; even his assassins have to drag him out of the mine to kill him—there is no time to theorize. He does acquire some theory along the trail, mostly from the sermons of the radical preacher the Reverend Moss Gatlin. Among the wisdom Rev. Gatlin passes on is the Marxist notion that "Labor produces all wealth. Wealth belongs to the producer thereof" (93). Webb's dynamite activities—which largely consist of blowing up mine property and railroad bridges—is an example of Mikhail Bakunin's propaganda of the deed. Still, Webb is not a scholar of the works of Marx and Bakunin. His actions are the spontaneous reaction to injustice created by economic liberalism, an example of what Polanyi describes as a countermovement—and not the result of any kind of organized ideology. He is a bomber. Later storytellers (myself included) add the adjective "anarchist."

Expanding on Polanyi's notion of the countermovement is the concept of the jacquerie as articulated by Michael Hardt and Antonio Negri in *Commonwealth*. Hardt and Negri define a *jacquerie* as "self-organized rebellion based on indignation" (236). According to Hardt and Negri, these jacqueries follow oppression worldwide. Like a countermovement, a jacquerie rises spontaneously. Unlike a countermovement, a jacquerie seems to be necessarily violent in nature. Like Webb, jacqueries largely lack a theoretical framework. Unlike Webb, jacqueries tend to be mass movements instead of a lone bomber (or a bomber who occasionally works with one or two others) roaming the mountains. Hardt and Negri note, "The central problem, though . . . is how to translate every moment of insurgency into a moment of government, how to make insurrection lasting and stable, that is, how to make the *jacquerie* effective" (*Commonwealth* 239). In other words, for self-organized, violent rebellion to compel positive change, it must link with other such movements resisting common oppressions. The jacqueries must further articulate their goals in order to move toward sustainable change.

One of the advantages of the encyclopedic breadth and intellectual depth of *Against the Day* is its ability to link jacqueries. These self-organized, violent rebellions follow the characters throughout the novel. Webb's son Frank experiences jacqueries in Mexico while running guns and fighting the various battles that historians have grouped together as the Mexican Revolution. For Frank, the jacqueries are unlinked. They move from one leader to another, each victorious leader becoming a mirror image of the tyrant he replaces. One of Webb's partners in crime, the Finn Veikko, also drifts from one jacquerie to another. He links them somewhat. This is demonstrated when the narrator explains, "[Veikko had] never seen much difference between the Tsar's regime and American capitalism. To struggle against one, he figured, was to struggle against the other" (83). Veikko gives the oppression a name: capitalism. Whether it is the aristocratic capitalism of the tsar or the plutocratic capitalism of the United States, Veikko recognizes common problems. Specifically, he finds the "same wealth without conscience, same poor people in misery, army and police free as wolves to commit cruelties on behalf of the bosses, bosses ready to do anything to protect what they had stolen" (83). In short, he finds the same oppression and exploitation of economic liberalism. Nonetheless, Veikko's propaganda of the deed is over in a flash. His actions create no sustainable change. The vagaries of the actions even leave a great deal of room regarding how the propaganda of the deed is interpreted. Finally, Webb's son Reef, his daughter-in-law Yashmeen, and his granddaughter Ljubica must navigate a series of competing jacqueries throughout the Balkans much later in the novel. All these jacqueries seem to be pawns in a chess match for various world powers; all are largely ineffective. In fact, Pynchon's choice of Mexico and the Balkans—two regions that remain volatile at the time of *Against the Day*'s publication, two regions that have wallowed under a couple of centuries of liberal, then neoliberal, oppression—invites the reader to investigate the danger of violent revolutions. Graham Benton, in his essay "Daydreams and Dynamite," observes in Pynchon's revolutionary character Ewball Oust "a familiar dilemma in any anarchist program—how to lash out at a corrupt system without capitulating to the very dehumanizing actions with which you have characterized your enemy" (204). The jacqueries in *Against the Day* beg similar questions. Specifically, if a revolutionary is to employ violent tactics, how does he subsequently separate the means of revolution from the ends of revolution? The jacqueries in *Against the Day* question the efficacy—and perhaps the morality—of violent resistance. These questions bear further exploration.

In her essay "The Religious and Political Vision of Pynchon's *Against the Day*," Katherine Hume reads suggestions of support for the implementation of violent resistance from Pynchon. Hume claims, "I too failed to register the seriousness with which Pynchon appears to support political violence because of my hostility to terrorism, but second and third readings persuade me that Pynchon is more aggressive here than in earlier novels, if only out of despair over lack of effective peaceful alternatives" (164). According to Hume, Pynchon's sympathetic portrayal of anarchist bombers, his privileging of the anarchists' arguments and rhetoric, and his juxtaposition of these portrayals with unambiguously negative portrayals of plutocrats all add up to somewhat of an endorsement of violent intervention. Graham Benton is less convinced. Benton argues, "While I do not believe . . . that Pynchon is clearly aligned with a call to violence as Hume suggests, I do see him pushing harder on the edges of one kind of anarchist agenda than in any other novel, if only to show more clearly what is at stake" (203). Benton also reads sympathetic portrayals of anarchist bombers, but his exploration of anarchism in the novel does not equate sympathy with endorsement, necessarily. The question of violence as a possible form of resistance emerges in contemporary theory that reflects many of Pynchon's views expressed in *Against the Day*. Hardt and Negri, whose criticism of neoliberalism and the subsequent formation of a neoliberal Empire aligns itself closely with Pynchon's criticisms, are not shy about an overt endorsement of violence. Hardt and Negri state:

> Gramsci has nothing in principle against armed struggle—and neither do we. The point is simply that arms are not always the best weapons. What is the best weapon against the ruling powers—guns, peaceful street demonstrations, exodus, media campaigns, labor strikes, transgressing gender norms, silence, irony, or many others—depends on the situation. . . . The first and most obvious criterion is, What weapons and strategy are most likely to be effective and win the struggle? (*Commonwealth* 368)

In other words, Hardt and Negri present no moral objection to violent uprisings. They defend these jacqueries as necessary, finding fault only in the difficulty of organizing them, taking them to the next level where sustainable positive change is possible.

The presentation of armed struggle in *Against the Day* is certainly more convoluted. The bomber Webb Traverse examines some of the complications:

> The tricky patch, it had seemed to Webb for a while now, came in choosing the targets [for his bombing activities]. . . . Lord knew that owners and mine managers deserved to be blown up, except that they had learned to keep extra protection around them—not that going after their property, like factories or mines, was that much better of an idea, for, given the nature of corporate greed, those places would usually be working three shifts, with the folks most likely to end up dying being miners, including children working as nippers and swampers—the same folks who die when the army comes charging in. Not that any owner ever cared rat shit about the lives of workers, of course, except to define them as Innocent Victims in whose name uniformed goons could then go out and hunt down the Monsters That Did the Deed. (84–85)

Through this meditation, the parameters the novel constructs around violent tactics begin to be established. Webb (if not necessarily Pynchon) is not morally opposed to killing some mine owners and their administration. He does recognize the difficulty in such acts. Specifically, mine owners—and the extremely wealthy in general—are well protected. As Vibe's would-be assassin Andrea Tancredi learns the hard way later in the novel, industrialists protect themselves by surrounding themselves with a private army. Going through a private army to attack a mine owner is dangerous business, possibly even suicidal.

On the other hand, Webb is morally opposed to killing workers. For him, it would exemplify the old problem of engaging in the behavior that he condemns: taking the life of the innocent. Webb also recognizes that he is fighting a rhetorical battle. His actions must be carried out in a manner that the media cannot turn against the workers.[5] The use of violence is further complicated when Webb acknowledges that "some of these explosions, the more deadly of them, in fact, were really set off to begin with not by Anarchists but by the owners themselves" (85). This highlights the absurdity—perhaps even the futility—of Webb's violent resistance. Through his actions of dynamiting rail lines and mine property, Webb is complicit in creating an atmosphere of increased violence against himself. It is one more example that a revolutionary's very tactics can and often will be turned against him.

Several anarchist characters in the novel express the notion that there are no innocent bourgeois. It would be a mistake to read this repetition as an endorsement, however, especially when one considers an event that occurs much later in the novel. Webb's son Reef sits in a Nice café with a fellow anarchist named Flaco. Flaco notes that the café is a good target for anarchist bombers. Reef responds, "I've got to where I like these cafés, all this to-and-fro of the city life—rather be out here enjoying it than worried all the time about some bomb going off" (850). Reef's response is complex. First, Reef is no member of the bourgeoisie. It is true that he has benefited from the money of the bourgeois Ruperta Chirpington-Groin through many of his travels in the novel. His relationship with her is a complex one, however, which seems predicated on his being sexually available for her, and her only responsibility to him seems to be taking care of his fiscal needs. In short, his time spent with Ruperta could be read more as a sex worker than as a member of the bourgeoisie. Reef is not exactly a member of the proletariat because he does not work an industrial job—or any job, for that matter. He is instead an example of what Pynchon defined as the preterite in *Gravity's Rainbow*. He is a character who exists outside the flow of mainstream society. And if Reef is not a member of the bourgeoisie, neither are several of Pynchon's characters who share a similar social position as Reef and roam in and out of similar cafés throughout the novel. Thus, the café in Nice and others like it in the novel are not exclusively bourgeois sites. When a bomb explodes in the café, it is not only an attack on the bourgeoisie. It is an attack on the café workers, the passersby, and the anarchists Reef and Flaco. To justify this bombing under the notion that there are no innocent bourgeoisie would require a revolutionary to expand the statement to: there are no innocent bourgeoisie or innocent employees of the bourgeoisie or innocent passersby in the vicinity of the bourgeoisie. Not only is this a far less catchy slogan, it is an extremely difficult argument to justify. Pynchon makes no attempt to justify it.

Pynchon's treatment of the bombing is telling as well. He employs very graphic imagery to describe the bombing itself. Among the detritus surrounding the explosion is "human blood everywhere, blood arterial, venous and capillary, fragments of bone and cartilage and soft tissue" (850). The specificity in this description—all the internal passageways that carry human blood have been severed so that the blood does not flow or spurt but it actually spills; even the tissue that holds the blood inside has been destroyed—highlights the material effects of the attack. The bomb destroys human lives down to the very blood, bone, and soft tissue. This description imprints the theory onto the act, takes it out of the abstract and into the concrete. Just as, throughout most of his oeuvre, Pynchon dismantles the fictions of liberal and neoliberal beliefs by representing material consequences of the economic system, this description of the bombing in the café in Nice dismantles theoretical revolutionary violence. It lays bare the consequences of the act. It connects the means of revolution with the ends.

To further enunciate this point, Pynchon follows the bomb scene with significant action. Reef and Flaco neither flee the scene of the bomb nor align themselves with the bombers. They certainly do not revel in the destruction the way Scarsdale Vibe did when Tancredi was murdered: flogging the corpses and dancing in celebration of a victory in a class war. Instead, they help the wounded, stop the bleeding when they can, and nurse the wounds it is possible for them to nurse. The combination of the graphic description of the material ends of anarchist bombing and Reef and Flaco's active reminder that any movement for social justice must be first about human well-being suggests that Pynchon's sympathetic portrayal of bombers does not equal an endorsement for bombs as legitimate tools of resistance.

Beyond the bombing, *Against the Day* explores the issues of armed struggle through a cast of characters densely populated with gunmen and action featuring their gunplay. Guns are presented as family heirlooms. The size, shape, and national origins of characters' guns are employed as devices to construct the characters' identities. Nearly every character over the age of four packs a gun and knows how to use it. Reef Traverse, for one, is fascinated with guns throughout the novel. At one point, he purchases an elephant rifle to hunt down Vibe. He does not use the rifle for that purpose, but he does use it to protect his future wife, Yashmeen, on the night when they first become a couple. Later, while Reef, Yashmeen, and their infant, Ljubica, struggle to flee the various jacqueries in the Balkans, they find themselves trapped between warring factions. They duck and cover during the shooting. Once the battle moves away from them, Reef leaves his wife and child to rush onto a battlefield that may still contain armed combatants to steal a machine gun off a corpse. Yashmeen recognizes this boyish fascination with guns as inherent in his personality. She explains this to her infant daughter.

The fascination expands to the whole generation of Traverses. When Kit is challenged to a duel in Göttingen, he insists on pistols as his weapon of choice. His German opponent—ironically named Günni—is horrified by the brutality of Kit's selection, by the deadly outcome that pistols ensure. Kit is unrelenting. As an American—and specifically an American from the mythical West of the nineteenth century—guns and gunplay form an integral part of his identity.

Likewise, when Kit and Reef's brother, Frank Traverse, finally meets his nephew (Reef's son) Jesse, the two Traverses bond over a discussion of the guns each is packing. In a strangely tender way, the guns save the two characters from the awkwardness of their first meeting. There is even a logic to both Frank and Jesse packing guns at that point. Earlier in the novel, Frank had reconnected with Jesse's mother and Frank's future wife, Stray, when she was running guns for Mexican revolutionaries. Part of her role in Ludlow—where Frank and Jesse do finally meet—is to run guns into the mining camp where striking coal miners are using the weapons to fend off the national guard.

The Traverse family's fascination with guns helps foreground the armed struggle that propels much of the action in the novel. The representation of this armed struggle—because it is in the hands of those whom traditional American histories tend to ignore or demonize—self-reflexively highlights the way in which bombs, guns, and their attendant violence permeate American culture at every level. Yet to better understand what Pynchon is doing with all this gunplay in the novel, it is helpful to return to Brian McHale's notion of genre poaching. Particularly through the character of Frank Traverse, Pynchon sculpts a pastiche of western dime novels. In a sense, Frank is a prototypical dime novel hero. He wanders throughout Colorado, New Mexico, and Mexico, fighting on the side of the disenfranchised. He wears his guns in plain view. He is quick to shoot. He is motivated at the core by a family vendetta. He is sworn to kill the men who have killed his father. All these are conventions of traditional westerns. The episodes in which Frank carries out the family vendetta, however, are a drastic deviation from traditional westerns. As McHale observes, "Messy and unsatisfactory, each episode ends in an anticlimax of one kind or another. These are hardly the sorts of stories that the dime novels conventionally tell about Wild West violence" ("Genre" 23). Indeed, when Frank kills Sloat Fresno (one of the two hired gunmen who killed Webb Traverse), the scene has almost no buildup. Two characters do not walk out onto Main Street at high noon. They do not look each other in the eyes and stare each other down. The plot of the novel does not race in an unyielding path toward their showdown. Instead, it happens by accident. Frank simply finds himself in a bar where Sloat Fresno is drinking. Frank does not contemplate his actions. He has, in fact, "no chance to rouse up any of those family emotions, none of that" (395). He simply draws, shoots, and kills Sloat before Sloat even realizes he is in a gunfight. Sloat "maybe never even recognized him" (395). The fact that Frank finds Sloat once Frank has stopped looking, the fact that the scene begins and ends in only a few sentences, and the fact that the showdown is less a fair fight and more a straight killing all combine to demonstrate the pointlessness of this act of vengeance. Nothing is accomplished by killing Sloat Fresno. Frank does not even feel better afterward. He feels worse, in fact. Even Frank's mother, Mayva, who had encouraged all three of her sons to avenge their father's death at the funeral, is ambivalent about the killing of Sloat. She compliments Frank for completing the act but seems to recognize that nothing has changed in the world now that Sloat is gone.

The futility of this showdown echoes Oakley Hall's western *Warlock*, which Pynchon famously praised. *Warlock* reenvisions the legendary showdown at the O.K. Corral in Tombstone. The Wyatt Earp character, named Clay Blaisedell in the novel, confronts the rogues who are disrupting the peace in the

Tombstone-esque town of Warlock. They have a shootout that is modeled after the gunfight at the O.K. Corral. Blaisedell kills some of the rogues and chases out the rest. Yet the gunfight occurs early in the novel. Unlike other popular representations of this showdown, Hall presents the gunfight not as the resolution of the problems the town—and, metaphorically, society—faces but as an ultimately futile attempt to solve problems. Instead, the town is faced with moving forward in the presence of Blaisedell, who presents additional problems. First, he has proven himself more deadly than anyone else in town. For this reason, townspeople come to fear and loathe him. Further, they need his protection as much as they resent his presence. Blaisedell, for his part, gradually comes to realize the trap in which he ensnared himself. The town suffers for their choice to settle their problems through the conventions of a dime novel. For much of the remainder of *Warlock*, the real problem confronting the town is the exploitation of the miners by outside corporate forces. In order to subdue striking miners, Blaisedell is expected to align himself with the very men he had been hired to kill at the beginning of the book. Clearly, Pynchon learned a few lessons from *Warlock*. He learned to represent the futility of hired gunmen, the messiness of real vendettas, and the exploitation of labor that mark the real issues of unrest in a community. Perhaps, most importantly, he learned to demonstrate how little is accomplished in a retributive killing. This is further evidenced in his portrayal of Scarsdale Vibe's assassination.

Frank finally meets Scarsdale in Trinidad, Colorado. The Colorado Coal Wars, which would later be resolved in events known as the Ludlow Massacre, have drawn both Frank and Scarsdale to town. Upon realizing that the man who hired gunmen to kill his father was within reach, Frank plots to murder Scarsdale. He confronts Vibe on the streets of Trinidad as Vibe is returning from lunch—thus apparently missing high noon by an hour or so. Otherwise, the scene is set up somewhat like a traditional western dime novel showdown. Frank does call out to Vibe. They both do have time to consider the act that they are about to engage in. They are even on the main street in town, with bystanders watching from a safe distance. The showdown is cut short, however, when Vibe's bodyguard Foley Walker decides to kill Vibe instead of Frank. The scene ends almost as quickly as it started. Walker unloads his clip into Vibe. Vibe falls in the snow. Frank blends back into the crowd. The antagonist of the novel is killed. Evil is vanquished. It even happens late in the novel, at a point that could be climactic, yet the murder is largely anticlimactic because nothing changes once Vibe is killed. He had been in Trinidad to inspire his fellow plutocrats to violently suppress labor activists in Colorado. Apparently, Vibe need not have bothered. The plutocrat John D. Rockefeller Jr. seemed perfectly inspired without the fictional Vibe to cheer him on. The Ludlow

Massacre went on even in a world without Scarsdale Vibe. Significantly, killing Vibe is ultimately a worthless act.

If Wall Street Is the 1 Percent, We're Everybody Else

Pynchon's act of situating the climax of the gunplay around the coal miners' strike in Ludlow in 1913 and 1914 is significant, also. Pynchon's representation of the events in Ludlow is faithful to the historical event. He employs the names of real people who were active in the event. His dates, places, and basic summary of actions all adhere fairly closely to the historical record. In Ludlow, Colorado, during what Howard Zinn described as "perhaps the most violent struggle between corporate power and laboring men in American history" ("The Ludlow Massacre" 184), coal miners were forced to engage in violent resistance when hired gunmen operating under the auspices of the National Guard attacked.[6] Pynchon clearly takes sides in this shootout. When Jesse Traverse and his friend meet the hired gunmen face-to-face, the narrator describes the boys recognizing in the gunmen "a level of evil neither boy had quite suspected in adults till now" (1010). The lieutenant in charge of the hired gunmen is described as a man "with a high forehead, lidless long eyes and mouth in a slit, a lizard's face" (1013). One of the miners declares the lieutenant to be "the devil" (1013). Contrasting these portrayals of the gunmen as villains, Pynchon represents the miners who shot back at the gunmen not only sympathetically but heroically. Nonetheless, Stray and Jesse, then later Frank, all must flee the scene of the strike when they are outnumbered by the corporate army and without hope of anything resembling a victory. As it is portrayed in the novel, the historical event at Ludlow ended poorly. The strike was called off without the coal miners' union gaining recognition. Several strikers, their wives, and their children were murdered. Neither Rockefeller nor any of his hired gunmen were ever convicted of a crime. The event is known to history—through what little representation it receives in traditional histories—as the Ludlow Massacre. It was a massacre. Pynchon's choice to situate this historical event as the climax for Traverse gunplay reinforces the idea that Pynchon's revolutionaries articulated in *Vineland:* if you cannot match Empire's armies with equitable, regimental strength, then it is best to find another path of resistance.

Howard Zinn's conclusion in his historical essay on Ludlow brings this argument back to the original concept of bilocation. Zinn argues, "If [the Ludlow Massacre] is read as a commentary on larger questions—the relationship of government to corporate power and of both to movements of social protest—then we are dealing with the present" (201). The history of the Ludlow Massacre can live in both places—it can bilocate—because it both is and is not commensurate with the present.[7] For example, nineteenth-century liberalism has distinctive differences from twenty-first-century neoliberalism. The economic liberalism that Polanyi describes in *The Great Transformation* is characterized by an almost religious faith in unregulated markets. Contemporary neoliberals do not seem to share this faith. As David Harvey demonstrates, contemporary neoliberals continue to preach this faith in unregulated markets and the "freedom" that accompanies them. In reality, markets are far from unregulated. As Hardt and Negri observe, "Neoliberalism . . . is not really a regime of unregulated capital but rather a form of state regulation that best facilitates the global movements and profit of capital" (*Multitude* 280). Contemporary neoliberals do not genuinely aspire to strip markets of regulation. Instead, they have created a network of national governments, multinational corporations, and supranational regulation agencies like the World Trade Organization that ensure all regulations should be sculpted to benefit the accumulation of capital at the expense of labor and workers. Harvey defines a neoliberal state as "a state apparatus whose fundamental mission was to facilitate conditions for profitable capital accumulation on the part of both domestic and foreign capital. . . . The freedoms it embodies reflect the interests of private property owners, businesses, multinational corporations, and financial capital" (7). Harvey's description of inextricable state and corporate interests matches both Zinn's reading of the Ludlow Massacre and Pynchon's representation of it.

Further, Wendy Brown argues, "Neo-liberal rationality, while foregrounding the market, is not only or even primarily focused on the economy; rather it involves *extending and disseminating market values to all institutions and social action*" (italics in original). This assessment seems almost a mirror image of Polanyi's criticism of economic liberalism as subverting all life to the logic of the marketplace. While important distinctions between liberalism and neoliberalism do exist, while the economic situation of the late nineteenth century does differ in many ways from the contemporary situation—primary among these differences being the stationary industrial labor predominant in the nineteenth century and fluid immaterial labor that is increasingly defining the twenty-first century—and while the modes of resistance differ between the nineteenth and twenty-first centuries, Pynchon's bilocation allows contemporary readers to view the two time periods through the same metaphoric piece of Iceland spar. Fredric Jameson states, "The historical novel can no longer set out to represent the historical past; it can only 'represent' our ideas and stereotypes about the past" (*Postmodernism* 25). I would expand this assessment to suggest that the way Pynchon historicizes and readers (myself included) interpret this historiography elucidates more about our current construction of culture than about any attempt we may make to understand the past.

For these reasons, so much of the criticism leveled at economic liberalism in both *Against the Day* and this chapter may also be read as a critique of neoliberalism. Many of the problems presented by Scarsdale Vibe and the plutocracy he represents can also apply to a growing twenty-first-century plutocracy. In his 2005 study *A Brief History of Neoliberalism*, David Harvey issues an alarm about wealth inequality. He argues that a contemporary plutocracy is approaching a commensurate share of the national wealth to that which was accumulated by robber barons of Vibe's ilk. Harvey further observes, "[T]he evidence strongly suggests that the neoliberal turn is in some way and to some degree associated with the restoration or reconstruction of the power of the economic elites. . . . [It is] a *political* project to re-establish the conditions for capital accumulation and to restore the power of the economic elites" (19). Since the "elites" Harvey describes are defined not only by their wealth but also by the inordinate amount of political power their wealth is used to purchase, plutocracy—by definition a ruling class of the extremely wealthy—is the proper word.

Published ten years after *A Brief History of Neoliberalism*, Thomas Piketty's *Capital in the Twenty-First Century* demonstrates that this wealth inequality continues to grow. Piketty states, "By 2010, the top decile's share of total wealth exceeded 70 percent, and the top centile's share was close to 35 percent" (349). Piketty's study found that wealth shares for the top 10 percent of wealth holders in the United States and for the top 1 percent of wealth holders were at their highest level in 2010 (the last year for which he provides data) since the Great Depression. The wealth shares of the top 10 and 1 percent are commensurate with 1870 and close to the rates during the years when *Against the Day* is set.[8] According to Piketty's conclusion, wealth inequality and the wealth shares of the top 10 and 1 percent continue to grow.

This contemporary class of "economic elites" is motivated by politics as much as economics, power as much as gain. In this regard, they can once again be bilocated to the "Gilded Age" of robber barons. Put succinctly, Emma Goldman, in her essay "Anarchism: What It Really Stands For," states: "While all anarchists agree that the main evil today is an economic one, they maintain that the solution of that evil can be brought about only through the consideration of *every phase* of life—individual, as well as the collective; the internal, as well as the external phases" (50). Goldman recognizes the same problem with economic liberalism as Brown articulates with neoliberalism: the infusion of marketplace logic into "every phase of life." Likewise, a contemporary analysis of *Against the Day*, which historicizes the time period when Goldman lived and the movement of which she was an instrumental part, must recognize how inextricably economics and politics are entwined and how the logic of the marketplace saturates every aspect of contemporary culture.

Just as Karl Polanyi narrowed the primary causes of two world wars and the rise of fascism to the failures inherent in the gold standard, Pynchon's critique in *Against the Day* can be narrowed to the unjust economic and power relations inherent in neoliberal ideology. While his antagonist Scarsdale Vibe may have been—in many ways—the classic nineteenth-century economic liberal who espoused a religious faith in the unregulated marketplace, neoliberalism shares no such genuine faith. Noam Chomsky, while discussing the roots of the Occupy movement, observes, "if, say, businesses believed in markets, they wouldn't do anything like the marketing they do today. If you take an economics course, they teach you that markets are based on informed consumers making rational choices. But business devotes huge resources to trying to create uninformed consumers who make irrational choices" (80). In other words, the executives of most multinational corporations—unlike Wade LeSpark in *Mason & Dixon*—do not have faith in Adam Smith's concept of an Invisible Hand. They instead steer markets through manipulative advertising, then try to make advertising's hand seem invisible.

Likewise, David Harvey demonstrates throughout *A Brief History of Neoliberalism* that faith in an unregulated marketplace is little more than a sales pitch for neoliberalism. The key to this sales pitch lies in the attractive notion of freedom. The pitch sells, essentially, the idea that a free marketplace means more freedom for everyone. Of course, the marketplace is not and cannot be free, and the freedom promised behind this pitch is dubious. Harvey observes, "What is so astonishing about the impoverished condition of contemporary public discourse in the U.S., as well as elsewhere, is the lack of any serious debate as to which of the several divergent concepts of freedom might be appropriate to our times" (183–84). In other words, freedom has come to mean the freedom of a few extremely wealthy individuals to establish rules ensuring their ability to continue accumulating wealth. This concept of freedom is problematic because it is freedom contingent on the exploitation of labor and land to serve the purposes of a handful of private hordes of wealth. This concept of freedom is predicated on the redistribution of wealth and power from the many to the few. Harvey's conclusion is similar to Polanyi's. Polanyi argues, "Clearly, at the root of the dilemma there is the meaning of freedom itself" (266). Like Harvey, Polanyi recognizes the complexity of the term *freedom*. According to Polanyi, a system of economic liberalism "means the fullness of freedom for those whose income, leisure, and security need no enhancing, and a mere pittance of liberty for the people, who may in vain attempt to make use of their democratic rights to gain shelter from the power of the owners of property" (265). In short, one person's freedom can be another person's bondage. Economic liberalism and neoliberalism ensure that a wealthy few gain the majority of freedom—as well as wealth and power—at the expense of the rest of humanity.

Heeding Harvey's call for a genuine discussion on freedom and Polanyi's interrogation of a freedom that only exists for a privileged few, the Occupy movement made explicit the bondage inherent in economic inequality. Michael Taussig observes this several times in his ethnography of Occupy, "I'm So Angry I Made a Sign." None of the signs sums up the neoliberal mythology of freedom more than one Taussig saw lying on the pavement: "Nobody is more hopelessly enslaved than those who believe they are free" (18). David Graeber expands on this discussion in *The Democracy Project*. Graeber recounts the earliest days of organizing for Occupy Wall Street and the conversations he had with other activists regarding slogans for the movement. Around the time of the conversations, Joseph Stiglitz had published his *Vanity Fair* article "Of the 1%, by the 1%, for the 1%." This article resonated with activist communities in general and with the Occupy Wall Street organizers specifically. Graeber concluded, "If Wall Street represents the 1 percent, then we're everybody else" (40). He sent an email dated August 4, 2011, suggesting the "99% Movement" to his fellow activists. By committee, the slogan grew to "We Are the 99%."

Noam Chomsky, reflecting on Occupy, suggests that the 99 percent rhetoric may be the greatest legacy of the movement. He claims, "Occupy lit a spark, and it's changed the substance, as well as the tone, of national discourse on crucial issues" (66). These issues are primarily economic inequality and, more broadly speaking, how economic inequality leads to disenfranchisement. The efficacy of this is best understood when recalling Astra Taylor's observation that the Occupy movement works best as theater.

Front and center on that stage was the consensus voting process. Though Occupy's hand signals were widely ridiculed in the mainstream press, the process led to feelings of empowerment among the protestors. Several activists wrote narratives about how and why they felt empowered. In "One No, Many Yeses," Marina Sitrin explains the choice to allow veto power to everyone in the movement, stating, "Most of us believe that what is most important is to open space for conversations—for democracy—real, direct, and participatory democracy" (8). Hena Ashraf, in "Claiming a Space for Diversity at Occupy Wall Street," recounts her experience wielding that veto power on the construction of the "Declaration of the Occupation of New York City." Ashraf and her companions felt marginalized by specific language in the declaration. They blocked the passage of the declaration, formed a working group, developed more inclusive language, and added it to the document. This time, the declaration passed by consensus. As a result, Ashraf and her companions "walked away realizing that we had spontaneously come together, demanded change, and created it in a movement we were in solidarity with" (35). This experience encouraged Ashraf and others to become more involved in the movement.

Ashraf's experience is part of the goal of consensus activism. In his handbook *Consensus*—which outlines the practices used by Occupy Wall Street—Peter Gelderloos concludes, "Rather than entering a situation in which they are pawns in political strategies developed by inaccessible leaders, activists who get involved with well-functioning consensus groups are rewarded with a sense of empowerment, and through that power develop a personal attachment to the struggle" (92). Consensus, in this regard, becomes freedom. More than consumables or unregulated marketplaces ever could, consensus affords freedom. Participants are enfranchised. Decisions are made cooperatively. Compromises are made, but consensus does not create winners and losers the way a voting system—or a plutocracy claiming to be a democracy—does. Instead, consensus demonstrates what real, participatory democracy looks like. Gelderloos claims that consensus is the most effective way for the 99 percent to effect change. Writing five years prior to the occupation of Zuccotti Park, Gelderloos theorizes, "People who see a protest organized through consensus are not likely to be terribly impressed. People who see health clinics, bookstores, childcare collectives, copwatches, and other groups running without leadership might begin to question the need for the bureaucracy and authoritarianism they have to put up with every day" (95). Chomsky comes to a similar conclusion when reflecting on the legacy of Occupy Wall Street two years after the protest, stating, "One of the real achievements of Occupy has been to bring people together to form functioning, supportive, free, democratic communities—everything from kitchens to libraries to health centers to free general assemblies, where people talk freely and debate" (67).

Fantasies of Freedom in *Against the Day*

Concepts of freedom are raised throughout *Against the Day*. The assassination of Scarsdale Vibe becomes significant when questioning these concepts. While the act itself is essentially pointless—killing Vibe did nothing to stop the massacre of striking miners in Ludlow—the pointlessness itself suggests that plutocrats do not need to be killed or even attacked. Instead, their neoliberal ideology must be dismantled. Wendy Brown argues, "[T]he Left need[s] to tap the desires—not for wealth or goods but for beauty, love, mental and physical well-being, meaningful work, and peace—manifestly unmet within capitalist order and to appeal to those desires as the basis for rejecting and replacing the order." Pynchon seems to work toward the same goal of replacing a concept of freedom meaning the freedom to accumulate goods with a freedom that creates more meaningful social relations.

In her examination of *Against the Day* in *Thomas Pynchon and the American Counterculture*, Joanna Freer suggests, "Pynchon tries to create an ecstatic experience of sorts in his reader, using the fantastical nature of his novels to tip them out of the grooves of their everyday patterns of thought, to send them on an imaginative journey, to displace them" (79–80). Freer argues that these moments of escape construct counternarratives and alternatives to the status quo. Building on this idea, we can see *Against the Day* constructing alternative possible societies, continuing the work that Pynchon began in *Vineland* and *Mason & Dixon*. In particular, *Against the Day* situates a vision for a better society—one that replaces the contemporary neoliberal one—with freedoms based on the concepts of nomadism, spiritual journeys, immaterial labor, intellectual inquiry, and community. His conclusions should by no means be read as a simple prescription for a new way to live, but instead a project of utilizing fiction to give form to ideas.

Nomadism is perhaps the most salient of Pynchon's concepts of freedoms that reject neoliberal ideology. The first lesson that the second generation of Traverse males (Reef, Frank, and Kit) learn is to sever any bonds that hold them fast to Colorado. They recognize that their father, Webb, had become tied to Colorado, to the mines, and to the exploitation therein. They recognize that the coal companies gain much of their power to exploit workers by tying the workers to the land. Nineteenth-century coal companies in Pennsylvania, West Virginia, and Colorado in particular were notorious for paying their workers not in cash but in company script, which could only be redeemed at company stores and was only paid after a certain amount of their wages were deducted to pay rent on their company housing. Thus, coal miners became wholly dependent upon the coal companies, not only for their wages but for their food, housing, and other consumables. Everything miners earned was returned to the company. Because the companies held this monopoly, they were able to profit off the workers (1) through low wages and (2) through inflated prices. While Webb attempted to dynamite himself out of this trap, his sons decided that the only way to avoid it was to refuse to work in the mines. They escape through vaguely criminal activities—gambling for Reef; gunrunning for Frank—or through education—Kit's pursuit of high-level mathematics. Their escape is further predicated on their completely severing any connection to a single place. Throughout the novel, the three Traverses live up to their name, covering much of North America, Europe, and Asia between them. Their journeys are not simply wandering, however. As Hardt and Negri explain, "Collective capital is increasingly faced with a mobile and flexible multitude. From the perspective of command and exploitation, this can only appear chaotic and disordered. The task facing capital is thus constantly to rebuild borders, reterritorialize the laboring populations, and reconstruct the fixed dimensions of social space." Further, "nomadism itself breaks down borders and threatens the territorial stability of capitalist control" (*Commonwealth* 244). In other words, when workers refuse to engage in the system of exploitation, capital must struggle to create a new system. The Traverses exemplify this concept. Their refusal to work steady jobs keeps them from being ensnared in the web of companies, company stores, and company script. Their refusal to buy land prevents debts to banks. Their nomadism allows them to live largely outside of capitalist commodity culture. The nature of their movements prevents accumulation, if for no other reason than the fact that people constantly on the move would have a great deal of difficulty moving the items they have accumulated, so they tend to accumulate less. This lack of accumulation represents a rejection of neoliberal ideology, which establishes a person's worth by the quantity and quality of the items he can hoard. For Reef, Frank, and Kit Traverse—as well as the wives they choose and the families they form—freedom becomes a state of being unbound to working and earning huge sums that simply lead to a vulnerability to being exploited.

In his essay "Setting Sail Against the Day," Heinz Ickstadt reads another level into this nomadism, particularly as it regards the characters of Reef Traverse and his wife, Yashmeen Halfcourt. Ickstadt states, "For Yashmeen and Reef Traverse the nomadic state is an Emersonian way of being *in* the world and yet 'unsettled'" (41). By evoking this Emersonian ideology, Ickstadt adds a spiritual element to the nomadism in the novel. Emerson famously declares that everyone should "enjoy an original relation to the universe" (35). Kit exemplifies this original relation to the universe in the spiritual sense that Emerson suggests. He travels east from Eastern Europe, venturing into Siberia to Lake Baikal, where he experiences an epiphany and envisions his own salvation. He continues from there to seek the Buddhist paradise of Shambala. For Kit, nomadism represents the freedom to seek a personal spirituality, his own unique relationship with a higher power. For Yashmeen and Reef, nomadism is more secular. They seek their own original relation to a world dominated by economics and politics. They have both been victimized, in a sense, by their socioeconomic status at birth. Yashmeen is not only a nineteenth-century woman and thereby subject to the cruelties of patriarchal society, she was also born a slave and purchased out of slavery by her adoptive father, Auberon Halfcourt. Thus, she was enslaved both figuratively and literally since birth. Reef is a working-class male from the industrial tradition of wage slavery and also from a specific branch of that tradition in which company stores and company script indentured workers into a close cousin of chattel slavery. The "freedom" of economic liberalism came from the bondage of people like Yashmeen and Reef. For the characters in the novel, however, freedom resides in the rejection of neoliberal ideology and, as much as possible, voluntary removal from neoliberal society.

The nomadism in the novel is dependent on the characters' ability to support themselves financially through their immaterial labor. According to Hardt and Negri, "In the final decades of the twentieth century, industrial labor lost its hegemony and in its stead emerged 'immaterial labor,' that is, labor that creates immaterial products, such as knowledge, information, communication, or an emotional response" (*Multitude* 108). Pynchon's bilocation situates this late twentieth-century phenomenon into his historical novel. His characters escape the hegemony of industrial labor through immaterial labor. This happens first through Kit Traverse, who leaves the coalfields of Colorado to pursue a degree in advanced mathematics—focusing specifically on vectors—from Yale University. Likewise, Yashmeen Halfcourt is able to distance herself from her childhood in slavery and gain some autonomy through her study of advanced mathematics, in her case not vectors but instead the Riemann zeta function. Dally Rideout pulls herself up from life as a homeless adolescent in New York and later in Venice through various forms of immaterial labor, primary among these forms being her work as a stage actress. Several other characters follow this pattern. They all represent cases of labor shifting from industry to information, from generating commodities to generating ideas and feelings. Perhaps most telling of these explorations into immaterial labor is the narrative arc of Dally's father, Merle Rideout.

Early in the novel, Merle Rideout and Webb Traverse bond over a discussion of dynamite and alchemy. Webb emerges from the conversation to continue his career as an anarchist bomber. This career ends in his torture and death. It is not clear if anything is accomplished by his acts of violent resistance. In all likelihood, his acts were futile and his death more sad than tragic. Merle, on the other hand, emerges from the conversation to pursue a career path in which his interests in chemistry, photography, and alchemy are employed in a variety of ways. He lives a nomadic existence, roaming from town to town, plying a variety of trades, each of which affords him the opportunity to nurture his intellectual curiosity. By the end of the novel, his intellectual curiosity leads him to team up with fellow nomad and immaterial laborer Roswell Bounce to invent a machine called the Integroscope. The Integroscope can be trained onto a photograph and follow the subject of the photo into her past and future. In Merle's words, the Integroscope "set free the images" (1037) in the photographs, taking them out of a moment frozen in time and allowing them to continue to move through time in whatever direction (past, present, subjunctive) they deem appropriate. For Merle, the invention is about connecting people to one another, understanding people's lives, histories, and directions and how their actions form their identities, and about finding people with whom one has lost contact. The scenes of the Integroscope in action in the novel demonstrate this purpose of Merle's. He uses it to help Lew Basnight find a woman whose life may be in danger. He also takes a photograph of the wife Lew is separated from at the beginning of the novel and allows Lew to see her again, animate the image, and find some closure thirty years later. For his personal purposes, Merle uses the Integroscope to find Dally once again and to reconnect with her (albeit in an ethereal way). Thus, through Merle's employment of his immaterial labor, he develops a technology that opposes the neoliberal ideology of accumulation. It is not an invention he sells or uses for financial profit. Instead, the technology is used to reconnect people, to solidify social relations.

Pynchon's exploration into immaterial labor is both complex and curious. Pynchon is often regarded as a bit of a Luddite. Many of his attacks have focused on technologies. *Gravity's Rainbow* traces the technology of the rocket and the rocket bomb as a way of suggesting that humans have a near-sexual love of death and are careening toward our own annihilation. *Vineland* lampoons television, fingering it as a major force in destroying sixties rebellion. Pynchon even wrote an essay for the *New York Times* entitled "Is It O.K. to Be a Luddite?" In the essay, Pynchon somewhat clarifies his stance on technology. He describes the original Luddites as resenting machines for two reasons: "One was the concentration of capital that each machine represented, and the other was the ability of each machine to put a certain number of humans out of work" (40). Perhaps, along these lines, one could summarize Pynchon's ambivalence toward technology as more a resentment of the neoliberal ideology of accumulation that was born and promulgated through the industrial revolution and for the attack these technologies have represented on working classes. The Integroscope exemplifies this ambivalence. The technology itself—like most technologies—is neither good nor evil. Merle uses it for positive purposes. It brings people together. Yet Merle also recognizes the negative potential of such a machine. He and Roswell hire Lew Basnight to protect them from nefarious forces that wish to steal the Integroscope and use the invention for purposes of surveillance, harassment, and power. While Merle and Roswell acknowledge the possibility that they are simply being paranoid by imagining others who will abuse the powers of the Integroscope, the context surrounding the invention suggests otherwise. They cite the historical example of Louis Le Prince, who invented the motion picture camera. Le Prince's mysterious disappearance and—at least according to Roswell Bounce—likely murder paved the way for the motion picture industry to profit off Le Prince's invention without sharing the profits with Le Prince. Beyond the possibilities of Merle and Roswell being murdered to allow corporate interests to profit off their technology, Pynchon has built another context surrounding corporate interests and technology.

Early in the novel, immediately after Scarsdale Vibe shoots the elderly woman in the hotel lobby, he meets with Yale professor Heino Vanderjuice. Vibe is concerned because Nikola Tesla has expressed his desire to develop a generating system that provides free electrical power to everyone. For Vibe, this desire is sacrilege. The electricity represents a commodity to Vibe. Taking this commodity out of the marketplace, giving it away rather than profiting off it, is antithetical to the economics of gain that define liberalism. Thus, Vibe seeks to counter Tesla's invention by having Professor Vanderjuice invent a method to diffuse this free electrical energy. Bounce's reference to Le Prince coupled with Vibe's intervention on behalf of the marketplace demonstrate the neoliberal perspective toward inventions and technology in general: that it must create commodities, that those commodities must be used for gain and accumulation, and that any commodities that do not satisfy these criteria must be absconded or sabotaged. Because this perspective not only exists but exists as the doxa, the liberating possibilities for immaterial labor and the technologies they invent must be approached with a certain amount of care.

Pynchon further explores the difficulties of immaterial labor as a means for rejecting a neoliberal society through his characters who pursue careers in the fields of immaterial labor. Danger arises not only from corporate interests and neoliberal ideology; it resides in the multitudes who constitute the resistance. As Katherine Hume observes of the protagonists in *Against the Day*, "We find no saints among those characters" (176). Indeed, regardless of the positive portrayal of Professor Vanderjuice throughout the novel, beyond the good he does for Kit while Kit studies at Yale, despite how much the Chums of Chance like and admire Vanderjuice, the fact remains that he takes Vibe's money and works to develop a system to counter Tesla's system of free electrical power for everyone. Similarly, Kit aligns himself with Vibe as a means of pursuing his career in immaterial labor. Vibe pays for Kit's Yale education in advanced mathematics. Kit feels as if he is a class traitor when he aligns himself with Vibe. Yale—as it is presented in the novel—represents so much of the neoliberal ideology that Kit opposes. Still, Kit takes the money and gains the knowledge that Vibe pays for and hopes to exploit. In one sense, the result of Kit's study of advanced mathematics is a form of resistance against Vibe and neoliberalism because Kit's field of study is not immediately exploitable in the short-term marketplace, which is the only type of knowledge that Vibe values. Kit produces no knowledge that Vibe can profit from. Subverting all value to the marketplace and systems of profits and losses, Kit represents a loss for Vibe. Kit's education is unrecoverable money spent by Vibe. When Vibe realizes this, he cuts Kit's funding. In fact, Vibe is so angered by this monetary loss that he sends Foley over to Germany to kill Kit. Luckily for Kit, this assassination attempt is never realized. Nonetheless, Vibe's partnership with Kit is illuminating. Kit's pursuit of advanced mathematics can be viewed as a metaphor for the ambivalence neoliberal ideology has with academics in general: the value of academics must be measured in terms beyond the marketplace. For this reason, his pursuit of knowledge that is not profitable in the short term can be seen as a form of resistance similar to his brothers' nomadism. Yet Pynchon complicates this notion even further later in the novel.

Kit finds himself in Italy during World War I. His study of vectors, which was worthless to Vibe because it could not be exploited in the short term, proves suddenly very profitable in the marketplace. Kit is employed to apply his knowledge of vectors to military aircraft design. Kit's passion for vectors applied to aircraft design modifies a warplane that one character, a pilot named Renzo, uses to dive-bomb his enemies. Renzo is a budding fascist. With Kit along for a test ride, he pilots his warplane into a controlled dive that terrorizes strikers at a weapons factory in Torino. At that point, Kit has a sort of epiphany that his immaterial labor, everything connected to it, "was all political" (1071). Further, Renzo's attack on the strikers, which is enabled by Kit's knowledge of vectors applied to a specific aircraft, is "the first and purest expression in northern Italy of a Certain Word that would not quite exist for another year or two" (1071), that Certain Word, of course, being fascism.

Dally Rideout's immaterial labor also provides a flawed example of a vision of a better future. While Dally's performances on the stage promote certain feelings and can be used as a form of activist theater, they are not employed for that purpose. Instead, she begins her acting career by performing in the role of a tourist who is kidnapped into white slavery in New York's Chinatown. The theater of which she is a part reifies racist notions about New York's Chinese American population. It represents the fear of the Yellow Peril that was so prominent in the late nineteenth and early twentieth centuries. One of Dally's main theatrical benefactors is R. Wilshire Vibe, Scarsdale's brother and the author, director, and/or producer of a variety of racist, sexist, and classist plays. Dally's rise to prominence on the London stage later in the novel leads not to any type of activism but instead to her offstage role as the mistress of weapons dealer and all around neoliberal villain Clive Crouchmas. Clive is so villainous, in fact, that he attempts to sell Dally into slavery when he believes she has betrayed him. Nonetheless, after she is economically autonomous enough to no longer need Clive, after she is married and largely independent, after his attempt to sell her into slavery, Dally has an extramarital affair with Clive. At no point, however, does Dally employ her immaterial labor as a means of resisting Empire. Thus, Pynchon blends human flaws—through Vanderjuice, Kit Traverse, Dally Rideout, and others—with technological exploitation to complicate the revolutionary potential of immaterial labor and intellectual inquiry. Both immaterial labor and intellectual inquiry can be effective means of resistance; both represent a problematic site to seek a vision for a better future. It is important to bear in mind, however, that Pynchon is not proposing simple solutions to confront Empire. Instead, like the Integroscope, which has the capacity to free its subjects and allow them to perform in the past, present, and subjunctive worlds, Pynchon's fiction explores the past, present, and subjunctive avenues for revolutionary ideas.

The problems that arise when Pynchon allows these revolutionary ideas to perform on their own, when he investigates where these ideas lead when they are set free, should not suggest the worthlessness of these ideas. Instead, Pynchon is substituting a flawed but improved future for a vision of utopia. As Katherine Hume concludes in the passage cited above, "We find no saints among those characters, but enough faith and enough decency to make them a functioning community" (176). Pynchon's clearest visions of a better future lie in his representation of these functioning communities, not only in *Against the Day* but in the two novels that precede it. *Vineland* ends by bringing together a multitude at the Becker-Traverse family reunion. The guests at the reunion are not necessarily biological family. They are, necessarily, a functioning and flawed community of resistance to Empire as it is constructed in that novel. The very same Jesse Traverse who is an adolescent revolutionary in *Against the Day* becomes the wise elder, quoting Emerson and shaping the meaning of rebellion within the novel. *Mason & Dixon* ends with the reconstituted family of Charles Mason subjunctively envisioning an America that fulfills its promises of democracy by granting enfranchisement to all its residents. Likewise, *Against the Day* resolves with explorations into community and family. One salient example of this exploration is represented when Reef, Yashmeen, and the third member of their relationship at this point in the novel, Cyprian Latewood, visit a community called Yz-les-Bains.

What It Means to Be an American

The representation of Yz-les-Bains connects Pynchon's representations of community with Wendy Brown's suggestion for confronting neoliberal ideology. Brown argues, "What remains for the Left, then, is to challenge emerging neo-liberal governmentality in EuroAtlantic states with an alternative vision of the good. . . . In its barest form, this would be a vision in which justice would not center upon maximizing individual wealth or rights but developing and enhancing the capacity of citizens to share power and hence, collaboratively govern themselves." The refuge at Yz-les-Bains presents a vision of a community that has removed itself from the neoliberal ideology of accumulation and replaced it with a vision of working together for the mutual benefit of everyone in the community. It is a refuge for anarchists and revolutionaries, a "venerable oasis without charge, though in practice even those against the commoditizing of human shelter were often able to come up with modest sums in a dozen currencies, and leave them with Lucien the concierge" (931). In representing Yz-les-Bains, Pynchon is careful to recognize that material needs exist even in anarchist refuges, that one cannot fully divest oneself of the marketplace. Even on the fringes of neoliberal society, money is necessary to some extent. Pynchon does not appear to oppose currency itself. He seems to oppose the hoarding of it that is valued by a neoliberal society of accumulation. Hoarding would be likewise troubling if the act were performed by anarchists at Yz-les-Bains who simply did not want to chip in to cover the common expenses of the community.

The residents of Yz-les-Bains are welcoming of the trio of Yashmeen, Reef, and Cyprian. The trio is engaged in a nontraditional, long-term sexual relationship with each other. This relationship is a divergence from traditionally observed heterosexual relationships between two partners, yet the residents of Yz-les-Bains make no effort to instill traditional requirements onto the trio. The message is clear: the multitude are welcome at this refuge. Difference is acknowledged but not used to divide the community. In fact, difference, because it is predicated on the rejection of those values that seek to divide communities and pit one subculture against another as a means of ensuring the power of the dominant culture, is a driving force for the enfranchisement of the multitude at Yz-les-Bains. The trio find a mirror image of their relationship when they encounter the former spy Ratty McHugh and his two suffragette wives. The wives further articulate the preconditions for community at the refuge: the acceptance of differences must include gender equity. As Jennifer Invert McHugh, one of Ratty's wives and a former classmate of Yashmeen's, explains about anarchism: "as long as women were not welcome, it never had a chance" (934). Instead, Yz-les-Bains is constructed on principles of differences and equity among the differences. This precondition is in line with Hardt and Negri's definition of the multitude as "singularities that act in common" (*Multitude* 105). It also matches Occupy's demonstration of horizontal networks rejecting a single issue, leader, or representative in favor of a practice of participatory democracy.

Yz-les-Bains both envisions this multitude and institutes classic anarchist beliefs. Residents observe no hierarchy. There is no chain of command. Economy exists, but it is an economy of social relations rather than of gain or accumulation. Labor exists, but it is not a commodity. Instead, residents recognize what tasks need to be completed to keep the community operating, and they perform those tasks. They work in common to support the community. Unlike Webb, who is labeled an anarchist bomber but does not have a clear understanding of anarchist theory, the residents at Yz-les-Bains have articulated their resistance. They oppose "tyranny over people to whom the land really belongs, land which, generation after generation, has been absorbing their labor, accepting the corpses this labor produces, along with obscene profits, which is left to other and usually whiter men" (935). In short, they oppose economic liberalism. They support a construction of the multitude that does not fall under a single unified belief system or homogeneous group that can be accurately labeled "the people," but instead is comprised of people who retain their differences yet work in concert against an economy of accumulation. They support a society that replaces the competition of capitalism with the cooperation of anarchism. They are, in a sense, Occupying one corner of the Alps.

At the heart of their resistance is their attempt to prevent the coming World War I. The residents' principal opposition to World War I is that, as Pynchon demonstrates in *Vineland*, warfare benefits national governments and corporate interests and attacks the rights of individuals. Ratty acknowledges that, if war should break out, "Anarchists would be the biggest losers, wouldn't they. Industrial corporations, armies, navies, governments, all would go on as before, if not more powerful. But in a general war among nations, every small victory Anarchism has struggled to win so far would simply turn to dust" (938). Indeed, Ratty's comment—no doubt bolstered by Pynchon's hindsight—is a prescient one. World War I did turn the anarchist movement to dust. Ratty further states, "A general European war, with every striking worker a traitor, flags threatened, the sacred soils of homelands defiled, would be just the ticket to wipe Anarchism off the political map" (938). Ratty's fears came to fruition, at least in the United States. Under Woodrow Wilson's Espionage Act, anarchists were frequently imprisoned for protesting the war. Prominent anarchists like Emma Goldman and Alexander Berkman were deported for publicly opposing conscription. Major anarchist publications were halted. J. Edgar Hoover attacked various anarchist headquarters. The movement was essentially killed by the war. Wilson, Hoover, and other members of the government used the war and fears of national security as justification for these attacks.

In order to attempt to prevent the coming war, Yashmeen, Reef, and Cyprian leave Yz-les-Bains for the Balkans, where they believe they can disarm a weapons system that will ensure an escalation of warfare. Obviously, the trio is unsuccessful in their larger attempt to prevent World War I. Nonetheless, their experiences at Yz-les-Bains and the hope it gives them to work for the common good seem to rejuvenate them. Cyprian finds the strength to return to the Balkans, where, earlier in the novel, he was nearly assassinated and where he ultimately undergoes a spiritual awakening. Yashmeen is likewise inspired. She leaves the refuge holding "on to a limitless faith that History could be helped to keep its promises, including someday, a commonwealth of the oppressed" (942). While History cannot keep its promise within the novel because that promise has not yet been realized in the world outside the novel, Yashmeen is able to find, within the fiction of the novel, somewhat of a commonwealth through her reconstituted family.

Yashmeen, Reef, and their infant daughter leave Cyprian in the Balkans and travel to Colorado, where they connect with Jesse, Stray, and Frank. The six form a strange family structure in which Jesse calls his uncle Frank "Pa" and his biological father "Reef," in which sexual histories and convoluted connections cause friction, in which jealousies initially simmer below the surface until Yashmeen and Stray realize that no husband-swapping will occur. The family structure grows when Yashmeen and Reef have another child. The family grows more complex when Yashmeen and Stray engage in a sexual relationship. Like Hume's assessment of the characters in the novel, this family is imperfect, but there is enough faith and decency among them to form a community. The family rejects neoconservative notions of family values that insist upon heterosexuality and recognize the patriarchal nuclear family as the only option. Instead, they operate as a community of mutual economic and emotional support, all working in common for mutual benefits.

Eventually, the Traverses' mode of resistance takes the form of removing themselves as far as possible from Empire. They settle in the Kitsap Peninsula of Washington State, where their means of financial support is vague and it is implied that their engagement with consumer commodity culture is minimal. Political violence takes a backseat to a project of working together to form a family and community. Webb's legacy as an anarchist bomber is referenced, but in a new context. When Jesse is asked to write an essay on what it means to be an American, Reef reaches for a pencil with "that look on his face, the same look his own father used to get just before heading off for some dynamite-related activities" (1076). In this moment, the pencil replaces dynamite for the Traverses. The violence inherent in attacking humans and property is rejected in favor of a project of using immaterial labor and intellectual inquiry to attack an ideology. Before examining what that pencil produces, it is important to return to the youngest of Webb's children, Kit.

Near the end of the novel, Kit and Dally Rideout get married and form their own type of nontraditional family. They become a couple with no children or extended community in sight. Unlike the residents at Yz-les-Bains or the Traverses in Kitsap, Dally and Kit's reconstituted family is not idyllic, and it is not removed from society. The couple have a much rockier terrain to cross. Their relationship is filled with infidelities, negligence, hurt feelings, and time spent in different cities, countries, sometimes even continents. In their final scene in the novel, they get back together. The narrator concludes their tale in the subjunctive, stating:

> May we imagine for them a vector, passing through the invisible, the "imaginary," the unimaginable, carrying them safely into this postwar Paris where the taxis, battered veterans of the mythic Marne, now carry only lovers and cheerful drinks, and music which cannot be marched to goes on uninterrupted all night, in the bars and *bals musettes* for the dancers who will always be there, and the nights will be dark enough for whatever visions must transpire across them, no longer to be broken into by light displaced from Hell, and the difficulties they find are no more productive of evil than the opening and closing of too many doors, or of too few. A vector through the night into a morning of hosed pavements, birds heard everywhere but unseen, bakery smells, filtered green light, a courtyard still in shade . . . (1082–83)

This impossibly long (technically never-ending because of Pynchon's ellipsis) sentence imagines for Kit and Dally the idyllic future that the reader supposes when the characters first meet. Significantly, even within the context of the novel, the idyllic future is a subjunctive one, one that exists in a Paris that will not go through the worldwide depression that did come along a few years after this scene, a Paris that does not get invaded and occupied by fascist Germany, a world in which the lovers can live without war weighing down their marriage. It is important to note that this idyllic future is not removed from society the way the residents at Yz-les-Bains are, the way the other Traverses are. For Kit and Dally, a vision of a better future is possible within city limits and adjacent to the marketplace that urban centers rely on. Kit and Dally are still part of the marketplace. They ride in taxis and buy bread at bakeries. And still the narrator bestows upon the scene a sense of optimism that, even as mired in a troubled past as the couple are, even with their history of mutual injuries inflicted mutually, a better future may exist, one in which they learn to work in common for mutual benefits. This underscores the subtleties of Pynchon's exploration into economic liberalism and neoliberalism. Just as his Luddite views do not attack technology so much as criticize the exploitation that accompanies technology, Pynchon's attack on neoliberalism is not an attack on commerce or even a marketplace. It is instead an attack on an ideology that privileges a marketplace over humans and extends the values of the marketplace to every aspect of society.

It is finally significant that Pynchon ends Kit and Dally's story in the subjunctive, asking the reader to read the imagined as true. In a self-reflexive manner, *Against the Day* asks its readers to perform a similar task: to use fiction as a way of understanding the ways in which neoliberalism grew from economic liberalism, what resistance movements have done to effectively confront it, what methods have failed, and what the real, material consequences have been. David Harvey concludes his *Brief History* by arguing, "The more neoliberalism is recognized as a failed utopian rhetoric masking a successful project for the restoration of ruling-class power, the more the basis is laid for a resurgence of mass movements voicing egalitarian political demands and seeking economic justice, fair trade, and greater economic security" (203–4). *Against the Day* performs this task. By bilocating liberalism and neoliberalism, anarchism and visions of a better future, it represents societies constructed from an ideology of the "freedom" of an unregulated market as failed utopia. The failure is tied to the exploitation of workers, the dehumanization of most of humanity, and the opulence of accumulation inherent in the economic system. Pynchon carefully dismantles the doxa of neoliberalism through the novel. The final stick of dynamite in the novel is tossed by young Jesse Traverse. The stick is not literal. It is instead his essay "What It Means to Be an American." Jesse writes, "It means do what they tell you and take what they give you and don't go on strike or their soldiers will shoot you down" (1076). This sentence is Jesse's entire essay. Pynchon, however, needs over a thousand pages of fiction to give this idea form, to take it from a sound bite to a meaningful call for rebellion.

CHAPTER 5

Inherent Vice and Being in Place

IN HER 2008 DOCUMENTARY *The Examined Life*, Astra Taylor interviews Michael Hardt as he rows the two of them around a pond in Central Park. Hardt discusses notions of revolution and democracy. He addresses the common notion of revolution: when one elite regime is forcefully removed and replaced by a new, hopefully better regime. He largely dismisses this notion, and he posits a second possibility, an idea "of revolution as just the removal of all of those forms of authority—state power, the power of capital—that stop people from expressing their natural abilities to rule themselves."

Hardt goes on to clarify that this form of revolution takes work, that it "really requires a transformation of human nature so that people are capable of democracy." This is a concept he later explores in greater depth in "Thomas Jefferson, or, the Transition of Democracy." In both the documentary and the essay, Hardt argues that real democracy—the rule by all—is a skill. It has to be learned, and it has to be practiced. As he tells Taylor while rowing around the pond in Central Park, "You can only learn democracy by doing it."

This notion feels remote for Hardt as he is surrounded by the wealth of upper Manhattan, flanked on one side by the old money of the Upper East Side and on the other by the relatively newer aristocracy of the Upper West Side (which, not incidentally, is the setting for Thomas Pynchon's *Bleeding Edge*). For Hardt, to speak of revolution on a beautiful day in Central Park seems a little absurd. Astra Taylor breaks her role as silent observer to ask, "Well, where would we pick that would be the revolutionary spot?"

Three years later, that spot would be Zuccotti Park. The occupation of the park in the heart of New York's financial district may not have been enough of an action to qualify as a revolution, but it was a revolutionary demonstration. In the park, occupiers demonstrated the notion of revolution that Hardt had posited. Inasmuch as they could, occupiers removed the power of capital and state power to create a space in which the skills of democracy could be learned and practiced.

Filmmaker Astra Taylor participated in the occupation of Zuccotti Park and documented her experiences in a series of short reflections, "Scenes from an Occupation." In one of her reflections, she discusses encountering "A young man, impersonating a carnival barker" who invited her to step up to a giant sheet of paper and write down how much she "was worth to the banks" (52). Taylor wrote down the total she still owed in student loan debt and walked away feeling a little sick. Despite all the hopefulness of this revolutionary moment and all the space created for humans to express their natural ability to rule themselves, the specter of debt haunted the occupation.

It's no mistake that debt hung over the Occupy movement. The movement was born out of the 2008 financial collapse and the subprime mortgage crisis. As capital floundered for new spaces to continue its insatiable need for growth in the twenty-first century, industries moved from producing goods to producing financial products. Much of the collapse can be tied back to risky financial products traded by banks that, until very recently, were forbidden by law to engage in this type of speculation. As mortgages and insurance companies covering those mortgages became risky investments, financial markets expanded their holdings in protected and insured products like student loans, encouraging the ballooning of student loan debt. As Taylor observes, the occupiers were not privileged college students or lazy, unemployed activists, not hippies or weirdos or slackers. Many were college graduates who'd been systemically excluded from the shrinking American middle class, who were struggling under a student loan debt that they may never have the opportunity to pay back. Taylor asks, "Would most people rather go back and live with mom and dad or camp somewhere like Zuccotti Park?" (53).

Among those who catalyzed the occupation of Zuccotti Park was David Graeber. Graeber teaches anthropology at the London School of Economics. He was in New York in the summer of 2011 to promote his book *Debt: The First 5,000 Years*.[1] While there, he participated in the initial planning meetings for the occupation. He stuck around for the occupation itself. Not coincidentally, debt and Occupy became inextricably entwined.

Between the time when Taylor and Hardt rowed around Central Park and the time when occupiers encamped in Zuccotti Park, Thomas Pynchon released *Inherent Vice* (2009). Several early critics of the novel dismissed it almost entirely. Tom LeClair called it "intellectually thin" (25), Richard Lacayo dubbed it "second-tier Pynchon" (60), and Mark Kamine ended his attack on the novel by simply stating, "I give up" (30). Other reviewers focused mostly on Pynchon's pastiche of crime novels, specifically Raymond Chandler's Philip Marlowe novels and the Coen brothers' *The Big Lebowski*.[2] Almost all the initial commenters on *Inherent Vice* missed its revolutionary potential. Doc Sportello, the novel's protagonist, is an early adopter of the notion of revolution explained by Michael Hardt. He seeks to remove state power and the power of capitalism and to reconceive notions of debt and community as a means of creating a democratic commons.

Rewriting Noir

Critics were not wrong to focus on Pynchon's pastiche in their early reviews of *Inherent Vice*. The book is as much a conversation as it is a novel. From the time of its release in 2009, critics observed the stylistic and structural similarities the novel shares with both Chandler's Philip Marlowe novels and the Coen brothers' *The Big Lebowski*. Some reviewers commended Pynchon for creating a pastiche of Chandler's work or for taking *The Big Lebowski* further. Other reviewers argued that Pynchon's blending of postmodern fiction and the tropes of a detective novel was a failed experiment. Louis Menand, writing for the *New Yorker*, took the opportunity to both commend and condemn this pastiche. Regardless of whether these early reviews praised or panned the novel, they all pointed toward the need for more complicated scholarship exploring the similarities and differences between *The Long Goodbye*, *The Big Lebowski*, and *Inherent Vice*. This exploration would lead specifically to the ways in which Pynchon's Doc Sportello rewrites both Chandler's Marlowe and the Coen brothers' Dude. Further, a deeper examination of Pynchon's interplay with the tropes of detective fiction and his meandering away from the form's conventions affords a deeper understanding of not only the novel but of the intersections between the novel and Occupy. Doc Sportello follows a business model with his private investigation company that suggests an alternative economic system from corporate consumer capitalism. Using David Graeber's *Debt* and Michael Hardt and Antonio Negri's *Commonwealth* as guides, it becomes clear that Doc is drifting away from notions of public and private property and into a living example of an economic system based on the commons. Further, while Hardt and Negri explore the abstract of love's political capabilities, and while previous discussions of Pynchon's other novels have investigated family as a site for redemption,[3] *Inherent Vice* takes the abstracts of love and family beyond politics and redemption and into a revolutionary alternative.

The first step in understanding deeper levels of the novel lies in an exploration into not only pastiche but the specific form of pastiche that Christian Moraru dubbed "rewriting." Discussions of postmodern pastiche typically refer to Frederic Jameson's definition of pastiche in *Postmodernism, or, The Cultural Logic of Late Capitalism*. Jameson writes: "Pastiche is, like parody, the imitation of a peculiar or unique, idiosyncratic style, the wearing of a linguistic mask, speech in a dead language. But it is a neutral practice of such mimicry, without any of parody's ulterior motives, amputated of the satiric impulse, devoid of laughter and of any conviction that alongside the abnormal tongue you have momentarily borrowed, some healthy linguistic normality still exists" (17). Several notions in this definition are key to understanding the stylistic significance of Pynchon's novel. First, true to Jameson's definition, Pynchon does, to some extent, wear the linguistic mask of Raymond Chandler. Pynchon maintains his comfortable third-person distance from the characters in the novel while Chandler chooses the more intimate first person for Philip Marlowe, yet Pynchon's third-person narrators are so dynamic and intrusive that the narrator himself seems to be a character in the novels. *Inherent Vice* continues this stylistic trend, albeit in a new manner. While the narrator of *Mason & Dixon* borrowed the style of eighteenth-century British novels, the narrator of *Against the Day* employed colloquialisms unique to post–World War I novels, and the narrator of *Vineland* seemed to be an old hippie explaining sixties rebellion to a generation born into Nixonian repression, the narrator of *Inherent Vice* borrows so much of both the journalistic style and noir flair of Chandler that he could be, well, not Chandler himself but a fairly convincing impersonation. Further, *Inherent Vice* does not seek Chandler as the source of its humor. Pynchon makes no jokes at Chandler's expense. Just as the narrator of *Gravity's Rainbow* reveled in building on the prose of Sax Rohmer's spy novels, the narrator of *Inherent Vice* seems to settle comfortably into his Raymond Chandler mask. He never breaks character or linguistically winks at the reader.

In fact, Pynchon's pastiche of Raymond Chandler is so complete that it can be read as a rewriting of, specifically, Chandler's *The Long Goodbye*. Christian Moraru, in his book *Rewriting: Postmodern Narrative and Cultural Critique in the Age of Cloning*, observes, "There are highly canonical, widely popular fictions that capture, even give birth to key myths of certain communities. At the same time, they acquire in the long run a communally 'mythic' weight through successive editing, teaching, reading, and related institutionalizing acts" (3). While *The Long Goodbye* may not be the most canonical text in university literature courses, the text is instrumental in giving birth to the myth of the rugged, individualistic American male who is guided by nothing more than his own moral compass. Chandler's novel has been edited and rewritten in numerous and diverse ways, from Haruki Murakami's reimagining of the novel in *A Wild Sheep Chase* to Robert Altman's adaptation of *The Long Goodbye* (which places the novel in a time machine and ships it to the 1970s) to Pynchon's *The Crying of Lot 49* (where we can envision Oedipa Maas as a sixties-style Marlowe, descending into a corrupt Southern California where she's entangled in moneyed machinations beyond her control and where solutions to the initial mysteries seem to be beside the point once the reader reaches the end). One of the most well-known rewritings of *The Long Goodbye* is the Coen brothers' film *The Big Lebowski*. Placing *Inherent Vice* in conversation with *The Long Goodbye* and *The Big Lebowski* helps elucidate the ways in which Pynchon incorporates pastiche and postmodern rewriting to approach revolutionary alternatives.

The Long Goodbye is perhaps Chandler's most powerful novel. It was the last original novel he wrote, and it was written at a time of both personal crisis (his wife was dying as he wrote it) and artistic crisis (he struggled to wrest his conception of the character of Philip Marlowe back from Humphrey Bogart's portrayal of him). *The Long Goodbye* became Chandler's attempt at the modernist "novel of the world." While it certainly fell short of Joyce's *Ulysses* and Faulkner's *Go Down, Moses* in both scope and richness of detail, *The Long Goodbye* quickly digresses from a murder mystery and drifts into larger investigations of the mass media, organized crime, big business, the justice system, and the legacy of World War II. Several representatives from each of these groups are given room to declaim in Chandler's novel. Detectives, lawyers, pulp authors, journalists, and even the media mogul Harlan Potter are all given space for their recitations examining how their society got to be in the mess that it was in. In this sense, Chandler realized the potential of the detective novel as a platform for cultural critique. He created, in a sense, a new kind of crime novel, one in which the detective may be able to use logic and deduction to solve the mystery at hand, but logic, deduction, observation, and the collection of a wealth of information are not enough to dig below the surface of any of life's significant mysteries.

In his essay "The Synoptic Chandler," Frederic Jameson tells a story about film director Howard Hawks and actor Humphrey Bogart drinking at a bar, arguing about the fate of a character from Chandler's *The Big Sleep*. They could not agree whether the character's death had been a murder, suicide, or some third thing. They called Chandler to ask him, and he could not remember, either. Jameson tells this story to suggest that, in a Raymond Chandler novel, the solution to the mystery is less compelling than the characters and episodes leading up to it. The Coen brothers utilize a similar resolution in *The Big Lebowski*. When the protagonist, the Dude, finally solves the mystery of the kidnapped girl, he calls his friend Walter to help him confront the criminal. The Dude explains his solution and, unlike the dramatic, finger-pointing scenes from Hercule Poirot novels, Walter acknowledges that the Dude has, in fact, solved the mystery. He then asks, "But how does all this add up to an emergency?" Further, once Walter and the Dude confront the criminal, he shrugs them off, saying, "You have your story. I have mine." In both cases, the anticlimactic nature of the solution is highlighted. Likewise, a reader of *Inherent Vice* can very easily forget that Doc is investigating the murder of Glen Charlock. She can forget who killed Charlock. She can even feel satisfied in her continued reading when Mickey Wolfmann, the character whose disappearance catalyzes the events of the novel, is found more than a hundred pages prior to the end. In all three cases, Chandler, the Coen brothers, and

Pynchon poignantly suggest that the solution of a single crime is never really the point.

On the larger scale, the abandonment of the typical crime fiction trope of an investigation leading to the meaningful detection of a significant truth becomes emblematic of Brian McHale's description of the shift from modern to postmodern concerns. In *Postmodernist Fiction*, McHale claims that postmodern fictions can be characterized by a "shift of dominant from problems of *knowing* to problems of *modes of being*—from an epistemological dominant to an *ontological one*" (10). All three works—*The Long Goodbye*, *The Big Lebowski*, and *Inherent Vice*—subvert the detective fiction trope of an epistemological truth at the end that reifies some grand narrative. They are instead more taken with little narratives exploring wealth and corruption in a Southern California that comes to represent, in some respects, a global marketplace.

Money and Complicity

In *The Politics of Postmodernism*, Linda Hutcheon argues, "[L]ess oppositional and less idealistic than the culture of the (formative) 1960s, the postmodern we know has to acknowledge its own complicity with the very values upon which it seeks to comment" (10). As a modernist novel preceding both the 1960s and postmodernism, *The Long Goodbye* largely ignores this issue of complicity. This ignorance can cause problems for a contemporary reader. While several leaders of society are given the room to critique their contemporary culture in *The Long Goodbye*, all these characters fail to reflect on their own role in creating or fostering this broken society. Everyone blames someone else without recognizing his own role. The novel ends at the moment when Marlowe's complicity is revealed, yet nothing in the narrative suggests that Marlowe is aware of his complicity. Further, if he does gain some awareness, the reader is deprived of the opportunity to see what Marlowe does with this awareness.

In *The Big Lebowski*, the Dude does not critique contemporary culture, and his complicity is comedic. When faced with the corruption of the extremely wealthy, the Dude goes along with it. This becomes one of his most famous moments of self-awareness in the film, as he says at the end, "The Dude abides." He willingly participates in the corrupt schemes he encounters. First, when he is employed to deliver a ransom to Bunny Lebowski's kidnappers, he steals the ransom and gives the kidnappers a suitcase full of dirty underwear. He feels betrayed when he finds out that he stole a suitcase with phone books instead of a million dollars. His betrayal is a punch line. He "threw a ringer for a ringer." This pattern continues throughout the movie. When the Big Lebowski denies the Dude a replacement rug, the Dude steals one. When wealthy heiress Maude Lebowski seeks the million dollars her father (the Big Lebowski) stole from her foundation to pay the ransom, and when pornographer Jackie Treehorn seeks the million dollars that Bunny Lebowski owes him, they both approach the Dude. The Dude offers to sell them dubious information. At no point does the Dude succumb to hand-wringing or frustration about his complicity. He just abides by it. The real complications of the Dude's complicity come from the plot. For every corrupt enterprise the Dude participates in, he loses a little more. In the end, he gains nothing. He still has no clear means of paying the rent that his landlord has been hounding him for throughout the film. His car is destroyed. He never gets his rug back, and the rug he steals is stolen from him. He never gains in any real way from his interactions with the wealthy and the corrupt. The narrator of the film, as he attempts to wrap everything up, can only laugh and shrug his shoulders.

Doc is different. At one key point in the novel, his ex-girlfriend Shasta explains to Doc how he is complicit in the system he seeks to critique. She tells him that he and the federal snitch Coy Harlingen are "peas in a pod.... Both of you, cops who never wanted to be cops. Rather be surfing or smoking or fucking or anything but what you're doing. You guys must've thought you'd be chasing criminals, and instead here you're both working for them" (313–14). Doc responds to this accusation of Shasta's by mentally cataloging his paying customers and recognizing that he has been working for the elements of society he views as most nefarious. His catalog reads like a description of Michael Hardt and Antonio Negri's concept of Empire. They are all members of the multinational corporations, governments, or supranational agencies that comprise a new sovereignty. Doc wonders, "Forget who—*what* was he working for anymore?" (314).

Doc need not analyze for whom he is working. He is already poignantly, sometimes painfully, aware. Unlike the unwitting Marlowe or Dude, Doc recognizes that he is being manipulated. He observes that Bigfoot is "hustling" him (274) and that he is "some dumb-ass sucker of a civilian PI who'll keep nosing on into the case" (284). Despite this recognition, Doc continues on. From a narrative standpoint, he need not. By the time Doc is genuinely manipulated by Bigfoot and the Golden Fang, the initial mysteries of the book have been solved. Glen Charlock's murderer has been (more or less) identified. Mickey Wolfmann has returned and his kidnappers have been identified. Even Shasta has returned home safely. The forces of the plot that propel the novel have been resolved. So why must Doc continue?

The answer to this question seems to lie in Hardt and Negri's assertion, "[W]e have to recognize that, regardless of how brilliantly and trenchantly we critique it, we are destined to live in *this* world, not only subject to its powers of domination but also contaminated by its corruptions" (*Commonwealth* vii). It is not enough to end *Inherent Vice* with a protagonist on the verge of realizing that he helps to create and is corrupted by the very world he criticizes (as Chandler ends *The Long Goodbye*). Instead, Doc must learn how to live in this contaminated world. He must find something to work for.

Examining the relationship the protagonists of *The Long Goodbye*, *The Big Lebowski*, and *Inherent Vice* have with money helps elucidate what Doc is working for. In "The Simple Art of Murder," Chandler states his detective "will take no man's money dishonestly" (18). True to this form, Marlowe accepts no dishonest money from his work in *The Long Goodbye*. Chandler suggests that the $5,000 bill that Marlowe's friend and first employer in the novel, Terry Lennox, sent him and the money that Marlowe's second employer, Eileen Wade, offered him was tainted. Marlowe would have thus become tainted by accepting this money. He rejects both payments. Nonetheless, Marlowe acts exactly as Terry Lennox, Eileen Wade, and the other wealthy, corrupt characters manipulate him to act. Marlowe is left with nothing at the end. His refusal to accept the money does not protect him from the corruption. He is still tainted for his complicity in the crimes. He is left without his friendship to Terry, which motivated him through much of the caper. Even his pride is in shambles.

The Dude's situation is far less complex in *The Big Lebowski*. He is willing to take money, sometimes even dishonestly. As I mention above, he plots to steal ransom money from the Big Lebowski, he tries to charge Maude Lebowski and Jackie Treehorn for information he does not have, and he steals a rug from the Big Lebowski. At one point in the movie, the Dude claims he "is not greedy. All the Dude ever wanted was his rug back." Yet he is greedy. He is willing to risk the life of a possibly (though improbably) kidnapped woman so he can pocket money that was stolen from a scholarship fund and earmarked for inner-city youth. If all he were genuinely concerned with were his rug, he could have simply washed the urine stain out with soap and water.

Doc eschews payment for different reasons. Unlike Marlowe, Doc has no delusions about his complicity. He knows he is complicit. Unlike the Dude, Doc does have the means of getting his hands on dishonest money, yet he rejects the payment. In fact, Doc's relationship with money is more complex than simply the acceptance or rejection of it. Almost every character who seeks to engage Doc's services, from Tariq Khalil to Hope Harlingen to Shasta herself, can't pay Doc. Doc accepts the cases, anyway. His acceptance of these cases intersects meaningfully with David Graeber's notions of communities that preceded or operate outside industrial marketplaces in *Debt*. Doc's rejection of Crocker Fenway's money exemplifies the revolutionary potential of Doc's business model. Both examples warrant a closer examination.

Doc and the First 5,000 Years of Debt

In *Debt: The First 5,000 Years*, David Graeber begins his anthropological investigation of currency-based economies with Adam Smith's myth of barter. As Graeber describes it, Smith's myth begins with human societies that inevitably evolve toward the division of labor. Once a tribe begins producing cobblers or arrow makers or potato farmers, these laborers naturally develop a currency in order to more equitably trade for their shoes or arrows or potatoes. In Smith's estimation, humans move from a state of nature to a state of capitalism. The problem, as Graeber points out, is that there is no evidence in human history of societies following this pattern. Graeber takes a more anthropological approach, investigating how early societies dealt with exchange, debt, and currency over the last five millennia.

Graeber finds that, in most human societies, "Barter is what you do with those to whom you are *not* bound by ties of hospitality" (33). In other words, most tribes or communities worked together and held property together. Graeber explains this practice by using an example of a walrus-hunting tribe of Inuits described in Peter Freuchen's *Book of the Eskimo*. In the example, Freuchen, a Danish anthropologist living with a tribe of Inuits, returns home from an unsuccessful hunt. A hunter who has had better luck gives Freuchen several hundred pounds of meat. Freuchen thanks the hunter and the hunter takes offense. For the hunter, this act is not something worthy of thanks; it is simply something humans do. Graeber concludes that, for the hunter and many humans living in societies preceding or outside of the global marketplace, "being truly human meant *refusing* to make such calculations, refusing to measure or remember who had given what to whom, for the precise reason that doing so would inevitably create a world where we began 'comparing power with power, measuring, calculating' and reducing each other to slaves or dogs through debt" (79). Returning to Smith's myth of barter, Graeber argues that, instead of humans developing currency so that a potato farmer who needs shoes can equitably trade with his cobbler, the cobbler would notice that the potato farmer needed shoes and give them to him. The potato farmer, when his crop came in, would share some of the crop with the cobbler. No specific calculations would be made. Bartering would be reserved for transactions with other communities not bound by the same ties of hospitality.

Doc Sportello, it would seem, comes from this tradition of exchange. When Tariq Khalil first approaches Doc, they establish credibility with each other. They have friends in common. They share a similar political outlook and socioeconomic class. They inhabit the same community. Through these connections, Doc feels bound by a communal tie to Tariq and accepts his case despite the fact that Tariq can't pay. Doc extends these communal ties to Hope Harlingen, who likewise shares acquaintances and political outlooks and communities with Doc. Doc even extends this to his ex-girlfriend Shasta. Though Shasta has recently spent time as the mistress of a land developer, she is folded back into Doc's community when she ascends his back stairs and reminds him of her Gordita Beach roots. Like the Inuit hunters and the imaginary cobbler, Doc recognizes a need in his community and meets that need without a specific currency or accounting. Likewise, when Doc needs information or weed or food or even Sauncho Smilax's legal services, his community provides those.

Graeber observes, "[W]hen we examine how economic life is actually conducted, in real communities and marketplaces, almost anywhere . . . one is much more likely to discover everyone is in debt to everyone else in a dozen different ways, and that most transactions take place without the use of currency" (22). Doc and his imagined community may not be so idealistic as to engage in these transactions through a revolutionary impulse. As Graeber observes, transactions without currency are more common among members of communities that lack access to currency and the means of enforcing debts. Nonetheless, Doc voluntarily enters into these arrangements, and they provide a counterexample to the rigid accounting of a global marketplace.

Graeber further explains the dangers of this type of rigid accounting. He observes that "these two elements—the violence and the quantification—are intimately linked" (14). Because barter tends to occur among strangers with no ties of hospitality, because debts are only valuable when the creditor has the means of enforcing payment, and because this enforcement typically takes the form of either violence or the threat of violence, Graeber notes, "it begins to be clear why there are no societies based on barter. Such a society could only be one in which everybody was an inch away from everybody else's throat; but nonetheless hovering there" (33). Doc, who got his nickname as a repo man—a debt enforcer—and who is not exactly a pacifist, nonetheless rejects the inherent violence in rigid accounting and quantification, instead practicing more communal forms of exchange. This runs directly counter to the actions of the novel's antagonists, Crocker Fenway and the Golden Fang.

Arrepentimiento

Doc's only real rejection of payment comes in his confrontation with a representative of the Golden Fang, Crocker Fenway. Unlike the examples above, in which Doc accepts nonpayment from Tariq, Hope, and Shasta as a means of practicing communal forms of exchange and fostering a more human community, Doc's rejection of Crocker Fenway's money signifies a larger rejection of bourgeois property and a rejection of the Golden Fang and the empire it represents.

In the novel, the Golden Fang is many things to many people. It is a boat. It is an international heroin ring. It is a tax dodge for dentists. It is a psychiatric hospital. It is an arms dealer. It is an organization more powerful than the Mob and the police, with the ability to mobilize the FBI. It is, in short, Empire as described by Michael Hardt and Antonio Negri. As in his previous three novels, Pynchon brings Empire down to human terms in *Inherent Vice*. Hardt and Negri argue, "The primary form of power that really confronts us today, however, is not so dramatic or demonic but rather earthly and mundane. We need to stop confusing politics with theology" (*Commonwealth* 5). Pynchon makes Golden Fang—which is metonymically Empire and what Hardt and Negri refer to when they discuss the "power that really confronts us today"—human. They are a network of businessmen who work in conjunction or at odds with one another in order to, as Crocker describes it, be "in place" (347). The amusingly named Crocker Fenway (a given name that calls to mind Betty Crocker, a surname that is mindful of Fenway Park) is the human face of Empire, the representative of Golden Fang, and the earthly and mundane man whom Doc confronts in the end. Their conversation is ostensibly about negotiating a handoff of the large amount of Golden Fang heroin that Doc unwittingly came into possession of. Crocker offers Doc money for the heroin. Doc says, "Suppose [the payment] didn't have to be in the form of, like, money?" (346). He negotiates instead for payment in the form of protection, the specific nature of which I discuss below. The resulting conversation moves to issues of property. Property is, of course, the chief concern of Crocker. He traffics in property. It is also a major theme in the novel. Pynchon repeatedly alludes to the "[l]ong, sad history of L.A. land use ... Mexican families bounced out of Chavez Ravine to build Dodger Stadium, American Indians swept out of Bunker Hill for the Music Center, Tariq's neighborhood bulldozed aside for Channel View Estates" (17). Likewise, the event that catalyzes the novel—the disappearance of developer Mickey Wolfmann—is essentially a matter of land use. Mickey is kidnapped because he has entered into a moment of personal crisis. Mickey articulates this crisis: "I feel as if I've awakened from a dream of a crime for which I can never atone, an act I can never go back and choose not to commit. I can't believe I spent my whole life making people pay for shelter, when it ought to've been free. It's just so obvious" (244). The result of this epiphany of Mickey's is a project he calls "Arrepentimiento. Spanish for 'sorry about that'" (248). Arrepentimiento is a housing development where anyone can go and live for free. If a person has the means to get to the house, she can live there. It would be, in a sense, an example of the Marxist common. Mickey's embrace of the commons threatens to undermine the core value upon which Empire is constructed.[4] For this reason, Golden Fang views Mickey's actions as a crime, and they remove him from society.

To understand why providing free housing would be a crime, it is helpful to return to Hardt and Negri's claim that "the concept of property and the defense of property remain the foundation of every modern political constitution" (*Commonwealth* 15). Hardt and Negri further argue that contemporary discussions of "fascism" focus on authoritarianism, yet "what is eclipsed or mystified, instead, is the daily functioning of constitutional, legal processes and the constant pressure of profit and property" (4). In other words, they argue that every modern republic is built on the premise of protecting private property and that this premise, more than mid-twentieth-century authoritarianism or repressive dictatorships, represents the primary barrier twenty-first-century democracy needs to overcome.

Inherent Vice expands the shift in Pynchon's oeuvre that began with *Vineland* and examines possibilities for resistance against Empire by moving the discussion from authoritarianism (as represented by Brock Vond in *Vineland* and Scarsdale Vibe in *Against the Day*) and toward the repressive aspects of property. Pynchon's exchanges regarding land use in *Inherent Vice* suggest that, in a republic built on John Locke's notions of the inalienable rights of life, liberty, and property, property eclipses all. In his essay "On the Pacific Edge of Catastrophe, or Redemption: California Dreaming in Thomas Pynchon's *Inherent Vice*," Rob Wilson observes, "All forces, from the LAPD to the Beach Boys, work on supporting Southland development, greed, excess, in suburban consensus" (221). Wilson calls this the "neoliberal counterconversion" in *Inherent Vice*, the rejection of ideas of life and liberty, of democracy, of people acting cooperatively to support the common good, all in favor of accumulating property in a privatized, corporate, consumer culture.

This notion is most salient in Doc and Crocker's conversation regarding property, not only in the words spoken, but in the act of the conversation itself. When one takes a step back and considers Crocker's decision to meet with Doc, it becomes clear that Crocker could have used violent means of retrieving the heroin from Doc rather than the peaceful alternative of meeting Doc in a restaurant. Crocker is part of Golden Fang, an organization with an incredible amount of resources at its disposal. Already in the novel, Golden Fang has mobilized a militia known as Vigilant California to kill Glen Charlock. They have also mobilized the FBI to kidnap Mickey Wolfmann. They could have acted like *Vineland*'s Brock Vond and sent the troops in to neutralize Doc. If their goal had been one of authoritarian control, violent means would have been used to subdue Doc and recover the heroin. Instead, their focus is on property. From this perspective, while a meeting in a restaurant will not send the powerful message that a violent attack would, it is more cost-effective. Power is not as important for Crocker Fenway as "being in place" (347) is. Being in place, for Crocker, means ownership of "[r]eal estate, water rights, oil, cheap labor" (347), the key elements that support global trade. Being in place means maintaining a system in which the global trade of multinational corporations works with governmental and supranational agencies to maintain the possession of property, regardless of the means by which that property was obtained. In this light, Doc's rejection of money as a form of payment from Golden Fang goes far beyond Marlowe's notion of rejecting money as a way of denying complicity. Doc's refusal of monetary payment is a rejection of a property-based economic system. His alternate request for payment is a move toward the common.

Hardt and Negri define the common as

> first of all, the common wealth of the material world—the air, the water, the fruits of the soil, and all nature's bounty—which in classic European political texts is often claimed to be the inheritance of humanity as a whole, to be shared together. We consider the common also and more significantly those results of social production that are necessary for social interaction and further production, such as knowledges, languages, codes, information, affects, and so forth. (*Commonwealth* vii)

Doc, in particular, demonstrates a world based on both the rejection of privatized land use and the embrace of shared land, language, knowledge, and information. His business model exemplifies this. As mentioned earlier, Doc accepts the cases presented to him by Shasta, Hope, and Talik with no expectation of payment. He does the same for Clancy Charlock and Coy Harlingen. In discussing this with Coy, Doc most directly addresses his ideology. Coy asks Doc when he needs to pay and Doc responds, "Whenever. Unless maybe you're one of these folks who believe information is money" (87).

This is an interesting and telling statement by Doc. As a private detective, he traffics in information. Just as Crocker has a vested interest in protecting the value of his property, Doc—according to the logic of late capitalism—has a vested interest in protecting the value of information. Yet he questions the notion of turning information into money. Instead, Doc trades information in a way that does not result in the accumulation of property for him. His immaterial labor does increase the overall wealth of his community in the sense that all the aforementioned clients lead richer lives based on the open exchange of information perpetuated by Doc. As Hardt and Negri observe, "Science would come to a standstill if our great accumulations of knowledge, information, and methods of study were not common" (*Multitude* 188). They further assert, "innovation requires common resources, open access, and free interaction" (338). Doc recognizes that, just as scientific innovations and the expansion of knowledge in multiple fields depends on openly sharing and contributing to our common knowledge, his role as a detective best serves the community when his accumulation of information is donated to the common.

As mentioned earlier, this seems to be a phenomenon of Gordita Beach. Doc personally benefits from other characters who share in this belief. He hires his lawyer, Sauncho, with no retainer and no monetary payment, yet Sauncho continues to represent Doc. Tito, a limousine driver and Doc's friend, gives Doc a fair amount of free rides. While Doc never pays Tito money for this, Tito is able to keep the lion's share of the money they stumble upon at a casino. Doc also obtains a great deal of free information from the nascent Internet enthusiast Fritz. When Doc claims he owes Fritz for this information, Fritz waves off payment (195). Instead, Doc, his clients, his lawyer, and his friends all contribute to a commonwealth of information that benefits them commonly, if not exactly equally. Doc's refusal of monetary payment from Crocker Fenway pulls Crocker into this system of the common. This commons is a revolutionary space. As W. J. T. Mitchell argues in "Image, Space, Revolution: The Arts of Occupation," "The commons is not an empty space that is simply free for the taking, but a battleground where the possibility of democracy and revolutionary change is contested" (111). Doc and his fellow Gordita Beach residents seem to intuit this. They live their lives in a space where democracy and systems of communal exchange are practiced. This reflects back to *The Examined Life*, in which Michael Hardt outlines a method of revolution as simply removing forms of authoritarian control and replacing them with more democratic alternatives.

Before exploring exactly how the commonwealth is beneficial, it is important to recognize that Doc does receive a significant monetary sum at the end of the novel. While he is in Las Vegas helping his client Trillium Fortnight find her lover, Puck Beaverton,[5] Doc bets the Mickey Wolfmann book, braving one-hundred-to-one odds to bet that Mickey was, in fact, kidnapped. Doc stakes a hundred dollars and wins. His receipt of the winning check leaves Doc, to some extent, in a financially stable place at the end of the novel. Doc is able to use the money to pay down all his debts. Since he spends so little money and appears to be living rent-free in an apartment owned by his aunt Reet, the leftover money could conceivably last Doc for several months. The money also demonstrates that, through Doc, Pynchon suggests an incremental move toward the common. Doc's recognition of his complicity carries with it the recognition that he does live in this world, which, for better or worse, requires a certain amount of money. He is not rejecting money entirely. Nor is he rejecting property entirely (which is highlighted by his love for his car). Instead, he is pushing for a world where the unquestioning faith in money and property is questioned, where labor benefits the common first and the individual second.

The fact that Doc made his money by betting the long shot is increasingly significant when one considers the nature of the bet. The odds-on money bets that Mickey Wolfmann kidnapped himself, that his philanthropy was a moment of weakness, and the kidnapping was a way of reneging his gift at Arrepentimiento. Doc, on the other hand, bets that even a real estate developer like Mickey Wolfmann could recognize the crime his life had been, reject that crime, and seek redemption. Further, Doc bets that it would take federal intervention supported by a network of international businessmen to make Mickey renege. In short, Doc's big payout came from his willingness to bet on the revolutionary potential of one of Empire's most entrenched businessmen.

Complicated Love and Possibilities in Gordita Beach

Doc's ability to bet on Mickey, coupled with his ability to trust Crocker Fenway, demonstrates the revolutionary potential of love that Hardt and Negri argue for in *Commonwealth*. Hardt and Negri state, "Bringing together these two faces of love—the constitution of the common and the composition of singularities—is a central challenge for understanding love as a material, political act" (184). I have discussed love in the constitution of the common, particularly with respect to Doc's business practices, above. The second notion to unpack in understanding the revolutionary potential of love is the composition of singularities that "compose new assemblages" (186). Hardt and Negri reject what they refer to as corrupt love, or love that forms units that isolate certain members from the rest of society. They cite, specifically, the corrupted love of nations through patriotism, or familial love when it leads to an isolated family unit. Instead, Hardt and Negri promote more politically powerful forms of inclusive love, of interpreting the notion to love thy neighbor as loving not only those who are close to us but those whom we view as the other. Doc's inclusive love can be viewed first in his relationship with Bigfoot Bjornsen. From Doc's perspective, Bigfoot should be a nemesis. Bigfoot takes every opportunity to frame, hassle, or manipulate Doc. Even so, Doc fosters a genuine affection for Bigfoot. Doc is considerate of Bigfoot's feelings and frequently does thoughtful, loving things for him. Bigfoot does not seem to share in Doc's affection (as demonstrated by Bigfoot repeatedly thrusting Doc into life-threatening situations), yet the fact that it is unrequited only makes Doc's love of the other more poignant. Of course, Doc's love extends well beyond Bigfoot.

When Doc negotiates with Crocker Fenway, he first asks for the release of Coy Harlingen so that Coy can be reunited with his family. This could be read as Doc negotiating for what Hardt and Negri refer to as a corrupted form of love because the release of Coy leads to the restoration of Coy to his nuclear family structure, complete with a husband, wife, and baby living in a suburban tract home. However, the family structure of a husband, wife, and baby is not necessarily isolating. Doc comes from one of these families. He seems to have healthy relationships with both of his parents. Additionally, Doc and his parents are not an isolated unit. His relationships with his aunt Reet and his cousin Scott, coupled with Doc's ability to extend his familial feelings to characters like Talil, Sauncho, and Shasta, suggest his openness rather than isolation.

Further, the Harlingens, with their history of heroin abuse and Coy's status as a rock star, are not exactly the traditional nuclear family. Hope Harlingen's phone call to Doc, in which she both thanks him and invites him to share time with this reunited family, coupled with Doc's first encounter with Hope, which was characterized by "kindness without a price tag" (39), all suggest that the Harlingens will not be an isolated family unit but rather part of the common that Doc works for.

Doc also negotiates with Crocker for a more general protection. As Doc tells his friend Denis, "I'm getting their word they won't hurt anybody. My friends, my family—me, you, a couple others" (349). This negotiation is significant first because it highlights Doc's conception of a community in which friends and family operate on the same horizontal level. When Doc seeks to protect his community, he looks out for those family members with whom he has a close relationship—his mother, father, aunt, and cousin. He also expands his horizontal network to include his ex-girlfriend Shasta, his friends and neighbors down at Gordita Beach, and potentially even his nemesis Bigfoot.

Herein lies the revolutionary potential of *Inherent Vice*. Hardt and Negri observe, "The real wealth, which is an end in itself, resides in the common; it is the sum of the pleasures, desires, capacities, and needs we all share" (*Multitude* 149). The wealth Doc works for in the end is the common. Nowhere is this exemplified more poignantly than in the final scene, when Doc drives down a Los Angeles freeway in a fog too thick to afford any real visibility. He and his fellow drivers learn they must band together if any of them are to survive. The competition that defines their lives, the quest for property and the nearly theological drive to maintain that property, is worthless. The hostile, cutthroat driving practices so familiar to drivers on Los Angeles freeways must be abandoned. Instead they must depend on the sight of people they cannot see, they must depend on their shared contributions, to make it through this alive.

There is hope for redemption in this moment. Doc fantasizes that it may last forever, that he may forever sustain this night of fog where property is worthless and a love of the other for the common good prevails.

Of course, this ending is as ambiguous as the fog that enshrouds it. In his essay "Under the Beach, the Paving-Stones! The Fate of Fordism in Pynchon's *Inherent Vice*," Doug Haynes reads the end in a far less hopeful light. Haynes concludes, "Indeed, by the end of Pynchon's narrative, collectivity has withdrawn into the somewhat meager form of a spontaneous caravan formed by cars in fog on an L.A. freeway, while utopian dreams have dwindled to an almost desperate desire for, to cite the novel's last sentence, 'the fog to burn away, and for something else this time, somehow, to be there instead'" (15). Haynes also reads *Inherent Vice* as a commentary on contemporary global capitalism. Specifically, he sees the novel as inhabiting the time when global marketplaces began their shift from the production sector to the financial one. This move, emblematized by Golden Fang in the novel, culminated in the world outside the novel with the global financial collapse of 2008 that, of course, triggered the Occupy movement, which so much of this study focuses on.

Despite seemingly contradictory conclusions, Haynes's reading of *Inherent Vice* is more of a companion to mine than a contradiction. The link between the two resides in Joanna Freer's summary of Pynchon's political project in *Thomas Pynchon and the American Counterculture*. Freer argues that Pynchon's "fundamental concern is with the oppression and exploitation of the masses by the powerful capitalist few and with methods of escaping or combating this" (95). In his reading of *Inherent Vice*, Haynes focuses on the oppression and exploitation of the masses; I focus on the methods of escaping or countering this. And while Haynes sees "utopian dreams" dwindling away, I provide no utopian dreams at all. I simply see hope for redemption. Nonetheless, Haynes's reading necessitates an additional examination of the oppression and exploitation within *Inherent Vice*.

As mentioned above, Brian McHale characterizes postmodernism as a shift from an epistemological dominant to an ontological one. Several critics of postmodernism observe that this shift affords those in power the capacity to exploit unstable notions of truth and create arguments that maintain a dangerous status quo.[6] This ties specifically into Pynchon's work through Casey Shoop's essay "Thomas Pynchon, Postmodernism, and the Rise of the New Right in California." Shoop posits that postmodernism's crisis of representation was exploited by Ronald Reagan in his 1966 campaign. Shoop states, "California was also the place where the Right reacted most powerfully to the crisis [of representation], offering counterprojections to recontain diversity within the logic of cold war binarism" (65). He explores this reaction with regard to *The*

Crying of Lot 49; many of his conclusions can translate to *Inherent Vice* and the Occupy movement.

When Crocker Fenway and Doc discuss the relationship between the Golden Fang and Doc's Gordita Beach community, they use concepts of landlords and renters to metonymically represent the two groups. Like Shoop's characterization of Reagan, Crocker divides the world into a paranoid "us" and a countercultural "them." Neither group can reconcile. One group, being "in place," can exploit and dehumanize the other group. This results in the other group constantly reacting, whether that reaction is a complicity with their situation or a revolt against it. These binaries can be extended in Occupy terminology to a 1 percent exploiting a 99 percent. In both cases, debt and the violence inherent in the enforcement of debt becomes the territory on which this battle occurs. In *Power Systems*, Noam Chomsky discusses this battle, suggesting, "We have a very class-conscious business class in the United States. They're always fighting a bitter one-sided class war and if they meet any opposition they will react" (69). Throughout *Inherent Vice*, the Golden Fang represents this very class-conscious business class, utilizing debt, property, and heroin to wage war on the 99 percent. Doc's demonstration of an alternative system of exchange and a practice of democracy in Gordita Beach accounts for only a very small resistance, just as several thousand protestors gathering in Zuccotti Park fall well short of a revolution. As Haynes suggests, utopian dreams dwindle.

In *The Democracy Project*, his reflections on Occupy, David Graeber recommends, "Perhaps instead of asking what the best political system is that our current social order could support, we should be asking, What social arrangements would be necessary in order for us to have a genuine, participatory, democratic system that could dedicate itself to solving collective problems?" (205). For Doc Sportello and *Inherent Vice*, this new arrangement entails moving away from a global marketplace and the violence of debt and establishing new practices of communal exchanges, more property in the commons, and a revolutionary concept of love. It is not utopian, and it is not perfect. Like so many subjunctive worlds in Pynchon's novels, Doc's vision is hampered by human frailties and flaws. Nonetheless, Doc's conception of Gordita Beach—and its expansion to places like Arrepentimiento and a foggy Los Angeles freeway—affords us a space to imagine a more just world beyond global, neoliberal capitalism.

CHAPTER 6

Bleeding Edge and Getting Constructively Lost

DURING AN EARLY SCENE in *Bleeding Edge* (2013), protagonist Maxine Turnow hears about an Internet space called DeepArcher. Justin, her friend Vyrva's husband, is one of the developers of the space. Maxine and Vyrva discuss Internet mogul Gabriel Ice's pursuit of the site and the major decision that Justin and his business partner, Lucas, must make between selling out or making DeepArcher open source. These conversations go far deeper than issues of how much money they can accumulate, descending into ideological territory about neoliberalism and accumulation on the one hand and participatory democracy on the other. Later, Justin invites Maxine into DeepArcher. Maxine enters the password-protected space. It is not exactly a video game and not exactly a website. It is a type of world that only really exists in a Pynchon novel—an imaginative representation of what the Internet could be. It is a safe space for coders to hide from corporate interests and share information. People have avatars they can control as they wander through the space. They can enter a seemingly limitless variety of worlds and talk to the other avatars they meet there. The world of DeepArcher comes into focus slowly for Maxine. She "recognizes from a thousand train and bus stations and airports . . . the smoothly cross-dawning image of an interior whose detail, for a moment breathtakingly, is far in advance of anything she's seen" (75). Maxine intuits that the program is pushing her toward boarding a shuttle, but she hesitates, enjoying the complexity and effluvia of the station around her. "'It's all right,' dialogue boxes assure her, 'it's part of the experience, part of getting constructively lost'" (76). Maxine continues to drift through DeepArcher, "after a while interested not so much in where she might get to than the texture of the search itself" (76).[1]

This moment when Maxine decides to get a little lost in DeepArcher may be one of the most direct moments of metacommentary in a Pynchon novel. It is as if the author is acknowledging to his readers that, yes, this novel takes place in New York in 2001, and, yes, it will have to discuss the attacks on the World Trade Center that year. Nonetheless, there is no reason to board the

{139}

shuttle and speed directly to September 11. Instead, there will be time to explore big questions about politics, economics, freedom, autonomy, and many other things along the way. So I will follow his instructions and enjoy the texture of the search.

In line with the rest of this book, my interest lies in the places where *Bleeding Edge* intersects with Occupy. After all, this is Pynchon's first—and, as of this writing, only—novel after Occupy Wall Street. Maxine's sons, Otis and Ziggy, would have been born around the same time as many Occupy activists. Some characters in the novel—March Kelleher, in particular, but many more—express political views very much in line with the activists who camped in Zuccotti Park. The literal and ideological common ground between Pynchon and the first Occupy protest is too compelling to bypass.

While speaking to activists encamped in Zuccotti Park, Slavoj Žižek complained, "[T]he ruling system has even oppressed our capacity to dream. Look at the movies that we see all the time. It's easy to imagine the end of the world. An asteroid destroying all life and so on. But you cannot imagine the end of capitalism" ("Don't Fall" 67). *Bleeding Edge* reclaims that capacity to dream. The reader knows that, while an asteroid is not on the way, two planes headed for the World Trade Center are. The impact will not destroy all life, but it will shake up the world in which the novel resides. Despite this, the focus of the novel moves away from the major violence of an asteroid or a terrorist attack and focuses more on the slow violence of neoliberal capitalism. The villains are not murderers per se. Nick Windust is both villain and murderer, and violence lingers at the margin of the novel. Capitalists, however, are the larger concern, the type for whom Windust really works. The true villain of the novel is hashslingerz CEO Gabriel Ice. A programmer named Driscoll Padgett says she would "Sooner lick the remains of a banana cream pie off of Bill Gates's face" than engage with Gabriel or hashslingerz. As she puts it, "they make fuckin Microsoft look like Greenpeace" (46). And the characters of *Bleeding Edge* position themselves in opposition not just to Ice. As Driscoll clarifies, during the dotcom boom, "the biggest winners were the men blessed with that ol' Wall Street stupidity, which in the end is unbeatable" (48). Yet even if the financial industry appears unbeatable, even if we can sooner envision an apocalypse than the fall of capitalism, capitalism seems to be failing, both inside the novel and outside of it. While reflecting on the roots of Occupy in *The Democracy Project*, David Graeber observes, "[W]e are left in the bizarre situation of watching the capitalist system crumbling before our very eyes, at just the moment when everyone had finally concluded no other system would be possible" (281–82). Naomi Klein expanded on this notion when she spoke at Zuccotti Park:

> Today everyone can see that the system is deeply unjust and careening out of control. Unfettered greed has trashed the global economy. And it is the trashing of the natural world as well. We are overfishing our oceans, polluting our water with fracking and deepwater drilling, and turning to the dirtiest forms of energy on the planet, like the Alberta tar sands. And the atmosphere cannot absorb the amount of carbon we are putting into it, creating dangerous atmospheric warming. The new normal is serial disasters, economic and ecological. (47)

In *Bleeding Edge*, the real disasters the reader and the characters brace themselves for are not terrorist attacks. They are serial economic catastrophes.

For the characters of the novel, the prevailing disaster is the dotcom crash. The detritus of the crash litters the novel. Most of the characters involved in the dotcom industry—coders like Driscoll, Justin, and Lucas; hackers like Eric Outfield—struggle to recover from the crash. Most of the characters involved in the "Wall Street" end of things—the venture capitalists, the developers encroaching on Maxine's neighborhood—have recovered. This divide illustrates a problem with contemporary capitalism; namely, wealth generated from labor shrinks while wealth generated from capital grows. When labor and productivity no longer lead to economic growth, when wealth is primarily generated from the money skimmed off the top of complicated financial instruments, the capitalist state that creates this situation seems fractured, teetering between one crisis and the next. Žižek, Graeber, and Klein all reference this fractured capitalist state. This divide between labor and capital also speaks to the reader, who experiences the events at least a dozen years from the novel's present day. In line with Klein's observation, the reader braces herself for "serial disasters" on the economic front. More of these disasters occurred during the twelve years between the novel's present and the novel's publication. In particular, the global recession of 2008 looms large. It is no wonder that Žižek, Graeber, Occupy, and Pynchon all seek to imagine an alternative to this type of capitalism.

Early in the occupation of Zuccotti Park, activists collaborated on a document entitled "Principles of Solidarity." The principles were "points of unity," ideas that the general assembly collectively supported through the consensus process. These principles were not demands of the protest. Occupy was not an act of civil disobedience advocating specific policy changes; it was an act of political disobedience rejecting the current conditions of political and economic sovereignty. Still, this assembly had ideas they wanted to confront and explore. Among them were "redefining how labor is valued . . . the sanctity of individual privacy . . . [and] endeavoring to practice and support wide application of open source" (Occupy Wall Street 25–26). Additionally, Marina Sitrin, reflecting on her experience at Zuccotti Park, states, "We all strive to embody the alternative we wish to see in our day-to-day relationships" (9). When these ideas are taken together, they shed light on a few significant aspects of *Bleeding Edge*. Starting with DeepArcher and moving through various subjunctive spaces, Pynchon envisions the alternatives many of us would like to see in our day-to-day lives. Like the general assembly's desire to redefine how labor is valued, Pynchon explores ways in which biopolitics maintains power over populations and the ways in which immaterial labor can simultaneously be complicit in maintaining that power and develop fissures at the foundation of it. Like the Occupy activists and through characters like Justin, Lucas, Vyrva, Maxine, and several other programmers who appear in the novel, Pynchon investigates privacy, open source, and the roles of a meaningful subject. This leads to a confrontation of neoliberal powers and a condemnation of twenty-first-century tech plutocrats embodied in Gabriel Ice. And, finally, Otis and Ziggy—the kids of the Occupy generation—create a compelling counternarrative in their occupation of DeepArcher, Zigotisopolis.

Neoliberal Villainy

Pynchon's critique of neoliberal capitalism begins early in *Bleeding Edge*. During the first day of action in the novel, Maxine's son Otis and Vyrva's daughter Fiona watch a cartoon with one of Otis's favorite television characters. Unlike the Tube in *Vineland*, where programming quells sixties rebellion and glorifies protofascists, Otis and Fiona's cartoon features "The Contaminator, in civilian life a kid who's obsessively neat about always making his bed and picking up his room but who, when out on duty as TC, becomes a lonely fighter for justice who goes around strewing garbage through disagreeable government agencies, greedy corporations, even entire countries nobody likes much, rerouting waste lines, burying his antagonists beneath a mountain of toxic grossness" (32). The Contaminator, then, is the first anti-Empire superhero. He attacks the networked power of national governments and multinational corporations by confronting them with the waste generated by their endless accumulation. The Contaminator's crusade invites a conversation with both the Occupy demonstrations and Hardt and Negri's exploration into resistance to Empire. While the superhero, the activists who participated in Occupy, and Hardt and Negri all confront a common injustice, the very fact that the Contaminator is a superhero runs counter to the ideas of Hardt and Negri's critical trilogy and the Occupy demonstrations. For Hardt and Negri and for the Occupy demonstrators, the solution to injustice would never be a single superhero. Hardt and Negri would have a multitude of crusaders for justice. They would form a horizontal network that respected all the participants' singularities while resisting a common injustice. The Occupy activists would build a system of participatory democracy and consensus to counter Empire. In both cases, the actions of the resistance movement would be more environmentally friendly than The Contaminator's. Still, The Contaminator is anti-Empire, and Otis's favorite cartoon mirrors the novel itself in casting the villains as greedy corporations and governmental agencies.

When Maxine's other son Ziggy returns home, he joins Otis and Fiona in a first-person shooter game that Justin and Lucas have developed. The game allows characters to roam around Manhattan, killing people in *Grand Theft Auto* style. Unlike *Grand Theft Auto*, the shooter's victims are not rival drug dealers, prostitutes, or the homeless. Instead, players target upper-middle-class people who flaunt their unexamined privilege: a wealthy woman who steals fruit from a street vendor, a mother hogging up the sidewalk with a twin stroller, loudmouths on cell phones, entitled bicyclists, an abusive dad in a business suit, and a line jumper. The poor, the homeless, those who cannot fend for themselves, and the preterite are all off-limits. The game is, instead, a small-scale class war against Upper West Siders.

This innocuous cartoon and video game lead into Maxine and Vyrva's conversation about the future of DeepArcher. Vyrva outlines Justin and Lucas's situation as the "Same old classic dotcom dilemma, be rich forever or make a tarball out of it and post it around for free, and keep their cred and maybe self-esteem as geeks but stay more or less middle income" (37). This is an interesting framing of the problem. Vyrva acknowledges and Pynchon highlights the fact that Justin and Lucas are already "middle income," and it is a high middle. Vyrva and Justin are residents of the Upper West Side, one of the most expensive neighborhoods in the United States. Their daughter attends a private school. There is no evidence in the book to suggest that Justin and Vyrva are struggling under the weight of rent or tuition. So the issue becomes one of, as Vyrva puts it, "a whole shitload of money crashing into our life right now" (38). Vyrva is hesitant to go after the money. She apologizes to Maxine for sounding like a hippie in her concerns. Maxine understands, saying, "Direction of flow, in or out, don't matter, above a critical amount, it's all bad" (38). Unlike the yuppies whom Ziggy, Otis, and Fiona shoot in their video game, unlike the villains of the novel, Maxine and Vyrva question the conventional wisdom of accumulation. They recognize their economic privilege. Specifically, they have enough money to sustain themselves in a relatively luxurious lifestyle. Should Vyrva chase that "whole shitload of money," it would only pay for different luxuries. She knows that. Maxine understands. She knows that her lifestyle and Vyrva's are not entitlements. Money can flow away from them; the next serial economic disaster can target them. Still, she views the possibility of going after the big payoff as something other than protection against the next disaster. It is instead a lifestyle change, one that's "all bad."

This takes on heightened importance when read against Immanuel Wallerstein's description of capitalism in *World-Systems Analysis*. Wallerstein claims, "We are in a capitalist system only when the system gives priority to the *endless* accumulation of capital" (24). He goes on to clarify:

> Endless accumulation is a quite simple concept: it means that people and firms are accumulating capital in order to accumulate still more capital, a process that is continual and endless. If we say that a system "gives priority" to such endless accumulation, it means that there exist structural mechanisms by which those who act with other motivations are penalized in some way, and are eventually eliminated from the social scene, whereas those who act with the appropriate motivations are rewarded and, if successful, enriched. (24)

This description characterizes neoliberal capitalism in an interesting light. First, we see that the point of capitalism is accumulation for its own sake. Economic growth is not a means to anything other than economic growth. The wealth is not used to create a more just society, to feed starving people, to heal the sick, to engage in any benevolent or social act, or to bring about any freedoms other than the freedom to accumulate more. It is its own end. Additionally, Wallerstein observes that capitalism "gives priority" to accumulation. This echoes Wendy Brown's definition of neoliberalism as a belief system in which "all dimensions of human life are cast in terms of market rationality." This is an ideology in which capital is an unquestioned positive, in which the market does not exist for us—we exist for the market. This means that we are rewarded for nurturing a system of endless accumulation and penalized for resisting it. With all this in mind, the classic dotcom dilemma that Vyrva, Justin, and Lucas wrestle with is also one of the most pressing questions facing all of us who live in a neoliberal society: What do we prioritize? On the one hand is endless accumulation. On the other hand is concern for a community, for those less fortunate, and for wealth we all hold in common.

Pynchon's characters engage with this question in a variety of ways throughout *Bleeding Edge*. Upper West Side lefty March Kelleher tells Maxine, "[L]ate capitalism is a pyramid racket on a global scale, the kind of pyramid you do human sacrifices up on top of, meantime getting the suckers to believe it's all gonna go on forever" (163). Pynchon positions her point of view as someone who saw her neighborhood and her family gentrified. The Lincoln Center and real estate developers moved in around her home, forcing out poorer, browner populations and leaving March as a revolutionary holdover from a very different time and tradition. Likewise, her daughter Tallis's Ivy League education put her in place to marry Gabriel Ice, and now March has a grandson named Kennedy whom Tallis and Gabriel are sending "to Collegiate. Where fuckin else. They want him seamlessly programmed into Harvard, law school, Wall Street, the usual Manhattan death march" (130). More than anyone in the novel, March has an unmitigated hatred for the actions of the 1 percent.

Maxine is less certain. True to her nature as an investigator, she gathers information and withholds judgment initially. Her fraud investigation agency is called "Tail 'Em and Nail 'Em." The narrator tells us, "[S]he once considered adding 'and Jail 'Em,' but grasped soon enough how wishful, if not delusional, this would be" (4). This afterthought should resonate with an audience that witnessed the subprime mortgage crisis that nearly bankrupted the United States in 2008. Unlike even the frauds who catalyzed the Enron and the savings and loan scandals before it, not one financier behind the subprime mortgage crisis was investigated, much less imprisoned. Instead, most were rewarded with gigantic buyouts or year-end bonuses. Maxine's frustration with this side of the financial industry is voiced more directly later in the novel when she tells Vyrva, "[I]n my business . . . what I see a lot of is innocent people making these deals with the satanic forces, for money way out of scale to anything they're used to, and there's a point where it all rolls in on them and they go under, and sometimes they don't come back up" (218). In this case, capitalists like Gabriel Ice are "satanic forces." Dealing with them is akin to selling your soul. Maxine is warning against the neoliberal ideology in which accumulation—"money way out of scale to anything they're used to"—is the point.

She is even more suspicious of the finance industry after the attacks on the World Trade Center. She and her ex-husband, Horst, discuss the stock market's activity surrounding the attacks. Horst is befuddled. He asks, "How could predicting market behavior be the same as predicting a terrible disaster?" Maxine replies, "If the two were different forms of the same thing." Horst does not want to hear this, dismissing it as "Way too anticapitalist for me" (320). Maxine's suspicions align with Naomi Klein's speech in Zuccotti Park. While the violence of global capitalism may happen more gradually over time, it leads to a series of disasters that rival terrorist attacks.

On the other hand, Maxine's actions throughout the novel are not those of an anticapitalist. She sends her sons to a private school. She shops recreationally. She was married to and spends much of the novel living with Horst, who is a commodities broker. She befriends various venture capitalists and even saves one from investing with Bernie Madoff, who is notorious for his multi-billion-dollar Ponzi scheme. And while these associations are not terribly problematic, her attraction to Nick Windust is. Windust is a neoliberal mercenary, someone who is dispatched to enforce the whims of national governments and organizations like the International Monetary Fund. His dossier reads like a collection of Empire's greatest hits. He was active in the military coup that unseated and assassinated Salvador Allende. He was "part of a cadre of old Argentina hands, U.S. veterans of the Dirty War who then stayed on to advise the IMF stooges that rose to power in its aftermath" (108). He lectured at the School of the Americas. He founded a neoliberal think tank. One of Hardt and Negri's criticisms of neoliberalism in *Commonwealth* is that "today's neoliberal economy increasingly favors accumulation through expropriation of the common" (138). Windust has a long history of that, working to take over "[w]ells that supply regional water systems, easements across tribal lands for power lines," and power plants that are privatized "for pennies on the dollar" (109). Windust represents the very disaster that Maxine sees in neoliberal capitalism, yet Maxine is uncontrollably attracted to him. Her relationship with him builds to the point in which they engage in sex that, for Maxine, is humiliating at best and rape at worst. Even afterward, like Prairie calling out for Brock Vond at the end of *Vineland*, Maxine yearns for Windust. Through these actions, both Prairie and Maxine demonstrate the attraction of hegemony. They are both unconsciously, fundamentally attracted to the authority they spend the rest of the novels resisting.

Maxine is certainly not the only character to demonstrate an ambivalence toward neoliberalism. March Kelleher, perhaps the most anticapitalist character in the novel, demonstrates a certain complicity with neoliberal capitalism through her meals with Maxine. Early in the novel, March refuses Maxine's invitation to go out to lunch. March refers to going out to lunch as a "[c]orrupt artifact of late capitalism" (115). So they go out to breakfast instead, despite the fact that no clear delineation is made between why breakfast is less corrupt than lunch. Then, later in the novel, they go out to lunch together.

Still, more than any other character, Maxine demonstrates our struggle and complicity with late capitalism. We are a part of it. It is the world we live in and the air we breathe. As Katherine Hume points out in her discussion of *Against the Day*, "We must quest within the world we have inherited" (180). Perhaps more to the point, as Linda Hutcheon writes in *The Politics of Postmodernism*, one of the conditions of our current cultural situation is our complicity in the very systems we critique (10). Nonetheless, our complicity does not preclude us from questioning the system and criticizing inherent injustices.

In contrast to March and Maxine is lawyer Chandler Platt. He works for the law firm Hannover Fisk (Pynchon loves his puns, especially when naming law firms) and seems to be making money hand over fist. He sits behind "a desk made of 40,000-year-old New Zealand kauri, more like a piece of real estate than a piece of furniture" (280–81). He is old friends with Eliot Spitzer, who would have been the attorney general of New York during the novel's present day. After the novel ends, the real-life Eliot Spitzer would go on to become governor of New York and later be forced to resign following a scandal with a prostitute. The desk and the friendship with Spitzer not only establish wealth and connections, they demonstrate his disregard for many of the concerns of the novel's characters, the activists at Occupy, and critics like Hardt and Negri. First, the 40,000-year-old kauri would hold real significance for native New Zealanders, yet Chandler dismisses the kauri's historical and cultural significance by appropriating the wood into a desk. Second, Eliot Spitzer, despite his record of prosecuting white-collar crime, ran his 1994 and 1998 campaigns for attorney general largely funded by the New York bank J. P. Morgan & Company (Finder B6). Not insignificantly, J. P. Morgan was one of the perpetrators of the subprime loan debacle that led to the 2008 economic collapse. Maxine visits Chandler because he seems to be, like Crocker Fenway in *Inherent Vice*, "in place." Chandler also has an intern working for him, an aspiring hip-hop artist named Darren, who gives Maxine a CD of his music. Chandler says, "I made the mistake of asking him once how he expects to make money. He said that wasn't the point, but has never explained what is. To me, I'm appalled, it strikes at the heart of Exchange itself" (283). In other words, Darren rejects, to some extent, the neoliberal belief that accumulation is its own end. Spreading his music to potential listeners is more important to Darren. This both confuses and appalls Chandler. His confusion likely resides in his unquestioned faith in accumulation. His disgust toward Darren's rejection points to another common theme in Pynchon's work.

Throughout both *Mason & Dixon* and *Against the Day*, the marketplace is presented in religious terms.[2] Pynchon returns to this theme through Chandler Platt. Immediately after expressing his disgust for Darren giving away free music, Chandler criticizes the Republican Party, saying, "This generation—it's almost a religious thing now. The millennium, end days, no need to be responsible anymore to the future. A burden has been lifted from them. The Baby Jesus is managing the portfolio of earthly affairs, and nobody begrudges Him the carried interest" (284). This is a complicated complaint from Chandler. On the one hand, he is critical of the religious terminology that has entered into the Republican Party platform; he fears for the future. Chandler's implied fear could be on ecological grounds. Much of *Bleeding Edge* resides under the specter of ecological catastrophe. As Naomi Klein expressed in her speech at Occupy and as Karl Polanyi discusses in *The Great Transformation*, treating land as a commodity leads to disaster (in Klein's terms) and annihilation (in Polanyi's). Chandler's criticism could simply be an economic one. He laments the loss of days when "you put in the work and took the money only after you'd earned it" (284). This could be read as a direct critique of the shady financial instruments that catalyzed the 2008 recession. Either way, Chandler dislikes the new "religious thing" of the Republican Party, its dismissal of future concerns, its faith in an apocalypse to render long-term planning moot, and its creation of serial disasters, be they ecological or economic. On the other hand, Chandler's criticism may be more nuanced. Perhaps he is not criticizing a religious approach to the marketplace. He is instead criticizing this particular religious approach. He still seems to have an unquestioned belief in accumulation, or in "principled greed" (284). When Darren gives away music, Chandler cannot imagine this to be something that may foster community ties similar to the way, say, Doc Sportello creates an alternative system of exchange in *Inherent Vice*. Nor can Chandler see music as a form of self-expression, a contribution to creating culture, and an end in itself. Coming from the tradition of neoliberalism, Chandler views music in particular and perhaps art in general as a commodity. In his view, Darren should be parlaying the commodity into the best possible position in the marketplace. The marketplace, after all, is where Chandler finds meaning. Further, though Chandler is critical of the new religion of the marketplace, he couches his criticism in religious terms of his own. He introduces the topic not by saying that the Republican Party has moved in a troubling direction or promulgated a dangerous platform. He instead says that it "has fallen on evil days" (284), a phrase with a distinctively religious undertone. In all likelihood, Chandler's critique of the Republican Party has less to do with it being religious but with the particular religion. He seems to object to Baby Jesus managing the marketplace instead of Adam Smith's Invisible Hand. The Invisible Hand, as both Wade LeSpark and Rev. Cherrycoke suggest in *Mason & Dixon*, is always and necessarily a faith-based construct.

The marketplace is presented in religious terms elsewhere in *Bleeding Edge*. After the attacks on the World Trade Center, Maxine visits her therapist, Shawn. He tells her, "The Trade Center towers were religious too. They stood for what this country worships above everything else, the market, always the holy fuckin market." When Maxine questions this idea, Shawn goes on to say, "It's not a religion? These are people who believe the Invisible Hand of the Market runs everything. They fight holy wars against competing religions like Marxism. Against all evidence that the world is finite, this blind faith that resources will never run out, profits will go on increasing forever, just like the world's populations—more cheap labor, more addicted customers" (338). Shawn's reaction to the attacks echoes a point Wallerstein makes in *World-Systems Analysis*: "The totally free market functions as an ideology, a myth, and a constraining influence, but never as a day-to-day reality" (25). The power of neoliberalism is the same as the power of a myth. In both cases, attractive stories trump evidence that would otherwise negate a belief system. In the case of neoliberal capitalism, the attractive story is that growth can be infinite, that labor and land can act like commodities, and that accumulation is so intrinsically valuable that it should take priority over all other concerns. In this mythical place, we should continue to build more cars and more roads to house them, we should produce more consumables made of and wrapped in plastic because oil is infinite, because the people who live and labor in oil-rich regions will peacefully abide by the laws of supply and demand, because the accumulation of these commodities is the most meaningful thing we can do with our lives. Of course, oil is not infinite, people cannot abide by the laws of supply and demand when they are in too great a supply and their market value does not provide enough for them to survive, and commodities are not meaningful. Thus, Shawn seems to suggest that the backlash to this myth was predictable, and that the choice of targets was meaningful. The religious war could be viewed, not as Muslims attacking a Christian country, but as the disenfranchised attacking the most prominent icons of neoliberalism. Shawn's disgust with the Taliban's attacks on Buddhist icons suggests that he does not endorse the attacks on the World Trade Center. His rant simply reminds the reader that we live in a neoliberal world. The ideology is so prevalent that we sometimes forget how flawed and faith based it can be.

The prevalence of neoliberal capitalist ideology has an impact on the kids in the novel as well. Of course, Otis and Fiona watch The Contaminator sabotage Empire, then they join Ziggy in a first-person shooter game. In both of these activities, they are engaging in prepackaged rebellion: watching a show or playing a game that someone else created. Using stuffed animals and a toy mall, the kids create their own imaginative space for rebellion.

Fiona's bedroom is overrun by the Beanie Babies her mother obsessively collects and by a large plastic dollhouse called "Melanie's Mall." Melanie is a "half-scale Barbie with a gold credit card she uses for clothes, makeup, hair-styling, and other necessities" (68). The doll, like Barbie, is a tool for teaching consumerism to young kids. The Beanie Babies are another way in which the next generation learns accumulation. These toys hark back to one of David Graeber's laments in *The Democracy Project*: "[T]he imagination, desire, individual liberation, all those things that were to be liberated in the last great world revolution, were to be contained strictly in the domain of consumerism" (281). According to the logic of neoliberal capitalism, freedom is often interpreted as the freedom to shop. Desire falls under the narrow scope of the advertising industry. Imagination is the purview of the entertainment industry. Otis and Fiona, two of the characters who share a generation with most of the activists who created the Occupy movement, are not sold on this idea of the transcendent properties of consumerism.

The mall is strangely compelling for Otis. He brings over more action figures—more dolls that teach consumerism—and introduces them to the world of the mall. Together, Otis and Fiona play games that "center on violent assault, terrorist shoplifting sprees,[3] and yup discombobulation, each of which ends in the widespread destruction of the Mall, principally at the hands of Fiona's alter ego the eponymous Melanie, in cape and ammo belts, herself" (68). The violence is cartoonish. Like the first-person shooter game, the destruction of the people at the mall is presented as harmless fun. Just as no character seemed to be using the video game to plan a shooting spree, Otis and Fiona do not appear to be planning a real terrorist attack through their Melanie's Mall games. Still, a real frustration with consumerism appears in this game. The fact that it occurs at the mall takes on more meaning when read in light of W. J. T. Mitchell's discussion of Occupy Wall Street. Mitchell discusses occupations that are neither liberating nor democratic. He observes that "capitalism . . . occupies public spaces with advertising (as in Times Square), or privatizes the agora and the village square by transforming it into the space of the shopping mall. (It is okay, of course, for the masses to camp out in front of Wal-Mart in order to grab the bargains available to the first customers)" (115). All occupations, then, are ideological. The occupation of Times Square is supported because it supports the mechanisms of neoliberal capital. Encampments leading up to Black Friday are welcome while encampments drawing attention to the wages of the workers inside result in mass arrests. Perhaps most compelling, Mitchell characterizes the shopping mall as a privatized agora. The marketplace that once invited discussions of Athenian democracy, that housed philosophers like Plato and Aristotle, has been reduced to a place for "clothes, makeup, hairstyling, and other necessities." Otis and Fiona react to this transformation by symbolically destroying the ideological tools of consumerism.

Biopolitics and Immaterial Labor

In many ways, Maxine and her friends are the perfect ciphers for exploring notions of labor and resistance at the beginning of the twenty-first century. In *The Democracy Project*, David Graeber observes, "There was a time when the paradigmatic politically self-conscious working-class American was a male breadwinner working in an auto factory or steel mill. Now it is more likely to be a single mother working as a teacher or a nurse. Compared to men, women are more likely to enter college, more likely to finish college, *and* more likely to be poor, the three elements that lead to a greater political consciousness"

(87). Maxine meets or coincides with this description. She is a single mother. She is a college graduate. She is not poor, but she is an outsider in the business world—a self-employed, unlicensed fraud investigator who survives by her wits. Like so many members of the Occupy movement, Maxine comes by her disillusionment with neoliberalism honestly. She is also poised at the forefront of a new form of resistance, provided she has some understanding of the mechanics of biopolitics and immaterial labor.

In *Society Must Be Defended*, Michel Foucault once again explores relations of power. As he does for much of his career, Foucault returns to ideas of discipline in *Society*. Discipline, for Foucault, focuses on the individual by separating the individual from society and developing various apparatuses to regulate her behavior. As societies move away from industrial production—which was what Foucault saw around him while he was delivering the lectures that became *Society Must Be Defended* in 1975–76—a new form of power begins to take shape. Foucault called this power "biopolitics." He envisions biopolitics as state power not enforced on individuals through various strategies of discipline but as state power enforced on a mass of individuals collectively. Foucault explains, "Biopolitics deals with the population, with the population as a political problem, as a problem that is at once scientific and political, as a biological problem and as power's problem" (245). Biopolitics, then, arises as a means of maintaining hegemonic power as economic production migrates from industrial production to more abstract forms of production. For Foucault, biopolitics oversaw more corporeal portions of society—birth rates, health care, fertility, and so on. In the years since his lectures, biopolitics has been broadened to information, affects, and other social relations. Within this broader definition, Maxine's work as a fraud investigator would be a part of biopolitical production. If she were a licensed investigator, her work would not really focus on the individual—"Jail 'Em," after all, was a bit delusional. Instead, fraud investigation would take on a more abstract form of production, producing the image, perhaps the illusion, that markets work, that investments can be treated honestly, that there is a form of power overseeing the exchange of financial products, that those who defraud this system will be discovered (if not exactly punished) and the system as a whole can continue. Maxine's role in relation to state power is more nebulous. As a licensed fraud investigator, Maxine would be more focused on producing the image or illusion of a stable financial industry. The industry itself, at least as it is presented in Pynchon's work, is largely faith based, and, as such, there must be some higher power overseeing it with an eye to fairness. This higher power would send out referees in the form of investigators who blow the whistle on the most egregious fouls. Maxine is not licensed, however. Her work does not create the illusion of a functioning system. Instead, because she is an unlicensed investigator, Maxine can be more focused on individuals, not in the sense of state discipline, but on a smaller scale, a scale that lends her a bit more autonomy.

Maxine's abstract production and engagements with biopolitics take on deeper meaning when developed with an eye toward immaterial labor. Maurizio Lazzarato examines this concept in his essay "Immaterial Labor." For Lazzarato, "Immaterial labor produces first and foremost a 'social relationship.' . . . Only if it succeeds in this production does its activity have an economic value. This activity makes immediately apparent something that material production had 'hidden,' namely, that labor produces not only commodities, but first and foremost it produces capital relations" (137). In other words, capitalism has moved beyond merely a system of producing commodities. We have long surpassed the point at which we have the capacity to produce all the material goods that the world's population needs. The next challenge in fostering the endless accumulation that is capitalism resides in creating desires, feelings, emotional attachments, identities, and various other affects connected to commodities or to markets. Immaterial labor does this work.

In *Commonwealth*, Michael Hardt and Antonio Negri observe, "Images, information, knowledge, affects, codes, and social relationships, for example, are coming to outweigh material commodities or the material aspects of commodities in the capitalist valorization process" (132). Most of the characters in *Bleeding Edge* demonstrate this shift. Almost no character in the book produces any material commodity. Instead, Pynchon's Upper West Side is populated by commodities brokers, computer programmers, business managers, lawyers, bankers, venture capitalists, journalists, private investigators, and the like. Outside of a few construction workers on Gabriel Ice's east Long Island summer home, nearly everyone in the novel works in immaterial labor. Within the context of a crime novel, Pynchon's characters shift our hegemonic views of discipline and justice.

First, we have Gabriel Ice as our primary villain. Nearly all of Gabriel's villainous activities are abstract. There are no mountains of cocaine like in *Scarface*, no piles of cash that the crooks can shower themselves in, no trucks needed to transport stolen goods. Nothing is material. Nothing is corporeal. Everything trafficked in, laundered, or stolen exists in the abstract world of the Internet. The money being moved is filtered through various online bank accounts. Only information is stolen or trafficked. All of Gabriel's bullying and "muscle" takes the form of money, legal documents, and the like.

Similarly, the characters on the outside of state power perform all their resistance in abstract or ideological forms. This connects with a fear Lazzarato explores in "Immaterial Labor." According to Lazzarato, "[E]mployers are extremely worried by the double problem [immaterial labor] creates: on the one hand, they are forced to recognize the autonomy and freedom of labor as the only possible form of cooperation in production, but on the other hand, at the same time, they are obliged (a life-and-death necessity for the capitalist) not to 'redistribute' the power that the new quality of labor and its organization imply" (135). Maxine exemplifies this. As a licensed fraud investigator, her job would require her to have the autonomy and freedom to actually investigate fraud, yet as an agent working under the umbrella of state power, her primary role would be less to seek out and expose fraudulent activities and more to promote the image that the market is working as it should. This double problem can be seen more clearly in Maxine's client Reg Despard. Reg is hired to make a documentary about Gabriel Ice. In order to do this, he requires a certain amount of access to Gabriel and hashslingerz. Reg also needs the autonomy and freedom to gather footage and construct a narrative. The danger of this, from Gabriel's perspective, is that this access and this autonomous narrative might expose some of Gabriel's criminal activities.

Hardt and Negri see revolutionary possibilities in this "double problem." They argue, "[T]he biopolitical process is not limited to the reproduction of capital as a social relation but also presents the potential for an autonomous process that could destroy capital and create something entirely new" (*Commonwealth* 136). Gabriel sees that Reg has this potential. Reg's documentary could destroy the hashslingerz brand and damage Gabriel's empire. This does not seem to be Reg's goal. He hires Maxine to find out what Gabriel is up to, hoping to use this information not to expose Gabriel but to protect Reg himself. Reg eventually finds protection by working for one of Gabriel's competitors, Microsoft. He calls Maxine to tell her about his new job, saying, "Yeah, the dress code takes some getting used to, all the breathing apparatus and stormtrooper gear" (348). Reg jokes about turning over to the dark side—the Empire in more ways than one—but does not seem to be positioning himself to "destroy capital and create something entirely new." Maxine and March Kelleher have different ideas about how to handle the information that Reg uncovers.

While filming for his hashslingerz documentary, Reg accidentally films footage that could be traced to a conspiracy connecting hashslingerz with the attacks on the World Trade Center. Reg gives this film to Maxine, and Maxine passes it on to March. March, with her *Huffington Post*–style blog, posts the footage at great expense to her personal safety. As the editor of this blog in a time when traditional journalism is failing, March is at the forefront of the revolutionary potential of immaterial labor. Lazzarato observes, "A polymorphous self-employed autonomous work has emerged as the dominant form, a kind of 'intellectual worker' who is him- or herself an entrepreneur, inserted within a market that is constantly shifting and within networks that are changeable in time and space" ("Immaterial" 139). Because she is self-employed and autonomous in a constantly shifting economy, March—like Maxine—has found room to work against the networked power of national governments and multinational corporations. She has the freedom that journalists at more entrenched publications, publications that function as examples of Louis Althusser's Ideological State Apparatuses, do not have. Specifically, March can share Reg's footage and cover stories that challenge Empire's hegemony. At great personal risk to herself, March does share this information. She broadens the conversation around the attacks on the World Trade Center and shifts focus away from the dominant narrative. She becomes, in a sense, the woman whom David Graeber predicts in *The Democracy Project*: an educated, politically conscious woman who actively works against an unjust system of power.

March's actions are reminiscent of women's role in the Occupy movement. In their study of women's roles in Occupy, Megan Boler, Averie Macdonald, Christina Nistou, and Anne Harris observed that Occupy's horizontal network provided more access to women activists. Occupy's practice of consensus empowered more women to speak. Once empowered, women took on various roles that fostered the movement. Boler and her colleagues described one of these roles as "adminning," explaining, "Adminning is a new way of performing leadership by taking responsibility for the logistics of information dissemination" (445). Admins ran various social media campaigns for regional Occupy groups. They worked as editors by posting original content, as curators by sharing information from other sources, and as journalists by writing pieces themselves. In these regards, March Kelleher represents an early version of an admin, using her autonomy and immaterial labor to challenge power systems.

Occupy Zigotisopolis

In all the above examples, characters in *Bleeding Edge* criticize and resist the power of Empire and the 1 percent. The criticism and resistance, by their very nature, are reactionary. However, Pynchon's novels tend to move beyond the reactionary and into visions of better worlds. *Vineland* has the Sisterhood of Kunoichi Attentives, *Mason & Dixon* has various expressions of the subjunctive, *Against the Day* has Yz-les-Bains, *Inherent Vice* has Doc's community at Gordita Beach, and *Bleeding Edge* has Zigotisopolis.

Zigotisopolis is an imaginary community that Maxine's sons create in DeepArcher. Maxine stumbles across it during her own forays in the space. She finds it rendered in a benevolently lighted palette taken from old-school color processes like the ones you find on picture postcards of another day. Somebody somewhere in the world, enjoying that mysterious exemption from time which produces most Internet content, has been patiently coding together these vehicles and streets, this city that can never be. The old Hayden Planetarium, the pre-Trump Commodore Hotel, upper-Broadway cafeterias that have not existed for years, smorgasbords and bars offering free lunches, where regulars hang around the door to the kitchen so they can get first shot at whatever's being carried in. (428)

This initial impression might lead to a dismissal of Zigotisopolis as another example of the nostalgia mode. It is cast in the light of old postcards. It presents a past that never was and the image of a world that, as Maxine observes, can never be. But the imagined city is more than that. Their choices are telling. The pre-Trump Commodore Hotel cannot be because Trump's construction project has already destroyed the original landmark. Smorgasbords and bars offering free lunches cannot be as long as we live in a society that prioritizes accumulation over social concerns. In this way, the "can never be" of Zigotisopolis revisits the novel's basic questions about ideology. Should we offer up the art of architecture to the altar of neoliberal capitalism? Should we support a culture that privileges accumulation—hoarding, really—over the basic needs of everyone? The latter question becomes more poignant when we consider it in light of Sarah van Gelder's reasons for occupying Zuccotti Park. She states, "We are seeing our ways of life, our aspirations, and our security slip away—not because we have been lazy or undisciplined, or lacked intelligence and motivation, but because the wealthiest among us have rigged the system to enhance their own power and wealth at the expense of everyone else" (3). Zigotisopolis, more than wishing nostalgically for a time that never really was, instead confronts the ideologies of our time and the destruction to which they lead.

Other places in Zigotisopolis are in direct conversation with earlier parts of the novel. Maxine witnesses in Zigotisopolis "the old Times Square, before the hookers, before the drugs, arcades like Fascination, pinball machines so classic now that only overly compensated yups can afford to buy them, and recording booths where half a dozen of you can jam inside and cover the latest Eddie Fisher single on acetate" (429). Again, the image is dripping with nostalgia, but it stands in contrast to Maxine's nostalgia for the dope dealers, pimps, and three-card monte artists earlier in the novel. Ziggy and Otis's Times Square also rejects what Maxine earlier calls "the forces of suburban righteousness [that] have swept the place Disneyfied and sterile" (51). The city that Ziggy and Otis envision, with its classic architecture, its resistance to the creative destruction of late capitalism, also stands in contrast to the current situation of Manhattan, which March Kelleher describes during her breakfast with Maxine. March complains, "Between the scumbag landlords and the scumbag developers, nothing in this city will ever stand at the same address for even five years, name me a building you love, someday it'll either be a stack of high-end chain stores or condos for yups with more money than brains" (115). Instead, Zigotisopolis is a "more merciful city" where "Ziggy has his arm over his brother's shoulder, and Otis is looking up at him with unhesitating adoration" (429). In this imagined space, even young brothers on the verge of adolescence get along.

The context of Zigotisopolis is also significant. It resides in DeepArcher after Justin and Lucas have decided to make the space open source. In response to the question that Vyrva raises in the beginning of the novel—whether to choose a system of endless accumulation or a world with concern for freedom and the commons—Justin and Lucas have chosen freedom and the commons. Their actions align with the ideology that March expresses admiration for earlier in the novel when she tells Maxine, "These kids are out to change the world. 'Information has to be free'—they really mean it" (116).

Wallerstein warns that choosing against endless accumulation comes with certain penalties. In the case of DeepArcher, turning it open source leads to the forces of capital occupying the space. Advertisements litter the early stations. Coders and corporations seek ways to monetize it. Still, Lucas holds out hope. He explains to Maxine, "These days you look at the surface Web, all that yakking, all the goods for sale, the spammers and spielers and idle fingers, all in the same desperate scramble they like to call an economy. Meantime, down here, sooner or later someplace deep, there has to be a horizon between coded and codeless. An abyss" (357). Hardt and Negri envision the revolutionary possibility in immaterial labor. March approaches this vision through her blog. Lucas yearns for it somewhere in the Deep Web.

Bleeding Edge presents a more ambivalent, more discursive approach to this revolutionary possibility. The Internet is presented more along the lines of Derrida's concept of the *pharmakon*. It is both the poison and the medicine. Like the immaterial labor that creates it, the Internet holds the potential to reinforce state power through the mechanism Foucault refers to as biopolitics, on the one hand, and it has the potential to completely revolutionize our economic and political relations, on the other hand. While March and Lucas focus on the latter, Pynchon gives voice to the former first through Maxine's father, who reminds Maxine, "You know where it all comes from, this online paradise of yours? It started back during the Cold War, when the think tanks were full of geniuses plotting nuclear scenarios . . . back then the Defense Department called it DARPAnet, the real original purpose was to assure survival of U.S. command and control after a nuclear exchange with the Soviets" (419). This historiography differs somewhat from the burgeoning Internet that Doc utilizes in *Inherent Vice*, which featured a fair amount of surveillance but was more envisioned as a simple information platform. In both novels, though, Pynchon presents the Internet as a product of state power.

His characters are not concerned only with the history of the Internet. Former hashslingerz IT guy Eric Outfield fears for its future. He complains, "We're being played, Maxi, and the game is fixed, and it won't end until the Internet—the real one, the dream, the promise—is destroyed" (432). This destruction, for Eric, entails turning the Internet into simply a series of sites that create and feed addictions to "shopping, gaming, jerking off, streaming endless garbage" (432) and otherwise keeping us distracted from the real problems that neoliberal capitalism presents.

While discussing the challenges of Occupy Wall Street, David Graeber laments, "It's a difficult business creating a new, alternative civilization, especially in the midst of the coldest, and most unfriendly streets of major American cities, full of the sick, homeless, and psychologically destroyed, and in the very teeth of a political and economic elite whose thousands of militarized police are making abundantly clear they do not want you to be there" (241). Zigotisopolis creates this new, alternative civilization in an online Manhattan. It is a small glimpse of possibilities, a small confrontation of ideologies. As with all of Pynchon's subjunctive spaces, it presents a glimmer of hope in the otherwise overwhelming neoliberal hegemony. There is a power in that alone: a power in demonstrating an alternative. It helps to reconstruct what Žižek characterized as our inability to dream or imagine a world beyond capitalism. Still, as with all of Pynchon's subjunctive spaces, it is incomplete and complicated.

CHAPTER 7

A Snappy 'Ukulele Accompaniment

IN ONE of the early biographical sources on Thomas Pynchon, author Jules Siegel details his friendship with Pynchon. As a narrator, Siegel is questionable at best. He recounts events for which he had no firsthand knowledge. He frequently has difficulties remembering what exactly happened. He blames his own selfishness and his heavy drug use for these lapses in memory. In the end, he presents a wonderful bit of memoir that paints a vivid portrait of Jules Siegel and keeps Pynchon shrouded in a veil of mystery.

Siegel also provides one specific description that is very useful to understanding Pynchon's work. Siegel describes Pynchon as someone who "could carry a tune well and made up ribald parodies of popular songs, which I seem to remember—surely I am imagining this—were accompanied on a ukulele" (122). With this statement, Siegel not only puts an 'ukulele in Pynchon's hands; he gives Pynchon a subjunctive 'ukulele, an 'ukulele that may be imagined but is taken as real.[1] Like the 'ukulele itself—which is simultaneously a tacky tourist souvenir and a genuine, rich instrument of indigenous culture—Pynchon's subjunctive 'ukulele works in complicated ways. At times, it can be read as a representation of the network of multinational corporations, national governments, and international financial institutions that Michael Hardt and Antonio Negri refer to as "Empire." At other times, it can represent the networked multitude that works in concert to resist this Empire. The 'ukulele makes an appearance in every novel Pynchon has written from *Gravity's Rainbow* onward. Perhaps because the 'ukulele references span across such a broad swath of Pynchon's oeuvre, it does not serve as a single metaphor. Exploring the multiple 'ukulele references in Pynchon's novels helps elucidate some of the more subtle points of Pynchon's politics. The 'ukulele provides both an image for and soundtrack to Pynchon's counternarrative against Empire and its attendant neoliberal ideology.

Before exploring the ways in which Pynchon uses the 'ukulele as a metaphor, it helps to understand this enigmatic little instrument better. In "A New History of the Origins and Development of the 'Ukulele, 1838–1915," John King and Jim Tranquada trace the origins of the 'ukulele back to the Portuguese colony of Madeira, where, for a few centuries, locals had played a small treble guitar called a machete. The machete was culturally significant for Madeirans. It factored heavily in their celebrations and festivals. Eighteenth- and nineteenth-century travelers to the island frequently reported hearing the machete at parties and other festive occasions. As food shortages and political instability drove several residents of Madeira to various parts of the United States, Europe, South America, and Hawaii, the machete followed. Perhaps for this reason, there may be truth to the legend that, upon the landing of the Madeiran ship *Ravenscrag* in Honolulu, passenger João Fernandes celebrated by erupting into song accompanied by a borrowed machete, thereby officially planting the seed of the 'ukulele in Hawaii. King and Tranquada cite several newspaper accounts of Madeiran immigrants playing machetes around Hawaii.

The machete took many forms before becoming the 'ukulele. The instruments varied in size, scale, and tunings. They had four, five, six, or eight strings. Before they earned the name 'ukulele, the small instruments could be grouped together, in the terms of one of the original 'ukulele luthiers, Jose do Espirito Santo, as "guitars of all sizes" (qtd. in King and Tranquada 9). Over the course of a generation, from the landing of the *Ravenscrag* in 1879 to the Panama-Pacific International Exposition in San Francisco in 1915, the instrument that evolved from the machete came to represent indigenous Hawaiian culture. King David Kalakaua frequently entertained foreign dignitaries with a group of musicians known as "The King's Singing Boys," who sang traditional Hawaiian songs in the Hawaiian language accompanied by the 'ukulele. The last monarch of Hawaii, Queen Lili'uokalani, famously wrote the bittersweet requiem for the island she was losing, "Aloha Oe," to be accompanied by the 'ukulele. Perhaps most significantly, local luthiers replaced the standard spruce or pine soundboards with the indigenous local hardwood koa. Koa wood was emblematic of Hawaiian culture. The use of koa soundboards, coupled with the distinctive Hawaiian re-entrant tuning, gave the 'ukulele its distinctive sound.

This specific history connects to Pynchon's politics in a variety of ways. Much of the site of resistance for Pynchon lies in reclaiming culture and identity from Empire. This reclaimed culture and identity is neither perfect nor pure. As Katherine Hume observes, "We must quest within the world we have inherited" ("Religious and Political Vision" 180). The sites of resistance must exist within Empire because Empire's expanse is so broad that there is almost no room outside of it. As I have mentioned in previous chapters, Hardt and Negri conceive of Empire as a sovereignty without a single sovereign. They reject from the outset "the idea that order is dictated by a single power and a single center of rationality *transcendent* to global forces, guiding the various phases of historical development according to its conscious and all-seeing plan, something like a conspiracy theory of globalization" (*Empire* 3). Empire is neither an individual authoritarian ruling with an iron fist nor a conspiracy of the excessively wealthy. It is instead better understood as a horizontal network of multinational corporations, national governments, and supranational financial institutions. Individual power among the humans composing the network shifts, with some individuals rising relative to others, some profiting immensely, and some falling out of power, yet the structure remains intact.

The 'ukulele emerged within the context of a nascent Empire. Hawaiians were faced with the violent overthrow of their islands by a network of corporate and government interests from within the United States. They could not combat this network's overpowering military and economic strength. They were forced to seek resistance in other ways. Specifically, they sought to sustain and validate their culture. The 'ukulele became the symbol for this Hawaiian culture. It does not matter that the 'ukulele had been born of a Madeiran instrument or that the 'ukulele had been in Hawaii for less than a generation before it became a cultural symbol. Hawaiians reclaimed the machete. They made it distinctly Hawaiian. They absorbed the horrors of colonization, the destruction brought by the introduction of a global marketplace to the island, and the hostilities of a military takeover, and came out of it with an 'ukulele. Obviously, this was not an equitable trade. On a literal level, the U.S. conquest of Hawaii is one more dark spot in the history of U.S. colonization of indigenous populations. On a metaphoric level, there is something hopeful in this little guitar and its evolution to a symbol of indigenous culture. It exemplifies Pynchon's site of resistance, because this is the challenge that Pynchon's novels confront: How do we survive Empire's colonization of our homeland, the domination of its markets, its militarization, its attack on our democracy, its privatization of our social safety net? And this is the answer the novels present: we fight on an ideological battlefield, we construct a culture that reclaims the artifacts of global capitalism and repurposes them, we answer the selfishness of economies of gain and accumulation with the mutual benefits of an economy of social relations. An examination of the 'ukulele in Pynchon's novels reveals this.

From *Gravity's Rainbow* Absurdity to *Vineland*'s Deliverance

The first notable example of the 'ukulele in Pynchon's novels appears in *Gravity's Rainbow*. Pynchon introduces Tyrone Slothrop through the character's workspace. British secret agent Teddy Bloat photographs Slothrop's cubicle. The reader gets a sense of who Slothrop is through the stuff gathered around his desk. Among the flotsam gathered there are "the scribbled ukulele chords to a dozen songs including 'Johnny Doughboy Found a Rose in Ireland' ('He does have some rather snappy arrangements,' Tantivy reports, 'he's a sort of

American George Formby, if you can imagine such a thing,' but Bloat's decided he'd rather not)" (18). The 'ukulele chords and songs they represent are telling. First, the portability of the 'ukulele is highlighted. The instrument is something that an American working with British military intelligence in London can carry with him. It can be a symbol of home for Slothrop. He can be an "American George Formby." The allusion to George Formby—the first among several in Pynchon's novels—further characterizes Slothrop. Formby was a former vaudevillian who rose to the height of his popularity during World War II. He became one of the highest-paid film stars in England in the 1940s. His films typically featured Formby playing comical songs on his banjolele. The banjolele is a hybrid instrument with neck, scale, and tuning of an 'ukulele and the body of a banjo. Formby used the banjolele to craft songs that were frequently silly, but, as evidenced by the economic injustice in "Why Don't Women Want Me?" and the opposition to hierarchy in "Our Sergeant Major," Formby's songs demonstrate real concern with class inequity. Teddy Bloat groans at the Formby reference (as, later, Doc Sportello of *Inherent Vice* will). Nonetheless, Pynchon, who himself is a popular cultural force concerned with class inequity and wont to break out into goofy songs, should not be too dismissive of Formby.

Slothrop is further characterized by the 'ukulele when Bloat also finds on Slothrop's desk "a busted corkscrewing ukulele string" (18), which suggests that Slothrop plays the 'ukulele with enough verve to break a string, and he does so at the office. This information introduces another significant aspect of Pynchon's use of the 'ukulele in his novels: it is supposed to be fun. Even the most talented ukulelists know that the instrument is not to be taken too seriously. There are serious aspects to the instrument. It is born of colonialism, global markets, and militarization (just as *Gravity's Rainbow* and Pynchon's other novels are), but it is also born of celebration, community, and cultural identity. It is an instrument further symbolic of times when one takes a break from the seriousness of life. By characterizing Slothrop as an American Formby, a guy who—though he works in military intelligence during a world war, in a city that is actively being firebombed—brings his 'ukulele to his office and plays goofy songs, Pynchon gives the reader an outline of what is becoming his distinctive style of fiction. Critics like Fredric Jameson refer to this as a postmodern blending of high and low culture. The terms *high* and *low*, however, present a troubling hierarchy. Perhaps it would be more appropriate to describe Pynchon's style as a mixture of the serious and the silly, the deadly and the absurd.

The serious and the silly, in this case, blend together all the aforementioned ideas: that Empire's reach is too expansive to escape, that resistance tends to be cultural and on a small scale. It is reminiscent of Michael Taussig's ethnography of Occupy Wall Street, "I'm So Angry I Made a Sign." Taussig describes the occupation of Zuccotti Park as a demonstration in the purest sense of the word. The occupiers were not simply protesting neoliberal capitalism, they were demonstrating an alternative to it. This alternative promoted a form of participatory democracy built around working toward consensus rather than simply voting. It featured a horizontal resistance movement in which the singularities of the participants are never sacrificed, much in line with Hardt and Negri's vision of a multitude. It demonstrated fun—Taussig describes a group of older women in the middle of Zuccotti Park knitting woolies and telling stories—and a good sense of humor, right down to the distribution of a "Lick My Goldman Sachs" bumper sticker. Similarly, Slothrop's 'ukulele demonstrates an alternative to the war office of which he is a part. It brings communities together in song. It celebrates life, ribald and goofy and passionate as it can be, instead of the death and destruction of the war and the v-2 bombs plummeting on the city. It conjures memories of an instrument built to culturally resist the ideology of colonial wars.

The deadly and the absurd blend in two later references to 'ukuleles in *Gravity's Rainbow*. First, Slothrop is vacationing on the Riviera when he witnesses Katje Borgesius in the clutches of an octopus, screaming for help. Slothrop races to the rescue. He is initially unable to disentangle Katje from the octopus's grip, and he fears that the last thing Katje will see will be his Hawaiian shirt, with its "vulgar-faced hula girls, ukuleles, and surfriders all in comic-book colors" (186). This representation of an 'ukulele—bastardized, reduced to an image on a gaudy tourist shirt—seems suddenly absurd to Slothrop. The 'ukulele is overshadowed by the other events in this scene, during which Slothrop is set up by a group of spies (with whom he thought he was working) and a well-trained octopus. But its absurdity, at least in Slothrop's mind, does not end here. Much later in the novel, when Slothrop sweats out a fever in occupied Berlin and feels as if he might die, he also wallows in self-deprecation. He tells himself, "And you are no knightly hero. The best you can compare with is Tannhauser, the Singing Nincompoop—you've been under one mountain at Nordhausen, been known to sing a song or two with uke accompaniment" (364). At what Slothrop feels is his lowest point, he constructs his identity with "uke accompaniment." By this point, Slothrop has traded his 'ukulele for the even more portable harmonica, yet the 'ukulele remains a part of his identity. It is the silliness to counterbalance the seriousness that surrounds him, here in the heart of the wreckage at the end of a world war. There is a sense of hopelessness that accompanies this 'ukulele, raising the question of where one finds any sense of celebration or hope among the annihilation of World War II.

The 'ukulele's final appearances in *Gravity's Rainbow* once again find that site for celebration, for silliness that is not absurd. In one specific scene, American soldiers and sailors, American women attached to the military, local German women, and an assembly of other displaced characters engage in a postwar party. According to Steven Weisenburger, author of *A Gravity's Rainbow Companion*, "In this episode the circular dancing of the gathered preterite forms a symbolic counterpoint to the mushroom cloud that will form eight thousand miles to the east" (255). In other words, while Empire accelerates its project of annihilation in the form of an atomic bomb dropped on Hiroshima, the multitude provides a counternarrative to this annihilation. They form together in a celebration of the multitude. Pynchon describes the scene: "Ukuleles, kazoos, harmonicas, and any number of makeshift metal noisemakers accompany the song, which is an innocent salute to Postwar, a hope that the end of shortages, the end of Austerity, is near" (593). The presence of 'ukuleles in Cuxhaven, Germany, at the end of the World War II seems odd. It is not impossible that the locals along the North Sea had 'ukuleles, or that American servicemen brought them from home. However, the 'ukuleles seem more subjunctive, a fictional device that the reader accepts to allow Pynchon to insert all that the 'ukulele represents into this scene. What, specifically, the 'ukulele represents in Slothrop's identity and in postwar celebrations remains underdeveloped in the context of *Gravity's Rainbow*.

Of course, music plays a huge role in the novel. In *The Art of Allusion*, David Cowart provides what may be the definitive study of music in Pynchon's first three novels. With respect to *Gravity's Rainbow*, Cowart analyzes the significance of Pynchon's explorations into classical music and the new forms of music composition that were emerging in Germany prior to the war. Cowart concludes, "Music like this is subversive because it forces the hearer to take views too dangerously close to perceptual freedom. He gains knowledge and ceases to be useful to those who would have him remain in ignorance, lulled by religious, patriotic, even economic lies, and willing to sacrifice what little he has—life itself—for the expediency of the state or the interests of the powerful" (92). In simpler terms, the music Slothrop and Weissmann discuss sows the seeds for rebellion. Once one has had a genuine encounter with the freedom that music promises, the constraints of state and economic power become dubious. Again, this is a small site for resistance. The music will not overthrow national governments or dismantle neoliberal Empire. It is not a panacea and does not lead to a utopia. It works better in line with Taussig's explanation of Occupy: it demonstrates an alternative on a personal level. Amid the overwhelming promulgation of Empire's ideology and perpetual warfare, we can stage moments free of aspirations to capital and the pursuit of material wealth.

We can find meaning outside the marketplace in song, in dance, and in communal gatherings.

Pynchon's later novels were written after the neoliberal takeover of the 1980s, during which Empire implemented a global program of privatization, deregulation, militarism, and free-market fundamentalism. This historical context impacts explorations into the 'ukulele as a motif. Beginning with *Vineland*, the 'ukulele can be read as somewhat transformative. It becomes both a reminder of the dubious nature of Empire and a shield to protect the multitude.

The first actual 'ukulele in *Vineland* appears in a flashback about Zoyd Wheeler's time as the in-flight musician on Kahuna Airlines. On one particular flight, intruders enter the aircraft. They have "elite-unit grace" (64), automatic rifles, and a purpose that, while it is not clear to the reader nor to the occupants of the flight, is clear to the pursuers. The passengers react to the intrusion by drinking heavily. Zoyd continues to play his keyboard. He is accompanied by a strange man "holding a banjo-ukulele of between-the-wars vintage" (65). The strange man accompanies Zoyd, performing the Pynchon original "Wacky Coconuts."

The strange man with the banjolele is later revealed to be Takeshi Fumimoto. Takeshi's accompaniment on "Wacky Coconuts" successfully disguises him from his pursuers, who leave the aircraft without their man. This scene is layered with significance. First, the banjolele serves as an appropriate representation of Pynchon's global perspective in the novel. It is an instrument born from a Madeiran machete, which evolved into a Hawaiian 'ukulele, yet with the body of an instrument created by enslaved Africans in the southern United States. The instrument was popularized by a British entertainer and is now in the use of a Japanese man. Pynchon's preterite—the disenfranchised people surviving in global commodity culture—are represented in every stage of the banjolele's evolution from Madeira to the Kahuna Airlines flight. Further, this global instrument serves as a shield to the elite-unit grace and advanced technology and weaponry of Empire. Takeshi is able to fend off a superior force with his silly and serious instrument and his silly song.

This site featuring the 'ukulele is helpful for expanding an understanding of Hardt and Negri's Empire in relation to the work of Pynchon. The example is a bit fantastical. The special forces unit boards the plane midflight the way pirates would have boarded ships mid-Atlantic during the seventeenth and eighteenth century. In all likelihood, this is not possible in the world we live in. Within the context of the novel, this invasion makes sense. Militarized groups working for a network of national governments and multinational corporations impose their presence and will on several of the characters. They are so ubiquitous that the reader does not bat an eye when these militarized forces invade a flying Kahuna Airlines plane. Further, because the unit is searching for Takeshi, an observant reader can infer for whom the forces are working. Takeshi has already proven himself to be a rogue insurance investigator, one who does not always allow his investigations to favor large corporations. He has no specific connection with any government agency. Thus, this militarized unit would also likely be privatized, working at the behest of some fraudulent multinational. Power is demonstrated to be more horizontal, shared by national governments and multinational corporations alike, both operating above international law or accords.

Takeshi wields his 'ukulele with comparable effectiveness a second time in the novel. After DL accidentally performs the death touch on Takeshi, he tracks her down at the Retreat of the Sisterhood of Kunoichi Attentives. Takeshi senses that he will not be able to walk unarmed into the retreat, so he arms himself with an 'ukulele purchased in San Francisco—perhaps only coincidentally the site where, at the Pan-Pacific International Exposition in 1915, the 'ukulele catalyzed its popularity in American culture. He travels to the retreat and finds himself "there in the perilous open, regarded no doubt over the sights of Uzis set on full automatic" (162). Takeshi responds to this armed confrontation by pulling out his 'ukulele and singing a goofy song called "Just Like William Powell." The song endears him to the Sisterhood. The weapons are dropped. He finds a way to work with the Sisterhood to counteract the effects of the death touch and to enter, with DL, into the business of karmic readjustment.

Just as Takeshi's first 'ukulele elucidates aspects of Empire, his second 'ukulele entertains a multitude. The Sisterhood deviates in some respects from Hardt and Negri's vision of a society beyond Empire. Hardt and Negri develop their work from a Marxist tradition, advocating a move away from private property and toward a Marxist commons. The Sisterhood exists within capitalist conventions. The similarities between the multitude and the Sisterhood lie instead in their almost Occupy-like demonstration of participatory democracy. When Hardt and Negri discuss the specifics of resistance from the multitude, they observe, "The most important organizational characteristic of these various movements is their insistence on autonomy and their refusal of any centralized hierarchy, leaders, or spokespeople" (*Multitude* 86). In other words, for a multitude to be successful, their means cannot be separate from their ends. They must be built around consensus and structured horizontally in a way that retains individuals' singularities. The Sisterhood is an excellent demonstration of this. Different sections of the facility have people in charge. For example, Prairie Wheeler spends a bit of time in charge of the kitchen. The power in this role is limited to creating recipes that effectively utilize the resources of the kitchen and please the residents. It is a consensus-based role. Prairie holds no real hierarchical power. The Sisterhood exemplifies Francesca Polletta's reflection on resistance movements in "Participatory Democracy's Moment." Polletta observes, "Leadership is often informal and collective. . . . But what we have seen in recent movements is something more deliberate. Decisions are made by General Assemblies that are open to all. Consensus, rather than voting, is standard. The watchwords are decentralization, participation, and autonomy" (80). The Sisterhood is a decentralized space. There is a sort of mother superior in the form of Sister Rochelle, but even her power seems to be more informal and collective. Everyone who is part of the Sisterhood is open to participate in a meaningful fashion. The organization places a high priority on autonomy. This is exemplified by DL's comings and goings. Sister Rochelle has a nurturing relationship with her and supports DL's business venture that, technically, is in competition with the Sisterhood's. Even the decision to lower the uzis in the presence of Takeshi and his 'ukulele is made by consensus.

The final instance of the 'ukulele in *Vineland* occurs in the hands of Hub Gates while he, Sasha, and Frenesi drive south to Los Angeles. As a nuclear family, Hub, Sasha, and Frenesi do not quite work out. Hub and Sasha divorce, unable to withstand the residual pressure of their blacklisting during the years of the House Un-American Activities Committee. Frenesi rebels against both parents, aligning herself with the fascists whom Sasha and her family had fought against for generations. Yet the narrator describes one halcyon moment between the three, "driving down to Hollywood, Sasha at the wheel, Hub with a uke from Hawaii singing 'Down Among the Sheltering Palms' to Frenesi the baby between them" (290). Before the pressures of Empire—demonstrated in this case by McCarthyism and the COINTELPRO-like government intervention that seduces Frenesi—overcome and divide this family, there is a moment of a hope, when the young couple and their baby daughter move into what they believe will be a better life. This moment is accompanied by Hub on the 'ukulele. This scene, coupled with Takeshi's 'ukuleles, demonstrates the *Vineland* use of the instrument: it is a weapon of peace, an instrument of transformation, a symbol of hope.

The Complex Representations of the 'Ukulele Post-*Vineland*

The 'ukulele plays a much smaller role in *Mason & Dixon*. One could assume that Pynchon avoids placing an 'ukulele into the narrative because the bulk of events in the novel occur a century prior to the legendary moment when João Fernandes disembarked from the *Ravenscrag* and erupted into what very well may have been the first performance of the 'ukulele in Honolulu. Pynchon, however, has never been an author to submit to the tyranny of chronology. He revels in anachronisms. For example, Mason and Dixon discuss a miraculous watch Dixon had received from his mentor, William Emerson. The watch seems to run on perpetual motion. Mason scoffs at this idea. He states, "Had I tuppence for ev'ry approach made to Bradley upon the Topick of Perpetual-Motion, I should be elsewhere than this,— recumbent I imagine upon some sand beach of the Friendly Isles, strumming my *Eukalely*, and attended by local Maidens, whom I may even sometimes allow to strum it for me" (319). Mason imagines an 'ukulele (or "*Eukalely*") more than 130 years before the term was first used in print. He imagines himself in Hawaii more than a decade before Captain James Cook arrived there and renamed them the Sandwich Isles. He also seems to make a joke that alludes to George Formby. Formby wrote a song titled "With My Little Ukulele in My Hand," which uses the term 'ukulele as a double entendre for a penis—at the end of the song, the narrator describes the birth of his son, singing, "I knew it was a boy for he had a ukulele in his hand, oh baby!"

As mentioned above, Pynchon revels in anachronisms, and they serve the purpose of bilocating his narratives both in the historical past and the present lens through which we, as readers, view the past. In her discussion of "historiographic metafiction," Linda Hutcheon points out, "[W]e can likely only know the past through our present" (73). Her further argument explains that our concept of the past is based not only on specious textual evidence but also on our decision to privilege certain facts over others in an attempt to impose contemporary interpretations onto past events. Hutcheon cites Pynchon as a creative force behind this historiographic metafiction. With this in mind, it is helpful to remember that Pynchon's historical works are always as much about the time period when they were written as they are about the time period they represent. In regard to *Mason & Dixon*, Pynchon wrote within the context of a neoliberal takeover. Superimposing this context over Mason's reference to the 'ukulele further places the instrument—along with Mason's dreams to live outside his current world of chartered companies and slave states—into the subjunctive realm of an imagined space beyond the grasp of Empire.

The other reference to the 'ukulele occurs earlier in the novel. Mason and Dixon sit on a front porch with their South African hosts, the Vrooms. A young man comes along to serenade the three adolescent Vroom girls. He plays a "diminutive three-string'd Lute" (80) that he describes as a "Fiji Islander's Guitar, first introduc'd there two hundred years ago by Portuguese Jesuits" (81). The actual instrument the young man plays could be any of a number of stringed instruments. Read in the light of Pynchon's repeated representations of the 'ukulele throughout his oeuvre, one could view this three-stringed lute born of the Madeiran diaspora as an early stage in the evolution of the 'ukulele. The instrument, after all, is forever changing and adapting to local cultures and tastes. The three strings of the instrument become more significant when considered in light of a specific passage in *Against the Day*.

Miles Blundell, one of the Chums of Chance in *Against the Day*, articulates one of the many meanings one can invest in the 'ukulele. His meditation on the 'ukulele serves as the most direct address regarding the 'ukulele as a metaphor in any Pynchon novel. Miles discusses:

> the widespread contempt in which ukulele players are held—traceable, we concluded, to the uke's all-but-exclusive employment as a producer of chords—single, timeless events apprehended all at once instead of serially. Notes of a linear melody, up and down a staff, being a record of pitch versus time, to play a melody is to introduce the element of time, and hence of mortality. Our perceived reluctance to leave the timelessness of the struck chord has earned ukulele players our reputation as feckless, clownlike children who will not grow up. (552)

Miles's meditation is loaded with meaning. First, he discusses the timelessness of a chord. A chord is created on a stringed instrument when a musician combines the first, third, and fifth note of a scale. For example, the full scale of the key of G, which is Takeshi's preferred 'ukulele key in *Vineland*, is G A B C D E F#. G is the first note in the scale, A the second, etc. Thus, the G would be first, B the third, and D the fifth. When Takeshi formed a G chord on his banjolele, he played a succession of the notes (starting from the top string) B, G, D, G in one strum. The notes combine to make the G chord. Only one of the G notes is necessary to form the chord, but since the 'ukulele has four strings, one note is repeated. This means that the young man in *Mason & Dixon*, with his diminutive three-string guitar from the Fiji Islands but of Portuguese descent, had all the strings necessary to play 'ukulele chords and therefore may have had one of the mutations in the evolution of the 'ukulele.

There is also the element of timelessness in the chord. Obviously, time does exist when one strums a chord on any stringed instrument. The sound created by the chord does blend at least three moments in time into one, creating an illusion of timelessness. This can be interpreted several different ways. Among them, one can explore Pynchon's relationship with time's relativity in both *Mason & Dixon* and *Against the Day*. Through his repeated discussion of clocks and watches in the former novel and his explorations into fourth-dimensional mathematics in the latter novel, Pynchon rejects the tyranny of time ticking away in an orderly fashion. Instead, Pynchon constructs a more complex view of time, one that is more relative, with moments expanding and contracting in irregular fashion. The past becomes something that does not exist as an objective moment in rational time but is instead a fiction created by memory, the perspective of the present, and the saturation of the imagination. The future races to meet characters in some instances and remains forever out of their reach in others. Like Billy Pilgrim, Kurt Vonnegut's protagonist in *Slaughterhouse-Five*, Pynchon's readers become unstuck in time, yo-yoing between the past, present, future, and subjunctive. The novels themselves, the fictional worlds they create, seem to exist forever in the present tense. They become as seemingly timeless as an 'ukulele chord.

Another way of interpreting Miles's meditation on the 'ukulele chord resides in Hardt and Negri's description of a multitude: "singularities that act in common" (*Multitude* 105). When Takeshi strikes a G chord, the D note remains a D, the B remains a B, yet these singularities work together to form a chord. In a sense, the D and B do become a G in that particular chord, but the D never loses its essence. It can be used again in a D chord, in a B chord, and in a number of other chords. By maintaining their individuality yet working together for a common sound, these notes work as a metonym for the concept of a multitude. In a more complete definition of the concept, Hardt and Negri explain: "The multitude is composed of innumerable internal differences that can never be reduced to a unity or a single identity—different cultures, races, ethnicities, genders, and sexual orientations; different forms of labor; different ways of living; different views of the world and different desires. The multitude is a multiplicity of all these singular differences" (*Multitude* xiv). In other words, by maintaining internal differences, the multitude need not choose between singularity and plurality. The multitude instead maintain their singularities but work in concert against the common exploitation of Empire. While the notes in an 'ukulele chord may not be specifically working against the exploitation of Empire, the fretboard of the 'ukulele expands the same metaphor as Pynchon's idealized site of the multitude in *Against the Day*, the anarchist retreat Yz-les-Bains. At the retreat, the characters recognize what needs to be done and do it. Their actions do not form identities that would then interpellate their social role. Instead, they work toward the common goal of sustaining the retreat without sacrificing their individuality or allowing any state apparatus to impose an identity upon them. Likewise, the notes on a fretboard are joined by whatever is needed to make a chord, then released with no loss of their singularity.

If one were to accept this interpretation as that which Miles is attempting to communicate in his meditation on 'ukulele chords, then his subsequent encounter with the nefarious Transgressor Ryder Thorn becomes more meaningful. Ryder brags to Miles that he has "learned a 'snappy' new arrangement of a Chopin nocturne" (552). In order to play this arrangement, Ryder would have to play a succession of individual notes—a melody—instead of chords. This melody would be a violation of the timelessness and multitude apparent in Miles's meditation on chords. As a plot device, this could signal to Miles that he must beware of Ryder. Ryder seeks to break the multitude and subject Miles once again to the tyranny of clock time—which, not incidentally, Ryder does seek to do and Miles does resist. This reading of melody in *Against the Day* has precedence in Pynchon's early novels, also. As David Cowart explains, Pynchon's "own metaphor for the love-death theme is 'melody'" (77). Within the context of *Against the Day*, the love would come in the timeless chords, the death in the element of time brought about through individual notes. This echoes back to *Mason & Dixon*, where the young man serenades the Vroom girls with his three-stringed lute. The three strings would provide all he needs to express love.

Pynchon's subsequent references to the 'ukulele in *Against the Day* and *Inherent Vice* follow the pattern established in *Gravity's Rainbow*, *Vineland*, and *Mason & Dixon*. As in the Cuxhaven scene in *Gravity's Rainbow*, the 'ukulele once again brings together the preterite in celebration in *Against the Day*. It does so for Kit Traverse while he is in Belgium, for Lew Basnight in London, and for picnickers at Candlebrow University in Ohio. As in *Vineland*, the 'ukulele accompanies scenes of hope, particularly for Miles Blundell, who carries his 'ukulele into the Chicago World's Fair, aspiring to join the presenters at the Hawaii exhibit in authentic Hawaiian music. As in *Vineland*, that hope is dashed by Empire's influence. The music at the Hawaiian exhibit is not authentic. It is a spectacle created as a commodity. Nonetheless, the 'ukulele itself remains that symbol of hope. As in *Mason & Dixon*, Pynchon presents the 'ukulele anachronistically. Professor Vanderjuice plays "a ukulele of some dark exotic wood trimmed with tortoiseshell" (324). The dark exotic wood would likely be mahogany, which is the common 'ukulele soundboard wood that is darker than koa. The mahogany combined with the tortoiseshell binding that characterizes early Martin 'ukuleles would suggest that Vanderjuice owns an 'ukulele made by the Martin company of Pennsylvania a few years prior to Martin actually making these 'ukuleles. This anachronism should be no problem for a veteran of the time travel conferences at Candlebrow University and a mathematician schooled in the fourth dimension as Vanderjuice is. The anachronism also rejects the death in the element of time brought about by melodies that Miles discusses with Ryder Thorn.

Finally, as in the 'ukulele's first appearance in *Gravity's Rainbow*, the instrument is referenced again in *Inherent Vice* to create another groan about George Formby. In the latter case, Doc's friend Jade describes the band Spotted Dick by saying, "You know the English ukulele player named George Formby?" Doc responds, "Sure, Herman's Hermits covered one of his." Jade says, "Well, these guys have covered everything else. I mean, try to be cool with it" (130). The song that Doc knows is "Leaning on a Lamppost." It is one of George Formby's hit songs, but it differs from the rest of Formby's oeuvre. Instead of a comical song that relies on humor to carry it, "Leaning on a Lamppost" is a tender love song. Spotted Dick, on the other hand, cover only the goofy songs. Since Formby recorded over a hundred songs, Spotted Dick have a near obsession with the goofy. Perhaps this is why Jade warns Doc away from their music.

Empire's 'Ukulele and the Multitude's

This warning serves as a fitting caveat to Pynchon's use of the 'ukulele as a metaphor. Clearly, Pynchon celebrates the 'ukulele. Clearly, he has no objections to comical songs, bawdy jokes, and working-class undertones, all of which characterize Formby's recordings. Clearly, when Jade warns, "Try to be cool with it," Pynchon has found a way to be cool with it. Nonetheless, Pynchon avoids absolutes. His representations of the 'ukulele, as well as his site for resistance residing in the multitude, are not dogmas. They are metaphors constructed to counter the neoliberal ideology of accumulation. There are problems with the metaphor. The 'ukulele itself is a fitting symbol for understanding these problems. 'Ukuleles simultaneously stand for an exoticized version of Hawaii as a paradise colonized by consumer commodity culture and as a genuine representation of the islands' indigenous culture. The meaning shifts. It is dependent on the context surrounding the symbol.

One of the problems of the 'ukulele is how easily it can be co-opted. According to King and Tranquada, the Panama-Pacific International Exposition in San Francisco in 1915 "launched a national craze for Hawaiian music and the 'ukulele" (22) in the United States. The exposition opened in February 1915. King and Tranquada report, "As early as September 1915 . . . Hawaiian manufacturers were complaining that mainland companies were fraudulently passing off their 'ukuleles as island-made" (25). The speed with which mainland companies misrepresented their products to associate them with the image of Hawaii demonstrates how quickly Empire is able to co-opt any aspect of reclaimed culture, rebrand that reclamation, and sell it back as a commodity. This pattern continues into the present.

The 'ukulele experienced a resurgence during the first decade of the twenty-first century. Much of this resurgence was fueled by the Internet, which expanded the availability of Hawaiian 'ukuleles and of 'ukulele instruction. YouTube allowed ukulelists to post videos of 'ukulele instruction and aspiring musicians to learn from them. Message boards on various websites also paved the way for numerous 'ukulele groups to form and strum together. In a sense, it became a microcosm of Hardt and Negri's vision of commonwealth. Communities gathered for purposes that existed outside the marketplace. They made music together. They shared information on how to make music. They did it all without charging a fee. In the case of the popular 'ukulele blog *Ukulele Hunt*, the creator engaged in these activities as a consciously political stand, advocating for reformed international copyright laws and an expansion of the creative commons through an increase of music in the public domain (Wood, "Why You Should Give a Crap About Copyright Terms").

Almost immediately, this craze was co-opted by Empire. The 'ukulele's popularity triggered the accelerated production of 'ukuleles of dubious quality constructed in Chinese factories, where, at least one 'ukulele company boasts, "[W]ork forces, at least for now, appear to be similar to western countries a hundred years ago, back when people appreciated just having a job.... [T]hey knew nothing of paid vacations, sick leave, workman's compensation, health insurance, temporary disability insurance, and whatever other incentives are now available to western workers." For this reason, the Chinese company can pay the workers "thirty times" less than comparable American workers ("Pono Frequently Asked Questions").

Further, King and Tranquada cite the Hawaiian Promotion Committee's lament that mainland business practices harm the music from the islands. A contemporary example resides in Israel Kamakawiwo'ole's version of "Over the Rainbow." Kamakawiwo'ole is rumored to have recorded the song to honor a friend of his who had recently died. Kamakawiwo'ole passed away before experiencing the phenomena that his recording would create. The song seemed to strike a nerve among mainland Americans. It became a posthumous hit for Kamakawiwo'ole. It also became a sensation for corporate America. Ben Sisario reports in a recent *New York Times* article, "The recording has been licensed more than 100 times to sell food, software, paint, bank services, lottery tickets and plenty else, and it shows no sign of slowing down." One of the reasons the song has been so popular in advertising campaigns resides in the humble, charming sound of the 'ukulele accompaniment. Because the 'ukulele is high pitched, because the re-entrant tuning produces such a distinctive sound, because it conjures orientalized images of an exotic island for mainland Americans, the instrument creates a soothing and trustworthy accompaniment to commodities that are environmentally hazardous (like paint) or ethically questionable (lottery tickets). The music can soften the edges around the industry responsible for triggering the Great Recession (bank services). The 'ukulele can even put a friendly face on contemporary plutocrats. Sally Ann Lasson, writing for the *Independent*, recently discussed her feelings about industrialist Warren Buffet playing the 'ukulele. According to Lasson, "It shows he's human. No other instrument could possibly convey this egalitarian message as succinctly as a uke." Herein lies the danger in the 'ukulele as metaphor. As soon as a newspaper reporter views her life and billionaire Warren Buffet's as "egalitarian," the 'ukulele is serving the interests of Empire. The inequality is further exemplified by the host of videos showing Buffet playing a cheap 'ukulele made under dubious working conditions in China.

Pynchon's final allusion to the 'ukulele reflects an ambivalence toward the instrument. No one in *Bleeding Edge* plays the 'ukulele. It brings no one together. It is not used to discuss time or resistance. It is mentioned only once. Maxine Tarnow has a conversation with Cornelia, the wife of venture capitalist Rocky Slagiatt. Cornelia describes her and Rocky's honeymoon in Hawaii as "heaven there, with ukuleles for harps" (279). As in the case of the corporate treatment of Kamakawiwo'ole's "Over the Rainbow," the 'ukulele is an exoticized prop for two New Yorkers in Hawaii. It is removed from its history and cultural significance and provides a simple background accompaniment to one pleasant event in a marriage that is already being defined by "What-have-we-done gazes" (279).

These problems mirror Hardt and Negri's criticism of postmodernism in *Empire*. Hardt and Negri claim that Empire has co-opted postmodernism as an ideology that promotes the exploitation of Empire. Hardt and Negri further argue that postmodernism's "politics of difference, fluidity, and hybridity in order to challenge the binaries and essentialism of modern sovereignty have been outflanked by the strategies of power" (138). In other words, Empire exploits the concepts of difference and hybridity to justify global commodity trade and the free exchange of markets. Postmodernism has not become the ideology of Empire. Empire continues to remain firmly entrenched in a neoliberal ideology that subjugates all aspects of human life to the logic of the marketplace. Since postmodernism is one of the aspects of life in a neoliberal society, it has also been saturated with the logic of the marketplace.

These co-optations—both with respect to the 'ukulele and postmodernism—are familiar to Pynchon. Thus, Pynchon's sites of resistance need to be explored in context and with complexity. For example, much of Pynchon's resistance lies in community and family, and both of these concepts have been co-opted by Empire. *Vineland*, which ends with Pynchon's vision of a reconstituted family and community system built up of nontraditional relationships and assemblages of disparate but comparably disenfranchised individuals serves to counter the narrow concept of "family values" promoted by George H. W. Bush in his presidential campaign. While Bush's views of family values had been reduced to the patriarchal values of the nuclear family, Pynchon expands his reconstituted families and communities to include the preterite, the multitude. Another example lies in the definitions of freedom. Pynchon is a great proponent of freedom, but he confronts the neoliberal definition of freedom, which is the freedom of markets, the freedom of the wealthy few to exploit the land and labor of most of humanity. Pynchon instead promotes a vision of freedom that is contingent on cooperation, on individuals working together for the mutual benefit of all. Thus, when I discuss Pynchon's site of resistance lying with family, community, and freedom, I must do so within the context of what these terms denote for Pynchon, and with the knowledge of how quickly and persistently these concepts are co-opted and redefined by governments and multinational corporations.

The best example of the necessity of welding the context to the concept lies at the end of *Against the Day*, when the character Jess Traverse summarizes what it means to be an American: "[D]o what they tell you and take what they give you and don't go on strike or their soldiers will shoot you down" (1076). While this works as a clever sound bite, for the statement itself to have real significance, the reader must be reminded of Pynchon's entire historiography of late nineteenth- and early twentieth-century economic liberalism, how the ideology was infused globally, the material effects it had on both land and labor, the devastation it imposed on millions of individual human lives, the ways in which it ravaged the globe from Mexico to the Balkans to tiny islands in the middle of the vast Indian Ocean, and how that ideology created the neoliberal ideology which has become hegemonic in contemporary society.

Finally, the 'ukulele, when it is tied to the context of Pynchon's novels and the hope he presents, becomes equally meaningful. It brings together communities in positive ways: to celebrate the end of a war (in *Gravity's Rainbow*) and hopefully the end of Empire's perpetual warfare (as discussed in *Vineland*); to aid intellectual inquiry (in *Against the Day*); to catalyze healthy, loving relationships (in *Mason & Dixon* and *Vineland*); to foster the construction of an identity as a fun, happy person willing to lend a hand, even to a spy being attacked by a trained octopus (in the case of Tyrone Slothrop); and, perhaps most importantly, to challenge every ideology that has become naturalized, right down to the tyranny of clock time itself (in the case of Miles Blundell's meditation).

A creed for the 'ukulele in Pynchon's novels lies in *Inherent Vice*, when Bigfoot Bjornsen describes Doc Sportello as someone who can "appreciate the distinction between child*like* and child*ish*" (213). Pynchon's vision of a better future lies in this characterization of Doc Sportello: someone who can take care of himself among the madness of contemporary society but never gives up that childlike sense of hope and wonder, never gives up that imaginative, subjunctive world that still can exist. A world that, like the 'ukulele, begins with the flawed situation Empire has placed us in, a situation that our own flawed complicity helps perpetuate, yet is still a world where the multitude can create a culture of reclamation. It is a world where we subvert the neoliberal ideology of accumulation with a counternarrative that has an 'ukulele as its metaphor. The counternarrative that tells us to have fun, sing goofy songs, join together in whatever family or communities work as long as they work for the mutual benefit of everyone, understand the context of contemporary society with all its flaws and all our flawed complicities, never sacrifice social relations for accumulation, and use any moments of respite to provide a counterbalance to the power of Empire.

CHAPTER 8

Occupy the Novel
A Conclusion

IN *VINELAND*, Pynchon creates his own type of supernatural—or, perhaps, preternatural—being: the Thanatoid. Thanatoids are the dead who walk among us. They are not ghosts. When DL makes the mistake of referring to them as such, Takeshi is quick to correct her. He tells her, "That word—around here it's a no-no" (173). Like ghosts, Thanatoids have been prevented from "their daily expeditions on into the interior of Death" (173). Unlike ghosts, Thanatoids are corporeal. The Thanatoid Ortho Bob eats a plate of ribs. Thanatoids have their own apartments, apartment complexes, villages, comedy roasts, and formal dances. They drive cars. Something about their preternatural state allows them to occasionally get those cars stuck in the tops of trees, but they still need a tow truck to get the cars back down. Like ghosts, Thanatoids can haunt those who have done them wrong. Unlike ghosts, Thanatoid hauntings seem to be monotonous and banal. They are more of a nuisance than a threat. Their problems are internal. Thanatoids, themselves, are haunted.

Similarly, Thanatoids are not zombies. They make zombie jokes like, "What does a Thanatoid do on Halloween? Put a fruit bowl on his head, two straws up his nose, and goes as a Zombie" (219). While they may be dead, corporeal, slow moving, and dim-witted, they do not follow the conventions of zombies. They do not eat brains. They do not turn the living into zombies by biting them. They do not trigger any type of apocalypse. Humans do not seek to kill them. Thanatoids pose much less of a threat. Moreover, Thanatoids can speak with the living. They can obtain and handle money, hire bands to play at the Thanatoid Ball, and hire DL and Takeshi to adjust their karma. As Weed Atman reveals late in the novel, "Thanatoids dream" (365).

They have souls, unlike zombies, and bodies, unlike ghosts, but like both zombies and ghosts, Thanatoids have died. The most prominent Thanatoid in *Vineland* is Weed Atman. The reader sees Weed get shot at the College of the Surf in the late 1960s. His death then is unequivocal. Yet his Thanatoid form continues to wander around Vineland in 1984. He is the dead who walks among the living, not haunting the living, not threatening them, sometimes employing them, and mostly just hanging out, watching the tube like other Thanatoids. Pynchon is not perfectly clear how a Thanatoid is created other than to suggest that they have died with some sort of karmic imbalance that is so strong they cannot continue on into the realm of death. Frequently, that karmic imbalance refers to their relationship with power and the marketplace. Among the Thanatoids are dentists, Vietnam veterans, and sixties activists seeking, in the words of Emerson as quoted by Jess Traverse at the family reunion, "Secret retributions [that] are always restoring the level, when disturbed, of the divine justice" (369). In this way, Pynchon's preternatural Thanatoids become the appropriate entryway into the conclusion of this book.

In a sense, Thanatoids predict the explosion of zombie stories at the start of the twenty-first century. Both tap into a fear that something is dead inside of us, yet we continue to move on. This is demonstrated poignantly in *Shaun of the Dead* when the protagonist, Shaun, awakes on the morning of a zombie apocalypse, goes to the local market, makes his purchase, and continues home before noticing that everyone around him is the walking dead. The humor resides in the common experience the audience shares of walking through public spaces and getting the sense that everyone around seems dead to the morning and in the common fear that we are not completely alive until we have gone to our local market or coffee shop and purchased our coffee, tea, soda, caffeine, high-fructose corn syrup, or other stimulant that awakens us from our living-dead state. Zombie movies have adopted a common trope that entwines a living-dead state with the marketplace. The characters in *Zombieland* fight their primary battles in spaces of conspicuous consumption—grocery stores, mansions—until the final, climactic scene in a theme park, where the living dead seem insurmountable. One of the most seminal movies about the living dead (though not exactly zombies) is *Army of Darkness*, in which an employee of a Walmart-like box store is transported back to the Middle Ages, where he accidentally raises the dead, then has to kill the creatures he called into existence. This confrontation with the marketplace happens again and again in movies about the living dead.

It is no coincidence that this genre has exploded after the neoliberal takeover of the 1980s. At the core of neoliberalism is a belief that endless accumulation is the primary goal of humankind. Grand philosophical questions about the meaning of life, about beauty, art, transcendent truth, spiritual depth, and so forth have all become sublimated. Meaning can be found in the marketplace. Our life is a commodity. We must get our money's worth out of it. Our art and our storytellers become images and narratives constructed to sell commodities. Meaning equals money.

Of course, we cannot help being skeptical about this. As Occupy activist David Graeber observed, we cannot help noticing that capitalism is crumbling around us. As Naomi Klein argued at Zuccotti Park, global consumer capitalism has polluted our air and water, created more carbon than the atmosphere can handle, developed a food supply that leads more to obesity than nourishment, and catapulted us from one disaster to the next. And on a personal level, we cannot help feeling that something about being human has been lost. We judge our values in relation to the marketplace, as if we were commodities instead of humans. When meaning equals money, our lives become fungible, our sense of both individuality and community crumbles. Like all the contemporary zombie stories—we fear that we are becoming the living dead ourselves, fighting that unevolved, slow-moving, dim-witted part of us that drags us through grocery stores and minimansions and theme parks, that haunts us from Walmart-like box stores. Or if we have not become zombies, we are lilting toward Thanatoid at least, with one eye always on the tube or a screen of some sort, gathering at freeway off-ramps in anonymous housing developments, adopting the personalities of the insomniac unavenged.

Since we cannot call DL and Takeshi to restore the karmic imbalances created by the neoliberal takeover, perhaps we can use Pynchon's post–*Gravity's Rainbow* novels as a heuristic, just as I have done with this book. We can begin by examining power and sovereignty as it has developed through global capitalism, understand it as networked among multinational corporations, national governments, and supranational economic institutions. Of course, Hardt and Negri's critical trilogy, *Empire*, *Multitude*, and *Commonwealth*, helps construct a foundation for understanding this new sovereignty. Of course, understanding goes far beyond Hardt and Negri and into recognizing new paradigms of labor, new conceptions of family and community, and deeper examinations into pseudoreligious faith in markets coupled with very material policies that ensure capital flows from the 99 percent to the 1 percent. The Occupy movement, likewise, works as a demonstration of how we can envision a better world beyond (or at least within) neoliberal capitalism. And, since neoliberalism gains and retains its power ideologically, perhaps the path to greater autonomy and more just societies lies in a deconstruction of that ideology. The next step, then, would be to apply these explorations of power and resistance in Pynchon's novels to other authors and works that cover similar territory.

What follows is less an analysis of specific works than an outline for applying the interpretive strategy I have used in this book to other contemporary novels. Because neoliberalism has become hegemonic and because so many major novelists confront neoliberal ideology, I hope that more scholars will utilize the theorists who laid the foundation for Occupy in their approach to contemporary literature.

Haruki Murakami

Thomas Pynchon and Haruki Murakami share several overlapping thematic elements throughout their novels. Murakami has even acknowledged that, after reading *V.*, he stopped reading Pynchon because their styles were too similar (Rubin 84). Both authors have written large, encyclopedic novels concerned with power on a global scale, war as a mechanism for attacking human rights, and the pervasive power of television. Placing the two authors in conversation with each other, even briefly in this conclusion, can be useful.

Like Pynchon in *Vineland*, Murakami explores the dehumanizing elements of the television throughout his oeuvre, but nowhere more directly than in his short story "TV People." "TV People" tells the story of an unnamed narrator, an advertising copywriter for an electrical-appliance manufacturer. One Sunday, while his wife is away with friends and he is wallowing in melancholy, three TV People arrive at his apartment, disrupt the order of the space, and install a television. As soon as it is installed, the narrator feels a shift in his world, "Almost as if I were riding backward on a roller coaster, wearing strong prescription glasses. The view is dizzying, the scale all screwed up. I'm thrown off balance, my customary world is no longer absolute. That's the way the TV People make you feel" (201). Unlike in *Vineland*, where the tube has the power to quell a rebellion, the TV People simply highlight the narrator's perceived insignificance. Once the television enters his life, he is perpetually distracted. He can no longer focus on conversations with his wife or meetings at work. Prior to the television, he typically read most evenings. Once the television is introduced, he can barely get through a page or two. The story ends with the narrator's wife vanishing. He responds by vanishing himself into the world of the television.

"TV People" thematically steers Murakami toward his masterpiece, *The Wind-Up Bird Chronicle*, which also tells the story of a disaffected salaryman (Toru Okada) whose wife vanishes. Toru's name means, literally, "to pass through." In this way, he harks back to the narrator of "TV People," who felt, once the television entered his life, as if he no longer has substance. The narrator even says, "I look at my hands half expecting to see clear through them" (202). Passing through Toru Okada is his brother-in-law, a scholar and politician who uses the television as a means to rise to power and control not only the general population's lives but, specifically, the lives of Toru and his wife. Murakami has stated explicitly that Noboru is a metaphor for television (Rubin 211). Toru's battle then becomes one with the power of television to make someone feel, as the narrator says in "TV People," "devastated, powerless, in a trance" (202). In a larger sense, Noboru Wataya and the television in Murakami's oeuvre is what Louis Althusser referred to as an Ideological State Apparatus.

The programming is, in a sense, intended to program the population. Ideology is presented in a way to suggest that it is not ideological at all. It is, instead, the natural state of affairs. It works to make people into meaningful subjects supporting the endless accumulation of neoliberal capital. When Noboru confronts Toru in *The Wind-Up Bird Chronicle*, he tells Toru, "From the first day I met you, I knew better than to hope you might amount to anything. I saw no sign of promise, nothing in you that suggested you might accomplish something worthwhile or even turn yourself into a respectable human being" (199). For Noboru, "amounting to something" or accomplishing "something worthwhile" translates to being a meaningful subject in relation to power in Japan: to working as a paralegal (the job Toru quit prior to the beginning of the novel), buying a house, taking his place as a salaryman. When Toru refuses this path, Noboru dismisses him as "garbage and rocks" (199), items that no longer have value in the marketplace.

If Noboru is to be seen as a metaphor for the television, then this scene, coupled with "TV People," suggests the ways in which television interpellates us as meaningful subjects. For the narrator of "TV People," he becomes isolated and powerless. His marriage ends. He is no longer able to read. His thinking becomes muddled. Yet he remains able to work in advertising. His immaterial labor makes him, to borrow Althusser's words, "*a (free) subject in order that he shall submit freely to the commandments of the Subject, i.e. in order that he shall (freely) accept his subjection*" (56, italics in original). Unlike the sixties activists in *Vineland*, the narrator of "TV People" was never part of an active rebellion, so the tube cannot quell his rebellion. He is subsumed by the television's power. He represents a disciplinary alienation. Foucault, throughout *Discipline and Punish*, examines ways in which institutions like prisons, mental hospitals, and the military separate individuals from their community, confront the aspects of the individuals' personalities that make them unique, and transform them into someone who can be useful and productive in terms of a bourgeois morality. The television replaces Foucault's disciplinary institutions yet performs the same work on Murakami's unnamed narrator. The narrator loses the aspects of his personality that make him unique, he is separated from his community (or at least family), and he becomes a more productive instrument of the marketplace. Toru, on the other hand, rejects his interpellation as a subject. He instead battles Noboru and the television. Unlike the activists in *Vineland*, Toru is neither part of a movement nor quelled by the tube. His resistance resides on a personal level.

Further, Toru's evolution as a character provides an alternative strategy for resistance. Unlike Pynchon's characters, who find strength in reconstituted families and communities, and unlike Occupy activists who gather in demonstration of a society built on participatory democracy, Toru turns inward. He finds an abandoned well, climbs down, and meditates. His meditations allow him to explore the impact of Japan's imperial history on the postwar generation, of which he is a part. They also allow him to dig deep into his psyche and analyze aspects of his personality that threatened his relationship with his wife. Toru's retreat down the well is not a rejection of society. He is not a monk fleeing to a cave solely in search of personal enlightenment. Instead, he follows the advice of his mentor, Mr. Honda. Honda tells Toru, "The point is, not to resist the flow. You go up when you're supposed to go up and down when you're supposed to go down. When you're supposed to go up, find the highest tower and climb to the top. When you're supposed to go down, find the deepest well and go down to the bottom. When there's no flow, stay still" (51). In other words, Toru takes a more holistic approach to his life in a neoliberal world. His career has made him feel empty, like a paralegal Thanatoid. His marriage is threatened by the presence of his brother: a politician, a television personality, and an Ideological State Apparatus in the flesh. His sense of self is blocked by his role in the shared history of his nation's involvement in the world wars of the first half of the twentieth century. To follow Honda's advice, Toru must react appropriately to his personal situation. He requires neither a social movement nor a reconstituted community. He needs instead to look inside himself and reconstruct his unique individuality outside of the influences of disciplinary mechanisms and Ideological State Apparatuses.

Much of Murakami's oeuvre deals with salarymen employed to perform immaterial labor who reject their interpellation as a subject. The same unnamed narrator serves as protagonist for four Murakami novels: *Hear the Wind Sing*, *Pinball 1973*, *A Wild Sheep Chase*, and *Dance Dance Dance*. Like the narrator of "TV People," he is a copywriter who has a problem with the women in his life vanishing. Unlike the narrator of "TV People," the protagonist of these four novels fights against the networked power of big advertising and television. In *1Q84*, both protagonists (Aomame and Tengo) reject the roles of corporate drone and escape to a world adjacent to our own, seeking something more meaningful in its subjunctive spaces. In *After Dark*, two students seek more dynamic options than moving into corporate Japan. Takahashi looks for hope in his music. Mari is not sure where to look. As in *The Wind-Up Bird Chronicle*, Mari must save a loved one who has been kidnapped by television. The pattern continues through most of Murakami's novels and several of his short stories.

Like Pynchon, Murakami presents power as networked between multinational corporations and national governments. Beyond being a metaphor for television, Noboru Wataya is a television pundit and a member of the National Diet. The villains of *A Wild Sheep Chase*—which, like *Inherent Vice*, can be read as a rewriting of Raymond Chandler's *The Long Goodbye*—are a media mogul and his would-be successor. The narrator of *Hard-Boiled Wonderland and the End of the World* is trapped between the warring factions of multinational corporations that seem to hold greater sovereignty over a slightly futuristic Japan than any national governments. In most of his novels, power can be read as a representation of what Hardt and Negri describe as Empire. The similarities between power in Murakami's fiction and power in Pynchon's fiction seem to shrink the geographical distance between the authors.

Of course, Pynchon and Murakami seek respite in different spaces. As I have discussed above, Pynchon frequently retreats to reconstructed family units, subjunctive spaces, or retreats like Yz-les-Bains in *Against the Day*, Zigotisopolis in *Bleeding Edge*, Gordita Beach in *Inherent Vice*, and the Sisterhood of Kunoichi Attentives in *Vineland*. Murakami's characters, on the other hand, retreat more inwardly. In *The Wind-Up Bird Chronicle*, Toru's uncle advises Toru to "start by thinking about the simplest things and go from there. . . . You ought to train yourself to look at things with your own eyes until something comes clear" (328). Most of Murakami's characters follow this advice. The narrator of *A Wild Sheep Chase* retreats to an abandoned cabin in remote Hokkaido where he meditates, jogs, reads, and plays guitar until he lures his nemesis out to that vulnerable space. The narrator of *Hard-Boiled Wonderland and the End of the World*, when he sees that he cannot reconcile with the warring corporations, retreats to an eternal space in his mind called "The End of the World." As mentioned above, Toru Okada goes down a well and meditates until he can find passage to his wife's spirit. In *Kafka on the Shore*, Kafka escapes his curse and finds respite in a secluded library.

The characters' journeys are not completely inward. Similar to Pynchon, all the characters seek to break from the isolating aspects of consumer capitalism and find spaces of real, human connection, places where characters can deal with the death of their best friend (*A Wild Sheep Chase*) or girlfriend (*Dance Dance Dance*), find love with a local librarian (*Hard-Boiled Wonderland and the End of the World*), reconcile with their wives (*The Wind-Up Bird Chronicle*), fall in love with their coprotagonist (*After Dark*, *1Q84*), or otherwise confront their loneliness. In other words, they find ways to live and be human, to not wallow in the living-dead world of Thanatoids and zombies.

Ali Smith

Between Pynchon's site of hope in communal spaces and Murakami's site of hope in internal examinations lies the hope in Ali Smith's novels. Like Pynchon and Murakami, Smith engages with the challenges of seeking meaning in a neoliberal society. This is perhaps most evident in a passage in her novel *There but for the* when nine-year-old Jennifer Young asks her mother, May, what human beings are for. When May does not understand the question, Jennifer clarifies, "What's the point of human beings? I mean like what are we for?" (172). By the age of nine, Jennifer has already been interpellated, has already learned to think of herself as a subject. The question itself is an artifact of late capitalism, an ideology in which humans are viewed as commodities. In Marxist terms, Jennifer demonstrates how, at the earliest ages, we have learned to think of ourselves in relation to our surplus value. As in much of Smith's work, the answers characters receive are not as compelling as the questions. The answers Jennifer receives are generic, condescending, or tautological. In the context of the chapter, which is entitled "For," Smith hints at the way language itself has become an ISA.

Many of the characters in the novel struggle with this question of meaning, with this interpellation of subjection. The character who catalyzes the events of the novel, Miles Garth, wrestles with these questions of meaning. His job is that of an "ethical consultant." In his own words, he does "work for firms who want to ensure they're ethically sound, or who would like to present themselves as more ethically sound" (86). He goes on to clarify that he investigates companies to find ways for them to be less ecologically damaging, to help communities, or, more frequently, to brand themselves in ways that suggest they are green and benevolent. He makes a joke, which ten-year-old Brooke repeats at a dinner party, that he is an "ethic cleanser" (86). The allusion to the euphemism "ethnic cleansing" invites the reader into Miles's internal battle. Throughout the novel, he is presented as a genuinely thoughtful and caring person. He has chosen a career that would ostensibly help make his world a better place. Yet by the time he attends the dinner party at the chronological beginning of the novel, he feels powerless, lost, and complicit.

Miles reacts to these feelings by occupying a room in his hosts' (the Lees) house. The occupation can be read as a political move similar to Occupy. *There but for the* is set in 2009 and was published two months prior to the occupation of Zuccotti Park. Nonetheless, when Miles takes over the room in the Lees' house, it seems to fit within the narratives of Occupy. The Lees live in a restored seventeenth-century home in an upscale neighborhood in Greenwich. They are not exactly members of the 1 percent, but they adhere fairly strictly to the ideologies of neoliberalism—to the point where, once Miles occupies their guest room, they will not break the door to the room down because it is a seventeenth-century door, far too valuable for such rough treatment. They have frequent dinner parties in which they invite token "others": black academics, gay men, a couple from the Middle East. Yet their core group of friends is white, wealthy, and heteronormative (if not exactly heterosexual). One of the Lees' closest friends is a drone dealer who brags that his drones are good for spying on protest meetings. The Lees themselves constitute a pun. Smith names them Genevieve and Eric Lee, or GenEricLee.

When his dishonest job and the neoliberal world and the dinner party become too much for Miles, he retreats to the Lees' guest room, locks himself in, and stays for several months. Word gets out about Miles's occupation. He becomes a bit of a folk hero to others who feel disaffected or disenfranchised. His silence makes him even more of an icon. Since he never outlines his demands, ideologies can be thrust upon him. Still, since Smith has already developed him as a caring, thoughtful person, Miles's retreat can be read closer to the retreats of Murakami's characters: a time when he can meditate, exercise, gather his thoughts, and envision a better way.

All this may suggest that *There but for the* would be Smith's most direct connection to the project of this study: criticizing Empire and constructing a multitude through an occupation. Several of the works in Smith's oeuvre would benefit from this type of reading, especially if placed in conversation with other global novelists like Pynchon and Murakami. Smith's *Girl Meets Boy* tells the story of two sisters. One, Imogen, is a copywriter charged with making the privatization of water politically palatable. The other, Anthea, is a free spirit who infects her sister with a rebellious streak. Several sections of the novel feature direct criticisms of Empire. As a copywriter, Imogen is promoted to the "Pure Dominant Narrative Department" (121), where she is expected to construct alternative narratives that reframe the ecological and human destruction caused by the multinational corporation she works for as something positive. Her boss explains that the company is doing nothing illegal. International treaties reinforce the legality of the devastation their corporation causes. Imogen responds to this untenable position by teaming up with Anthea, Anthea's partner, and Imogen's colleague and lover to create a resistance movement that confronts global capitalism. Taking a page from Pynchon's playbook, Smith ends the novel within a subjunctive space envisioning reconstituted families as part of the counternarrative to Empire.

Similarly, one could explore the global power underlying Smith's *Hotel World*, the reconstituted families and another occupation in Smith's novel *The Accidental*, and the sophisticated ways that Smith folds gender and sexuality into the discussion of neoliberal capitalism and the resistance to it.

Now Everybody

In his monograph *Pynchon's Postnational Imagination*, Sascha Pöhlmann makes an argument for taking Pynchon studies beyond postmodernism and into more postnational realms. He defines the postnational "as anything that works towards dismantling the hegemony of nation-ness as a metanarrative" (8). Doing so both frees Pynchon from the constraints of postmodern categorization and places Pynchon in a global conversation. By (1) following Pöhlmann's advice and (2) building off the heuristic I have created in this book, we could use Pynchon studies as the launching pad for examining power and resistance in the contemporary novel. I have given two brief examples of how this would work if it were applied broadly to the oeuvres of Haruki Murakami and Ali Smith. Several more possibilities exist. Pynchon's exploration into late capitalism as a religion would be enlightening in conversation with Paul Murray's novels. In Murray's *Skippy Dies*, an elite Catholic boarding school in Dublin shifts its focus when the priest who was headmaster is replaced by an economics teacher. The school remains a place of worship, but the reverence transitions from Christianity to neoliberalism. Murray continues this investigation into pseudoreligious capitalism in *The Mark and the Void*, his satire of the banking industry after the recent global recession.

The ecological impacts of neoliberalism in Pynchon, which I touch on in the *Mason & Dixon* and *Against the Day* chapters above, could be further explored when read in conversation with the science fiction–inspired "An Orison of Somni-451" chapters of David Mitchell's *Cloud Atlas*. Mitchell's entire oeuvre can be examined through the lens of neoliberal capitalism applied here. Kiran Desai's criticisms of treating land and labor as commodities in both New York and eastern India in her novel *The Inheritance of Loss* would be another welcome addition to the conversation. Sampath's retreat into the guava orchard in Desai's *Hullabaloo in the Guava Orchard* could even be read as another literary occupation. These themes continue to arise in the works of contemporary authors like Paul Beatty, Margaret Atwood, Chang-rae Lee, Dave Eggers, and many others.

In "How to Put the Rights of People and Nature over Corporate Rights," Occupy activists Thomas Linzey and Jeff Reifman argue, "If the Occupy Movement is to succeed over time, it must follow the lead of community rights building efforts that have begun to dismantle the body of law that perpetually subordinates people, community, and nature to wealthy corporate minorities" (70–71). Theorists like David Harvey, Wendy Brown, Slavoj Žižek, Immanuel Wallerstein, and Michael Hardt and Antonio Negri all claim that, in order to take these steps, to think in terms of communities and wealth in common, we must first confront the neoliberal ideology of endless accumulation. One place to stage this confrontation can be in the works of contemporary novelists. Pynchon and the host of other novelists I mention here provide the inventive worlds that allow us to cast off the shackles our contemporary culture clasps on our imaginations and to envision ways of living outside the confines of global consumer capitalism. Hopefully, these new paradigms take us away from our fears of becoming the living dead and allow us to live more human lives.

NOTES

Chapter 2. *Vineland* and the Insomniac Unavenged

1. Pynchon is obviously conscious of this irony. For a more complicated view of this, see Pynchon's introduction to the fiftieth-anniversary edition of Orwell's *1984*.

2. In *A People's History of the United States, 1492–Present*, Howard Zinn describes several of these free speech protests that occurred from 1909 to 1912 in cities like Spokane, Fresno, Aberdeen, and San Diego (324–25).

3. Not incidentally, Reef Traverse would be Prairie's great-great-grandfather.

4. Captain John Yossarian, the protagonist in *Catch-22*, is haunted by the awkward diction the military uses with regard to his friend Dunbar. Dunbar did not disappear. He was disappeared, suggesting that some outside force led to Dunbar's disappearance. Likewise, Minoru seems to have *been* disappeared, i.e., some force of Empire seems to have taken Minoru out of the equation.

5. Karl Polanyi demonstrates the destructive results of viewing land and labor as commodities in *The Great Transformation*. See, in particular, Polanyi's chapter "Popular Government and Market Economy."

6. It is important to qualify this notion of a "failed" movement. I do not wish to imply that all sixties student activism failed. I disagree with that notion. As exemplified below with the quotation from Ralph Waldo Emerson, sixties student activism performed important work in balancing injustices in our society. I use the term "failed" simply to denote the failure of the violent wing of the student movement.

7. While students at Cornell University, Thomas Pynchon and Kirkpatrick Sale collaborated on a musical entitled *Minstral Island*. The manuscript for the musical is housed in the archives at the University of Texas.

8. Technically, members of the Weather Underground were killed in the explosion. Sale's history treats the Weather Underground as a faction of the SDS that splintered away from the core group and distinguished itself by incorporating direct, violent action against the power structure.

9. In *Against the Day*, a young Jess Traverse takes up arms against the Colorado National Guard at Ludlow.

10. A further problem of violent resistance to Empire that *Vineland* does not explore, though it is important to acknowledge, is the impossibility of separating violent means from violent ends. Pynchon saves this exploration for *Against the Day*. Reading the two novels as a conversation with each other regarding methods of resistance allows for a more complete view of Pynchon's arguments.

11. The gender implications of Pynchon situating his site of resistance with a sisterhood should not be ignored. However, a deeper analysis of this would only serve to mirror the main arguments presented by Molly Hite in "Feminist Theory and the Politics of *Vineland*."

Chapter 3. *Mason & Dixon* and the Ghastly Fop

1. To verify historical dates and occurrences, I have relied largely on Charles Mason's journal and Edwin Danson's book, *Drawing the Line*. I also consulted Louis C. Kleber's "The Mason-Dixon Line" and Charles Clerc's *Mason & Dixon & Pynchon*.

2. Like Benjamin's storyteller, Cherrycoke "combine[s] the lore of faraway places, such as a much-traveled man brings home, with the lore of the past, as it best reveals itself to natives of the place" (85). Cherrycoke becomes the *postmodern* storyteller by rejecting the role Benjamin places on the storyteller—that of someone giving counsel. In fact, one of the difficulties scholars have with *Mason & Dixon* is the lack of direct counsel or the depth of ambiguity within the book. Also unlike Benjamin's storyteller, who disappears because of the rise of the novel's popularity, Cherrycoke self-reflexively embraces the novel and several of the various possibilities the form affords. He even lets the fictional novel *The Ghastly Fop* tell his story for a couple of chapters.

3. I am borrowing David Cowart's definition of the subjunctive: "the imagined as true" (344).

4. Edwin Danson's *Drawing the Line* also mentions this incident in Dixon's life. According to Danson, at least the Dixon family believed the incident to be based in fact.

5. By no means is Lewis alone in this interpretation. Brian Thill surveys several critics with whom Lewis's reading is in agreement.

6. It is not clear which revolutionary. Pynchon writes the conversation as quick exchanges of dialogue. Most statements do not feature dialogue tags, so it is not always clear to the reader who is speaking. I assume that Captain Volcanoe says this, but I cannot be certain of that assumption.

7. Samuel Thomas, Adam Lifshey, Tony Tanner, and Christy L. Burns, among others.

8. See, for example, Karl Polanyi's *The Great Transformation*, which argues that the notion of a self-regulating marketplace is an impossibility because it is dependent on labor, land, and money acting as commodities, though labor, land, and money are by definition not commodities and never act as such. Polanyi additionally portrays the belief in this self-regulating marketplace as an almost spiritual faith.

9. My source for Channing's call for a uniquely American literature as well as much of the discussion of *Hobomok* is Carolyn L. Karcher's *The First Woman in the Republic*.

10. Though, I must add, I do not read Hobomok's disappearance at the end in this way.

11. Or perhaps bisexual. Pynchon does not clarify.

Chapter 4. *Against the Day* and a World Like Ours, with One or Two Adjustments

1. I use the term *economic liberalism* to describe an ideology based on the belief that a self-regulating free-market society can and should exist. While it may be a bit confusing because liberal and liberalism can often denote a political view drifting toward the left in American society, I am not using the term *liberal* with that connotation in this essay. Many use the term *capitalism* to express economic liberalism. Because the term *capitalism* is so emotive and carries so many different connotations, I will attempt to avoid using it when I mean liberalism or neoliberalism. I use the specific term *economic liberalism* because much of this chapter relies on Karl Polanyi's analysis of economic liberalism in his book *The Great*

Transformation. A more familiar term that denotes essentially the same concept would be *classical liberalism*, referring to the ideology promulgated by eighteenth- and nineteenth-century economists like Adam Smith and David Ricardo.

2. Polanyi uses this term: "[L]eaving the fate of soil and people to the market would be tantamount to annihilating them" (137).

3. See, specifically, Jeffrey Severs's "'The abstractions she was instructed to embody': Women, Capitalism, and Artistic Representation in *Against the Day*," in which Severs traces Dally Rideout's journey through Hell and toward some form of autonomy.

4. "De-doxify" is Linda Hutcheon's term.

5. This assumes, of course, that the media disproportionately represents the views of the wealthy. This is certainly the case in the early twenty-first century, when a handful of extremely wealthy corporations control more than 90 percent of the media in the United States. It was likely the case in Colorado in the late nineteenth and early twentieth centuries. This is evidenced by a letter that Howard Zinn unearthed while researching the Ludlow Massacre of 1914. In the letter, a vice president of Colorado Fuel and Iron—John D. Rockefeller Jr.'s corporation and the coal company that was actively waging war against its workers—assures Rockefeller, "Another mighty power has been rounded up on behalf of the operators by the getting together of fourteen of the editors of the most important newspapers in the state" ("The Ludlow Massacre" 192). Rockefeller's VP in Colorado was not unjustified in believing that he had the press in his pocket. Zinn's survey of newspapers as far away from Colorado as the *New York Times* demonstrates that the press had almost no sympathy for the strikers.

6. Zinn demonstrates that the majority of the "National Guardsmen" involved in the Ludlow battles were not, strictly speaking, National Guardsmen but employees of the Baldwin-Felts Detective Agency and various other strongmen hired by John D. Rockefeller Jr.'s Colorado Fuel and Iron and enlisted in the service of the National Guard solely for the purpose of subjugating the striking miners.

7. Perhaps I would be more accurate to claim that it lives in three places: it trilocates, so to speak, because Zinn's essay was written in and addressing 1970. I choose not to make that detailed of a distinction, mostly because I do not see the relevance in doing so.

8. See Piketty's graph, figure 10.5, page 348 of *Capital in the Twenty-First Century*.

Chapter 5. *Inherent Vice* and Being in Place

1. At International Pynchon Week in Durham, 2013, Doug Haynes gave a lecture on the intersections between Graeber's *Debt* and Pynchon's novels. While Haynes focuses mostly on other works by Pynchon, I owe him a debt of gratitude for alerting me to the benefits of applying Graeber's ideas to Pynchon's novels.

2. See McLaughlin, Lacayo, Flusfeder, Menand, Kirn, and Sheffield, among others.

3. See N. Katherine Hayles's essay "'Who Was Saved?': Families, Snitches, and Recuperation in Pynchon's *Vineland*."

4. Nonetheless, it is interesting to note that Crocker Fenway agrees, in principle, with Mickey's belief that land ownership is dishonest. Crocker tells Doc, "People like you lose all claim to respect the first time they pay anybody rent" (346), which suggests that Crocker understands that the ownership of land is dubious at best and he cannot respect anyone whose actions would suggest a complicity in this dubious system.

5. Trillium is another nonpaying client. However, Doc's contribution to the common does not really help Trillium. While she is reunited with her lover, Puck beats her to the point of hospitalization.

6. Hardt and Negri among them. See *Empire* (137–58).

Chapter 6. *Bleeding Edge* and Getting Constructively Lost

1. I have previously discussed some of the ideas I am discussing here in my review of *Bleeding Edge* on *The Nervous Breakdown*.

2. See both my *Mason & Dixon* and *Against the Day* chapters above.

3. Which is perhaps a nod to the Great South Coast Plaza Eyeshadow Raid in *Vineland*.

Chapter 7. A Snappy 'Ukulele Accompaniment

1. The proper traditional pronunciation of the first syllable of 'ukulele sounds like "oo." The apostrophe preceding the first "u" signifies that traditional pronunciation, phonetically "oo-koo-lay-lay." When using that pronunciation, it is an 'ukulele. A more common and colloquial pronunciation adds a phonetic "y" to the first syllable, making it sound like "you" or "you-koo-lay-lay." When using the colloquial pronunciation, it is a ukulele. While writing this piece, I use the traditional spelling. When citing others, I use whichever spelling the author used.

WORKS CITED

Althusser, Louis. *On Ideology*. 1971. Brooklyn, N.Y.: Verso, 2008. Print.
Altman, Robert, dir. *The Long Goodbye*. United Artists, 1973. DVD.
Arrighi, Giovanni. *Adam Smith in Beijing: Lineages of the Twenty-First Century*. New York: Verso, 2007. Print.
Ashraf, Hena. "Claiming Space for Diversity at Occupy Wall Street." In *This Changes Everything: Occupy Wall Street and the 99% Movement*. Ed. Sarah van Gelder and the staff of *Yes! Magazine*. San Francisco: Berrett-Koehler, 2011. 33–35. Print.
Babb, Valerie. *Whiteness Visible: The Meaning of Whiteness in American Literature and Culture*. New York: New York University Press, 1998. Print.
Benjamin, Walter. *Illuminations*. Trans. Harry Zohn. New York: Schocken, 1969. Print.
Benton, Graham. "Daydreams and Dynamite: Anarchist Strategies of Resistance and Paths for Transformation in *Against the Day*." In *Pynchon's* Against the Day: *A Corrupted Pilgrim's Guide*. Ed. Jeffrey Severs and Christopher Leise. Newark: University of Delaware Press, 2011. 191–213. Print.
Bleecker, Ann Eliza. "The History of Maria Kittle." In *Women's Early American Historical Narratives*. Ed. Sharon M. Harris. New York: Penguin, 2003. 1–35. Print.
Bluestein, Gene. "Tangled Vines." *Progressive* 54.6 (June 1990): 42. Print.
Boler, Megan. *Feeling Power: Emotions and Education*. New York: Routledge, 1999. Print.
Boler, Megan, Averie Macdonald, Christina Nistou, and Anne Harris. "Connective Labor and Social Media: Women's Roles in the 'Leaderless' Occupy Movement." *Convergence: The International Journal of Research into New Media Technologies* 20.4 (2014): 438–60. Print.
Boyle, T. Coraghessan. "The Great Divide." *New York Times Book Review* (1997): 9. *Academic Search Premier*. EBSCO. Web. 1 June 2011.
Brown, Wendy. "Neo-Liberalism and the End of Liberal Democracy." *Theory & Event* 7.1 (2003): n.p. Web. 5 May 2011.
Burns, Christy L. "Postmodern Historiography: Politics and Parallactic Method in Thomas Pynchon's *Mason & Dixon*." *Postmodern Culture: An Electronic Journal of Interdisciplinary Criticism* 14.1 (Sept. 2003). *Project Muse*. Web. 9 June 2010.
Carswell, Sean. "Destroying Mothers: The Emma Goldman Papers Project." *Clamor* 19 (Mar./Apr. 2003): 50–53. Print.
———. "Getting Constructively Lost: A Review of Thomas Pynchon's *Bleeding Edge*." *The Nervous Breakdown*. 13 Sept. 2013. Web. 8 Jan. 2016.
Chandler, Raymond. *The Long Goodbye*. 1953. New York: Vintage, 1992. Print.
———. *The Simple Art of Murder*. 1950. New York: Vintage, 1988. Print.
Child, Lydia Maria. *Hobomok and Other Writings on Indians*. 1824. Piscataway, N.J.: Rutgers University Press, 1986. Print.

Chomsky, Noam. *Power Systems: Conversations on Global Democratic Uprisings and the New Challenges to the U.S. Empire.* New York: Metropolitan Books, 2013. Print.

Clerc, Charles. *Mason & Dixon & Pynchon.* Lanham, Md.: University Press of America, 2000. Print.

Coen, Joel, dir. *The Big Lebowski.* Prod. Ethan Coen. Universal Studios, 1998. DVD.

Cowart, David. *The Art of Allusion.* Carbondale: Southern Illinois University Press, 1980. Print.

———. "Attenuated Postmodernism: Pynchon's *Vineland*." In Greene, *The Vineland Papers*, 3–13. Print.

———. "The Luddite Vision: *Mason & Dixon*." *American Literature: A Journal of Literary History, Criticism, and Bibliography* 71.2 (June 1999): 341–63. Project Muse. Web. 9 June 2010.

Cunningham, David. *There's Something Happening Here: The New Left, the Klan, and FBI Counterintelligence.* Berkeley: University of California Press, 2004. Print.

Danson, Edwin. *Drawing the Line: How Mason and Dixon Surveyed the Most Famous Border in America.* New York: Wiley, 2001. Print.

Dean, Jodi. "Claiming Division, Naming a Wrong." In *Occupy! Scenes from Occupied America.* Ed. Astra Taylor, Keith Gessen, and editors from *n+1*, *Dissent*, *Triple Canopy* and *The New Inquiry*. Brooklyn: Verso, 2011. 87–92. Print.

Derrida, Jacques. *Dissemination.* Trans. Barbara Johnson. Chicago: University of Chicago Press, 1981. Print.

Desai, Kiran. *Hullabaloo in the Guava Orchard.* New York: Grove, 1998.

———. *The Inheritance of Loss.* New York: Grove, 2006.

Downing, David B. "World Bank University: The War on Terror and the Battles for the Global Commons." Author's private collection, ms.

Emerson, Ralph Waldo. *Nature and Selected Essays.* 1836. Ed. Larzer Ziff. New York: Penguin, 1982. Print.

Finder, Alan. "THE 1998 CAMPAIGN: THE MONEY; Spitzer Concedes That His Father Has Helped to Pay for Campaigns." *New York Times* 28 Oct. 1998: B6. Print.

Fleischer, Ruben, dir. *Zombieland.* Sony Pictures, 2009. DVD.

Flusfeder, David. "Chandler in Flares." *New Statesman* 3 Aug. 2009: 42–43. Print.

Formby, George. *George Formby: England's Famed Clown Prince of Song.* JSP, 2004. CD

Foucault, Michel. *Discipline and Punish.* Trans. Alan Sheridan. 1977. New York: Vintage, 1995. Print.

———. *"Society Must Be Defended": Lectures at the Collège de France, 1975–1976.* Trans. David Macey. New York: Picador, 1997. Print.

Foxx, Redd. *In a Nutshell.* King, 1975. Record.

Franklin, Benjamin. *The Autobiography of Benjamin Franklin.* 1784. New York: Penguin, 2003. Print.

Freer, Joanna. *Thomas Pynchon and the American Counterculture.* New York: Cambridge University Press, 2014. Print.

Gelderloos, Peter. *Consensus: A New Handbook for Grassroots Social, Political, and Environmental Groups.* Tucson: See Sharp Press, 2006. Print.

Goldman, Emma. *Anarchism and Other Essays.* 1917. New York: Dover, 1969. Print.

Graeber, David. *Debt: The First 5,000 Years.* Rev. ed. Brooklyn: Melville House, 2014. Print.

———. *The Democracy Project.* New York: Spiegel and Grau, 2013. Print.

Greene, Geoffrey. *The Vineland Papers: Critical Takes on Pynchon's Novel*. Elmwood, Ill.: Dalkey Archive Press, 1994. Print.

Hall, Oakley. *Warlock*. 1958. New York: New York Review Books, 2006. Print.

Harcourt, Bernard E. "Political Disobedience." In *Occupy: Three Inquiries into Disobedience*. Ed. W. J. T. Mitchell. Chicago: University of Chicago Press, 2013. 45–92. Print.

Hardt, Michael. "Introduction: Thomas Jefferson, or, the Transition of Democracy." In *The Declaration of Independence*, by Michael Hardt and Thomas Jefferson. New York: Verso, 2007. vii–xxv. Print.

Hardt, Michael, and Antonio Negri. *Commonwealth*. Cambridge, Mass.: Harvard University Press, 2009. Print.

———. *Empire*. Cambridge, Mass.: Harvard University Press, 2001. Print.

———. "The Fight for 'Real Democracy' at the Heart of Occupy Wall Street." *Foreign Affairs*. 11 Oct. 2011. Web. 26 Jan. 2012.

———. *Multitude: War and Democracy in the Age of Empire*. New York: Penguin, 2004. Print.

Harvey, David. *A Brief History of Neoliberalism*. New York: Oxford University Press, 2005. Print.

Harvey, David, Michael Hardt, and Antonio Negri. "Commonwealth: An Exchange." *Artforum* 48.3 (Nov. 2009): 210–21. Korotonomedya. Web. 14 June 2010.

Hayles, N. Katherine. "'Who Was Saved?': Families, Snitches, and Recuperation in Pynchon's *Vineland*." In Greene, *The Vineland Papers*, 14–30. Print.

Haynes, Doug. "Under the Beach, the Paving-Stones! The Fate of Fordism in Pynchon's *Inherent Vice*." *Critique* 55.1 (2014): 1–16. Print.

Heller, Joseph. *Catch-22*. 1961. New York: Dell, 1990. Print.

Hite, Molly. "Feminist Theory and the Politics of *Vineland*." In Greene, *The Vineland Papers*, 135–53. Print.

Hughlett, Mason A., ed. *The Journal of Charles Mason and Jeremiah Dixon*. Philadelphia: American Philosophical Society, 1969. Print.

Hume, Katherine. "The Religious and Political Vision of Pynchon's *Against the Day*." *Philological Quarterly* 86.1/2 (2007): 163–87. Print.

Hutcheon, Linda. *The Politics of Postmodernism*. New York: Routledge, 1989. Print.

Ickstadt, Heinz. "Setting Sail Against the Day: The Narrative World of Thomas Pynchon." In *Against the Grain: Reading Pynchon's Counternarratives*. Ed. Sascha Pöhlmann. Amsterdam: Rodopi B.V., 2010. Print.

Jameson, Fredric. *Postmodernism, or, The Cultural Logic of Late Capitalism*. Durham: Duke University Press, 1991. Print.

———. "The Synoptic Chandler." In *Shades of Noir: A Reader*. Ed. Joan Copjec. New York: Verso, 1993. 33–56. Print.

Jhally, Sut, dir. *Advertising and the End of the World*. Northampton, Mass.: Media Education Foundation, 1998. DVD.

Jones, Malcolm. "Pynchon's Shaggy Dog Story." *Newsweek* 115.2 (1990): 66. Print.

Kamine, Mark. "Pynchon Up Close." *The New Leader* May/June–July/Aug 2009: 29–30. Print.

Karcher, Carolyn L. *The First Woman in the Republic: A Cultural Biography of Lydia Maria Child*. Durham: Duke University Press, 1994. Print.

King, John, and Jim Tranquada. "A New History of the Origins and Development of the 'Ukulele, 1838–1915." *The Hawaiian Journal of History* 37 (2003): 1–32. Print.

Kirn, Walter. "Drugs to Do, Cases to Solve." *New York Times Book Review* 23 (Aug. 2009): 9. Print.

Kleber, Louis. "The Mason Dixon Line." *History Today* 18.2 (1968): 117–23. Print.

Klein, Naomi. "The Most Important Thing in the World." In *This Changes Everything: Occupy Wall Street and the 99% Movement*. Ed. Sarah van Gelder and the staff of *Yes! Magazine*. San Francisco: Berrett-Koehler, 2011. 45–49. Print.

Lacayo, Richard. "Magical Mystery Tour." *Time* 17 Aug. 2009: 60. Print.

Lasson, Sally Ann. "Duke of Uke: Why Is One of London's Quaintest Ukulele Shops Facing Closure?" *The Independent*, 9 July 2011. Web. 19 July 2011.

Lazzarato, Maurizio. "Immaterial Labor." In *Radical Thought in Italy: A Potential Politics*. Ed. Paolo Virno and Michael Hardt. Minneapolis: University of Minnesota Press, 1996. 132–46. Print.

———. *The Making of the Indebted Man: An Essay on the Neoliberal Condition*. South Pasadena: Semiotext(e), 2012. Print.

LeClair, Tom. "For a Good Time, Read Tom." *American Book Review* Mar./Apr. 2010: 25. Print.

Leithauser, Brad. "Any Place You Want." *New York Review of Books* 37.4, (15 Mar. 1990): 7–10. Print.

Leonard, Sarah. "Scenes from an Occupation." In *Occupy! Scenes from Occupied America*. Ed. Astra Taylor, Keith Gessen, and editors from *n+1*, *Dissent*, *Triple Canopy* and *The New Inquiry*. Brooklyn: Verso, 2011. 83–98. Print.

Lewis, Barry. "Teaching Pynchon's *Mason & Dixon*." *Explicator* 67.3 (Spring 2009): 154–57. Print.

Lifshey, Adam. "Bordering the Subjunctive in Thomas Pynchon's *Mason & Dixon*." *Journal x: A Journal in Culture and Criticism* 9.1 (Autumn 2004): 1–15. Print.

Linzey, Thomas, and Jeff Reifman. "How to Put the Rights of People and Nature over Corporate Rights." In *This Changes Everything: Occupy Wall Street and the 99% Movement*. Ed. Sarah van Gelder and the staff of *Yes! Magazine*. San Francisco: Berrett-Koehler, 2011. 70–73. Print.

Locke, John. *Two Treatises of Government*. 1690. New York: Cambridge University Press, 1988. Print.

Lyotard, Jean-François. *The Postmodern Condition: A Report on Knowledge*. 1979. Trans. Geoff Bennington and Brian Massumi. Minneapolis: University of Minnesota Press, 1984. Print.

Mattessich, Stefan. *Lines of Flight: Discursive Time and Countercultural Desire in the Work of Thomas Pynchon*. Durham: Duke University Press, 2002. Print.

McHale, Brian. *Constructing Postmodernism*. New York: Routledge, 1993. Print.

———. "Genre as History: Pynchon's Genre Poaching." In *Pynchon's Against the Day: A Corrupted Pilgrim's Guide*. Ed. Jeffrey Severs and Christopher Leise. Newark: University of Delaware Press, 2011. 15–28. Print.

———. *Postmodernist Fiction*. New York: Methuen, 1987. Print.

McLaughlin, Robert L. "Book Review." *Review of Contemporary Fiction* Annual No. 3: 163–64. Print.

Menand, Louis. "Soft-Boiled." *New Yorker* 85.23 (2009): 74–75. Print.

Mendelson, Edward. "Levity's Rainbow." *The New Republic* 9 & 16 July 1990: 40–46. Print.

Mitchell, W. J. T. "Image, Space, Revolution: The Arts of Occupation." In *Occupy: Three Inquiries into Disobedience*. Ed. W. J. T. Mitchell. Chicago: University of Chicago Press, 2013. 93–130. Print.

———. "Preface." *Occupy: Three Inquiries into Disobedience*. Ed. W. J. T. Mitchell. Chicago: University of Chicago Press, 2013. vii–xv. Print.

Moraru, Christian. *Rewriting: Postmodern Narrative and Cultural Critique in the Age of Cloning*. Albany: SUNY Press, 2001. Print.

Morrison, Toni. *Playing in the Dark: Whiteness and the Literary Imagination*. New York: Vintage, 1993. Print.

Murakami, Haruki. *1Q84*. Trans. Jay Rubin and Philip Gabriel. New York: Vintage, 2012. Print.

———. *After Dark*. Trans. Jay Rubin. New York: Knopf, 2007. Print.

———. *Dance Dance Dance*. Trans. Alfred Birnbaum. New York: Kodansha, 1994. Print.

———. *Hard-Boiled Wonderland and the End of the World*. 1985. Trans. Alfred Birnbaum. New York: Vintage, 1993. Print.

———. *Hear the Wind Sing*. Trans. Alfred Birnbaum. New York: Kodansha, 1987. Print.

———. *Kafka on the Shore*. Trans. Philip Gabriel. New York: Vintage, 2005. Print.

———. *Norwegian Wood*. 1987. Trans. Jay Rubin. New York: Vintage, 2000. Print.

———. *Pinball, 1973*. Trans. Alfred Birnbaum. New York: Kodansha, 1985. Print.

———. "TV People." In *The Elephant Vanishes*. Trans. Alfred Birnbaum. New York: Knopf, 1993. 195–216. Print.

———. *A Wild Sheep Chase*. 1982. Trans. Alfred Birnbaum. New York: Vintage, 2002. Print.

———. *The Wind-Up Bird Chronicle*. 1994. Trans. Jay Rubin. New York: Vintage, 1998. Print.

Murray, Paul. *The Mark and the Void*. New York: Farrar, Straus and Giroux, 2015. Print.

———. *Skippy Dies*. New York: Farrar, Straus and Giroux, 2010. Print.

Occupy Wall Street General Assembly. "Principles of Solidarity." In *This Changes Everything: Occupy Wall Street and the 99% Movement*. Ed. Sarah van Gelder and the staff of Yes! Magazine. San Francisco: Berrett-Koehler, 2011. 25–26. Print.

Olster, Stacey. "The Way We Were(n't): Origins and Empire in Thomas Pynchon's *Mason & Dixon*." In *American Fiction of the 1990s: Reflections of History and Culture*. Ed. Jay Prosser. London: Routledge, 2008. 107–99. Print.

Palmeri, Frank. "General Wolfe and the Weavers: Re-envisioning History in Pynchon's *Mason & Dixon*." In *The Multiple Worlds of Pynchon's* Mason & Dixon. Ed. Elizabeth Jane Wall Hinds. Rochester, N.Y.: Camden House, 2005. 185–98. Print.

Piketty, Thomas. *Capital in the Twenty-First Century*. Trans. Arthur Goldhammer. Cambridge, Mass.: Harvard University Press, 2014. Print.

Pöhlmann, Sascha. "Introduction: The Complex Text." In *Against the Grain: Reading Pynchon's Counternarratives*. Ed. Sascha Pöhlmann. Amsterdam: Rodopi B.V., 2010. Print.

———. *Pynchon's Postnational Imagination*. Heidelberg: Universitätsverlag Winter, 2010. Print.

Polanyi, Karl. *The Great Transformation: The Political and Economic Origins of Our Time*. 1944. Boston: Beacon, 2001. Print.

Polletta, Francesca. "Participatory Democracy's Moment." *Journal of International Affairs* 68.1 (Fall/Winter 2014): 79–92.

"Pono Frequently Asked Questions." *Koolauukulele.com*. Ko'olau Guitar and Ukulele Company, n.d. Web. 19 July 2011.

Pynchon, Thomas. *Against the Day*. New York: Penguin, 2006. Print.

———. *The Crying of Lot 49*. 1966. New York: Harper, 2006. Print.

———. *Gravity's Rainbow*. 1973. New York: Viking, 1987. Print.

———. "The Heart's Eternal Vow." *New York Times*. Apr. 10, 1988. Print.

———. *Inherent Vice*. New York: Penguin, 2009. Print.

———. "Is It Okay to Be a Luddite?" *New York Times*. 28 Oct. 1984. p. BR1. Print.

———. "A Journey into the Mind of Watts." *New York Times Magazine*, 12 June 1966, pp. 34–35, 78, 80–82, 84. Print.

———. *Mason & Dixon*. New York: Holt, 1997. Print.

———. "Mortality and Mercy in Vienna." *Epoch* 9.4 (Spring 1959). Print.

———. "Nearer My Couch to Thee." *New York Times*. June 6, 1993. p. BR3. Print.

———. *Slow Learner*. New York: Holt, 1984. Print.

———. *V.* 1964. New York: Harper, 1999. Print.

———. *Vineland*. 1991. New York: Penguin, 1997. Print.

Rafferty, Terrence. "Long Lost." *The New Yorker* 19 Feb. 1990: 108–12. Print.

Raimi, Sam, dir. *Army of Darkness*. Universal Studios, 1992. DVD.

Robertson, William Preston. *The Big Lebowski: The Making of the Coen Brothers Film*. New York: Norton, 1998. Print.

Rubin, Jay. *Haruki Murakami and the Music of Words*. London: Harvill, 2002. Print.

Rushdie, Salman. "Still Crazy After All These Years." *New York Times* 14 Jan. 1990: BR1, 36–37. Print.

Sale, Kirkpatrick. *SDS*. New York: Random House, 1973. Print.

Schaub, Thomas Hill. "*The Crying of Lot 49* and Other California Novels." In *The Cambridge Companion to Thomas Pynchon*. Ed. Inger H. Dalsgaard, Luc Herman, and Brian McHale. New York: Cambridge University Press, 2012. 30–43. Print.

Sedgwick, Catherine Maria. *Hope Leslie, or, Early Times in the Massachusetts*. 1827. New York: Penguin, 1998.

Severs, Jeffrey. "'The abstractions she was instructed to embody': Women, Capitalism, and Artistic Representation in *Against the Day*." In *Pynchon's* Against the Day: *A Corrupted Pilgrim's Guide*. Ed. Jeffrey Severs and Christopher Leise. Newark: University of Delaware Press, 2011. 215–38. Print.

Sheffield, Rob. "The Bigger Lebowski." *Rolling Stone* 6 Aug. 2009: 38–39. Print.

Shoop, Casey. "Thomas Pynchon, Postmodernism, and the Rise of the New Right in California." *Contemporary Literature* 53.1 (2012): 51–86. Print.

Siegel, Jules. "Who Is Thomas Pynchon and Why Did He Take Off with My Wife?" *Playboy* Mar. 1977: 97, 122, 168–70, 172, 174. Print.

Sisario, Ben. "Ukulele Crazy." *New York Times* 17 Apr. 2011. Web. 19 July 2011.

Sitrin, Marina. "One No, Many Yeses." In *Occupy! Scenes from Occupied America*. Ed. Astra Taylor, Keith Gessen, and editors from *n+1*, *Dissent*, *Triple Canopy* and *The New Inquiry*. Brooklyn: Verso, 2011. 7–11. Print.

Smith, Ali. *The Accidental*. New York: Anchor, 2005. Print.

———. *Girl Meets Boy*. New York: Canongate, 2007. Print.

———. *Hotel World*. New York: Anchor, 2001. Print.

———. *There but for the*. New York: Anchor, 2011. Print.

Smith, James McCune. *The Works of James McCune Smith: Black Intellectual and Abolitionist*. Ed. John Stauffer. New York: Oxford University Press, 2006.
Smith, Shawn. *Pynchon and History: Metahistorical Rhetoric and Postmodern Narrative Form in the Novels of Thomas Pynchon*. New York: Routledge, 2005. Print.
Solomon, Eric. "Argument by Anachronism: The Presence of the 1930s in *Vineland*." In Greene, *The Vineland Papers*, 161–66. Print.
The Sonics. "Skinny Minnie." Rec. 1966. *Boom*. Norton, 1999. CD.
Star Wars: Episode V—The Empire Strikes Back. Dir. George Lucas. Perf. Mark Hamill, Harrison Ford, and Carrie Fisher. Lucasfilm, 1980. Film.
Sterne, Laurence. *The Life and Opinions of Tristram Shandy, Gentleman*. 1759. Ed. Melvin New et al. New York: Penguin, 2003. Print.
Stiglitz, Joseph. "Of the 1%, by the 1%, for the 1%." *Vanity Fair* 30 Apr. 2011. Web. 8 Jan. 2016.
Swift, Jonathan. *A Tale of a Tub and Other Works*. 1704. Cambridge: Cambridge University Press, 2010. Print.
Tanner, Tony. *The American Mystery: American Literature from Emerson to DeLillo*. New York: Cambridge University Press, 2000. Print.
Tate, J. O. "Sufferin' Succotash." *National Review* 30 Apr. 1990: 59. Print.
Taussig, Michael. "I'm So Angry I Made a Sign." In *Occupy: Three Inquiries into Disobedience*. Ed. W. J. T. Mitchell. Chicago: University of Chicago Press, 2013. 3–44. Print.
Taylor, Astra. "Scenes from an Occupation." In *Occupy! Scenes from Occupied America*. Ed. Astra Taylor, Keith Gessen, and editors from *n+1, Dissent, Triple Canopy* and *The New Inquiry*. Brooklyn: Verso, 2011. 1–98. Print.
———, dir. *Examined Life: Philosophy Is in the Streets*. Zeitgeist Films, 2010. Film.
Thill, Brian. "The Sweetness of Immorality: *Mason & Dixon* and the American Sins of Consumption." In *The Multiple Worlds of Pynchon's* Mason & Dixon. Ed. Elizabeth Jane Wall Hinds. Rochester, N.Y.: Camden House, 2005. 49–75. Print.
Thomas, Samuel. *Pynchon and the Political*. New York: Routledge, 2007.
Thoreen, David. "The Fourth Amendment and Other Modern Inconveniences: Undeclared War, Organized Labor, and the Abrogation of Civil Rights in *Vineland*." In *Thomas Pynchon: Reading from the Margins*. Ed. Niran Abbas. Madison, N.J.: Fairleigh Dickinson University Press, 2003. Print.
van Gelder, Sarah. "Introduction: How Occupy Wall Street Changes Everything." In *This Changes Everything: Occupy Wall Street and the 99% Movement*. Ed. Sarah van Gelder and the staff of *Yes! Magazine*. San Francisco: Berrett-Koehler, 2011. 1–12. Print.
Vonnegut, Kurt. *Slaughterhouse-Five*. 1969. New York: Dial, 2005. Print.
Wallerstein, Immanuel. *World-Systems Analysis*. Durham: Duke University Press, 2004. Print.
Weisenburger, Steven. *A Gravity's Rainbow Companion: Sources and Contexts for Pynchon's Novel*. Athens: University of Georgia Press, 1988. Print.
Williams, Raymond. "Advertising: The Magic System." In *Cultural Studies Reader*. Ed. Simon During. New York: Routledge, 1999. 410–23. Print.
Wilson, Rob. "On the Pacific Edge of Catastrophe, or Redemption: California Dreaming in Thomas Pynchon's *Inherent Vice*." *boundary 2* 37.2 (2010): 217–25. Print.
Witzling, David. "The Sensibility of Postmodern Whiteness in *V.*, or Thomas Pynchon's Identity Problem." *Contemporary Literature* 47.3 (2006): 381–414. Print.
Wood, Alastair. "Why You Should Give a Crap About Copyright Terms." *Ukulelehunt.com*. 3 Nov. 2010. Web. 10 June 2014.

Wright, Edgar, dir. *Shaun of the Dead*. Universal Studios, 2004. DVD.
The Yes Men. Dir. Chris Smith. Los Angeles: MGM Home Entertainment, 2005. DVD.
Zinn, Howard. "The Ludlow Massacre." In *The Zinn Reader*. Ed. Howard Zinn. New York: Seven Stories, 1997. 183–202. Print.
———. *A People's History of the United States, 1492–Present*. Rev. ed. New York: Harper Perennial, 1995. Print.
Žižek, Slavoj. "Don't Fall in Love with Yourselves." In *Occupy! Scenes from Occupied America*. Ed. Astra Taylor, Keith Gessen, and editors from *n+1*, *Dissent*, *Triple Canopy* and *The New Inquiry*. Brooklyn: Verso, 2011. 66–70. Print.
———. "Introduction: The Spectre of Ideology." In *Mapping Ideology*. 1994. Ed. Slavoj Žižek. Brooklyn, N.Y.: Verso, 2012. 1–33. Print.

INDEX

Against the Day (Pynchon): anarchism in, 90, 93–100, 116–20; bilocation, 15, 81–82, 103–4; capitalism as quasi-religious belief in, 147; complicity in, 26; countermovements in, 94; economic liberalism in, 81–94, 174; freedom in, 16, 108–9; guns in, 100; Ludlow Massacre, 102–4; multitude in, 116–20; narrator, 124; neoliberalism in, 81–82, 91–94, 110, 115; nomadism in, 109–11; political violence in, 26; power system in, 9; 'ukulele in, 168–70, 174; Western genre in, 101–3; Yz-les-Bains, 3, 115–19, 154, 169
Althusser, Louis, 21, 51, 154, 179–80
Altman, Robert, 124
anarchism, 16; in *Against the Day*, 90, 93–100; as countermovement, 94–95
Arab Spring, 7, 21
Army of Darkness (Raimi), 177
Ashraf, Hena, 107–8

Bakunin, Mikhail, 95
Barlow, Joel, 71
Benjamin, Walter, 49, 188n2
Benton, Graham, 96–97
Berkman, Alexander, 117
Big Lebowski, The (Coen brothers), 17, 122–28
Big Sleep, The (Chandler), 125
biopolitics, 28, 45–47, 142, 150–54
Bleecker, Ann Eliza, 71
Bleeding Edge (Pynchon): biopolitics in, 142; capitalism as quasi-religious belief in, 147–49; complicity in, 146; Empire in, 142–43; freedom in, 149; immaterial labor in, 142; multitude in, 142–43;

power system in, 10; resistance in, 17–18; 'ukulele in, 173; Zigotisopolis, 17–18, 142, 154–57
Bogart, Humphrey, 125
Boler, Megan, 46, 64, 70, 154
Boyle, T. C., 58
Bretton Woods, 9
Brown, Wendy, 9, 86, 104–5, 108, 115–16, 144, 185–86
Buffet, Warren, 173
Burns, Christy L., 60, 66, 68, 188n7
Bush, George H. W., 40

Casas, Bartolomé de las, 71
Chandler, Raymond, 122–28; *The Big Sleep*, 125; *The Long Goodbye*, 17
Channing, W., 69–70
Child, Lydia Maria, 70
Chomsky, Noam, 42, 106–8, 138
Claire, Voltairine de, 86
Coen, Joel and Ethan, 17, 122–28
commonwealth, 172
consensus, 107–8, 166
Cooper, James Fenimore, 69–70
Cowart, David, 163, 170, 188n3
Crying of Lot 49 (Pynchon): cultural context, 8; ending, 19; New Right in, 137–38; power system in, 9; mentioned, 31, 85, 124
Cunningham, David, 37, 42

Dean, Jodi, 87, 91
Derrida, Jacques, 156
Desai, Kiran, 18
Downing, David B., 12

economic liberalism, 16, 51–52, 188n1; in *Against the Day*, 81–94, 174

{199}

Emerson, Ralph Waldo, 41, 110, 177, 187n6
Empire: in *Bleeding Edge*, 142–43; chartered companies, 49–54; control over intellectual inquiry, 53–54; co-optation of 'ukulele, 171–74; definition, 9, 27–28, 39; in *Inherent Vice*, 127, 130–35; in *Mason & Dixon*, 52; perpetual state of warfare, 32–35, 163–65; postmodernism, 73; mentioned, 10, 19, 67, 158, 178, 182
Examined Life, The (Taylor), 20, 121, 134

Falk, Candace, 86
Faulkner, William, 125
Flynn, Elizabeth Gurley, 86
Formby, George, 161, 167, 170–71
Foucault, Michel, 151, 156, 180
Foxx, Redd, 57
Franklin, Benjamin, 54–55, 70–71
Freer, Joanna, 109, 137
Freuchen, Peter, 129

Gelderloos, Peter, 108
Goldman, Emma, 86, 105, 117
Graeber, David, 22, 76–79, 107, 122–23, 128–30, 138, 140–41, 149–50, 154, 157, 177–78, 189n1
Gravity's Rainbow (Pynchon): Counterforce, 8, 29; cultural context, 8; ending, 20, 115; impact of, 3–4; narrator, 124; opening, 49; power system in, 9, 34; preterite, 12, 99, 164; 'ukulele in, 160–63, 170, 174; mentioned, 31, 53, 83, 112

Hall, Oakley, 101–2
Harcourt, Bernard, 1, 20–23
Hardt, Michael, and Antonio Negri: biopolitics, 45–46; the common, 123, 133–35, 146; commonwealth, 172; definition of Empire, 9, 27–28; definition of multitude, 10–11, 28–29, 72, 116; discussion of Thomas Jefferson, 77–78; Empire in *Bleeding Edge*, 142–43; Empire in *Inherent Vice*, 127, 130–35; Empire's perpetual state of warfare, 32–35; "The Fight for 'Real Democracy' at the Heart of Occupy Wall Street," 11; Harvey's criticism of, 19; immaterial labor, 111–15, 152–54, 156; jacqueries, 95–100; love, 135–38; multitude in *Against the Day*, 169–70; multitude in *Vineland*, 165–66; neoliberalism, 104, 185–86; nomadism, 109–10; nostalgia, 40–41; postmodernism, 73, 173; slavery, 57–58, 61; types of revolution, 20–21, 121, 134; mentioned 23, 52–53, 142, 158, 178, 182

Harris, Anne, 154
Harvey, David, 8, 86, 104–7, 120, 185–86; criticism of Hardt and Negri, 19
Hawks, Howard, 125
Hawthorne, Nathaniel, 71
Hayles, N. Katherine, 20, 41, 43, 189n3
Haynes, Doug, 137, 189n1
Hite, Molly, 23, 35, 42, 187n11
Hoover, J. Edgar, 117
Hume, Katherine, 97, 113, 115, 118, 146, 159
Hutcheon, Linda, 17, 35, 125, 146, 167, 189n4

Ickstadt, Heinz, 110
immaterial labor, 17, 28, 45–47, 111–15, 133, 142, 150–54, 156
Industrial Workers of the World, 26, 28, 187n2
Inherent Vice (Pynchon): alternative system of exchange, 133–35, 148, 154; the common in, 123, 133–35; complicity in, 26; critical reception, 122–23; debt in, 129–30; ending, 136–38; Golden Fang as Empire, 130–35; Internet in, 157; narrator, 124; power system in, 9–10; resistance in, 17; similarities with Chandler novels, 122–28; similarities with *The Big Lebowski*, 122–28; 'ukulele in, 170–71, 174–75
International Monetary Fund, 24, 146
Irving, Washington, 71
"Is It O.K. to Be a Luddite?" (Pynchon), 112

Jameson, Frederic, 104, 123–25, 161
Jefferson, Thomas, 54–55, 77–78, 121
Jhally, Sut, 67–68
Johnson, Samuel, 71
Joyce, James, 125

Kalakaua, David, 159
Kamakawiwo'ole, Israel, 172–73
Karcher, Carolyn L., 69–70, 188n9
King, John, 158–60, 171–72
Klein, Naomi, 91, 140–41, 145, 147, 178

Lasson, Sally Ann, 172–73
Lazzarato, Mauricio, 63, 152–54
Le Prince, Louis, 112–13
Lewis, Barry, 58, 188n5
Lifshey, Adam, 68, 188n7
Lili'uokalani, 159
Linzey, Thomas, 185
Locke, John, 55, 132
Long Goodbye, The (Altman), 124
Long Goodbye, The (Chandler), 17
Ludlow Massacre, 39, 102–4, 189n5
Lyotard, Jean-François, 65

Macdonald, Averie, 154
Marx, Karl: alienation, 63; commons, 12, 14, 17, 23, 40, 42, 53, 131–32, 156, 165–66; mentioned, 45, 95, 183
Mason & Dixon (Pynchon): anachronism in, 80, 167; capitalism as quasi-religious belief in, 147–48; chartered companies, 49–54; complicity in, 26, 50, 54, 59, 64; economic liberalism, 51, 63; genres, 83; narrator, 124; power system in, 9, 14–15; representations of Empire, 52; slavery in, 57–64; subjunctive, 49, 60, 64, 154; succeeding *Vineland*, 5; 'ukulele in, 166–68, 170, 174
Mattessich, Stefan, 42
McHale, Brian, 24–25, 65, 68, 83, 101, 125, 137
Melville, Herman, 6
Menand, Louis, 123
Mitchell, David, 18, 185
Mitchell, W. J. T., 3, 12, 134, 150

Moby-Dick (Melville), 6
Moraru, Christian, 17, 123–24
multitude: in *Against the Day*, 116–20, 169–70; in *Bleeding Edge*, 142–43; definition of, 10–11, 28–29, 72; in *Gravity's Rainbow*, 163; in *Mason & Dixon*, 72; in *Vineland*, 12, 41–48, 164–65; mentioned, 19, 158
Murakami, Haruki, 18, 124, 178–82
Murray, Paul, 18, 185

Negri, Antonio. *See* Hardt, Michael, and Antonio Negri
neoliberalism: Brown's definition, 104; debt, 63; as doxa, 86–88; "The Fight for 'Real Democracy' at the Heart of Occupy Wall Street," 11; Harvey's definition, 104; privatization, 42; quasi-religious belief, 66–67, 92–94, 147–49; in relation to academics, 114; in relation to innovation, 113; revolution, 8, 23–25, 164, 167, 177; slow violence of, 140; tenet of endless accumulation, 144–47; mentioned, 2, 10, 27, 76, 81
1984 (Orwell), 26, 187n1
Nistou, Christina, 154

Occupy Movement: *Against the Day* similarities, 81–82, 106–8, 116–20; *Bleeding Edge* similarities, 140–42; community building, 185–86; consensus, 107–8; critique of capitalism, 91; debt, 63, 121–23; as demonstration, 162–63, 178; economic inequality, 87, 107; first days, 1–3; *Inherent Vice* similarities, 121–22; lack of leadership, 22, 46–47, 77, 142–43; *Mason & Dixon* similarities, 75–79; as political disobedience, 21–23; *There but for the* similarities, 183–84; undemocratic occupations, 150; *Vineland* similarities, 41–48; women's roles in, 154
Olster, Stacey, 51–52, 62–63
Orwell, George, 23; *1984*, 26, 187n1
"Over the Rainbow" (Kamakawiwo'ole), 172–73

Palmeri, Frank, 54
participatory democracy, 2, 7, 11, 78–79, 165–66
Piketty, Thomas, 105, 189n8
Pöhlmann, Sascha, 6, 185
Polanyi, Karl, 10, 25, 35, 42, 75, 84, 87–94, 104, 106–7, 147, 187n5, 188n8
political disobedience, 20–23, 141
Polletta, Francesca, 18, 166
Pynchon, Thomas: alternatives to capitalism, 140; anarchist leanings, 76–79; awards, 4; conception of power, 9; criticism of capitalism as quasi-religious belief, 66–67, 92–94, 147–49, 185; criticism of neoliberalism, 119–20, 174; family values, 40–41, 116–20; freedom, 108–9, 174; "Is It O.K. to Be a Luddite?" 112; political violence, 16, 26, 38–39, 96–103, 187n10; preface to *1984*, 26; private property, 132; reaction to Ludlow Massacre, 103; shift in oeuvre, 27; subjunctive, 15, 64, 157; *Warlock* influence, 101–2. See also individual works
Pynchon Notes, 5

Reagan, Ronald, 23–24, 35, 42
Reifman, Jeff, 185

Sale, Kirkpatrick, 37, 187n7
Schaub, Thomas Hill, 20
Scott, Walter, 69
Sedgwick, Catharine Maria, 70
Severs, Jeffrey, 83, 189n3
Shaun of the Dead (Wright), 177
Shoop, Casey, 137–38
Siegel, Jules, 158
Sisario, Ben, 172
Sitrin, Marina, 107, 141–42
Slaughterhouse Five (Vonnegut), 169
Smith, Adam, 66, 81, 84, 88, 129, 148
Smith, Ali, 18, 182–84; *There but for the*, 183–84
Smith, Shawn, 24, 41
Solomon, Eric, 43
Sterne, Laurence, 71

Stiglitz, Joseph, 107
subprime mortgage crisis, 145–47
Swift, Jonathan, 71

Tanner, Tony, 57, 60, 68, 73, 188n7
Taussig, Michael, 2, 107, 162
Taylor, Astra, 1, 63, 77, 79, 107; *The Examined Life*, 20, 121, 134
Tesla, Nikola, 113
Thatcher, Margaret, 23
There but for the (Ali Smith), 183–84
Thill, Brian, 58–60, 188n5
Thomas, Samuel, 23, 44, 47, 51, 76, 188n7
Thoreen, David, 24–25, 32
Tom Swift, 83
Tranquada, Jim, 158–60, 171–72

'ukulele: in *Against the Day*, 168–70, 174; arrival in Hawaii, 159; banjolele, 161, 164; in *Bleeding Edge*, 173; Chinese manufacturers, 172; co-optation by Empire, 171–74; in *Gravity's Rainbow*, 160–63, 170, 174; in *Inherent Vice*, 170–71, 174–75; Madeiran origins, 158–59; in *Mason & Dixon*, 166–68, 170, 174; pronunciation, 190n1; symbol of Hawaiian culture, 159–60; in *Vineland*, 164–66, 170, 174
"Under the Rose" (Pynchon), 7, 29

V. (Pynchon): ending, 20; power system in, 9; Whole Sick Crew, 8, 29
van Gelder, Sarah, 155
Vineland (Pynchon): Becker-Traverse reunion, 3, 12, 14, 23, 39–44; Chipco as Empire, 30–31; complicity in, 35–36; critical reception, 4–5; cultural context, 8, 24; ending, 19, 115, 173–74; Great South Coast Plaza Eyeshadow Raid, 25–27, 43; multitude, 12–14; narrator, 124; People's Republic of Rock and Roll, 22, 38; political shift, 7; political violence in, 38–39; power system in, 13–14, 34; resistance in, 13–14; Sisterhood of the Kunoichi Attentives, 14, 23, 44–48, 154, 164–65; television in,

24–25, 178–82; Thanatoids, 176; 'ukulele in, 164–66, 170, 174; villain, 86
Volcker, Paul, 23
Vonnegut, Kurt, 169

Wallerstein, Immanuel, 144, 148, 156, 185–86
Warlock (Hall), 101–2
Washington, George, 54, 56–57, 70
Weisenburger, Steven, 163
Williams, Raymond, 67–68

Wilson, Rob, 132
Wilson, Woodrow, 117
World Trade Organization, 11, 60

Xiaoping, Deng, 23

Yes Men, The (Chris Smith), 60–61, 76

Zinn, Howard, 103
Žižek, Slavoj, 75–77, 140–41, 157, 185–86
Zombieland (Fleischer), 177

www.ingramcontent.com/pod-product-compliance
Lightning Source LLC
Chambersburg PA
CBHW011745220426
43666CB00018B/2900